The Wittgenstein Reader

The Wittgenstein Reader

Edited by

ANTHONY KENNY

BLACKWELL
Publishers

Copyright © Basil Blackwell Ltd, 1994

First published 1994
Reprinted 1994, 1995, 1996

Blackwell Publishers Ltd
108 Cowley Road, Oxford, OX4 1JF, UK

Blackwell Publishers Inc.
238 Main Street
Cambridge, Massachusetts 02142, USA

British Library Cataloguing in Publication Data
A CIP catalogue record for this book is available from the British Library.

Library of Congress Cataloging-in-Publication Data
Wittgenstein, Ludwig, 1889–1951.
[Selections. 1994]
The Wittgenstein reader / edited by Anthony Kenny.
p. cm.
ISBN 0–631–19361–8. — ISBN 0–631–19362–6 (pbk.)
1. Philosophy. I. Kenny, Anthony John Patrick. II. Title.
B3376.W561 1995
192—dc20   94–3778
                                                    CIP

Typeset in 11 on 13 pts Plantin by
Pure Tech Corporation, Pondicherry, India
Printed in Great Britain by T. J. Press Ltd, Padstow, Cornwall

This book is printed on acid-free paper

Contents

Acknowledgements   vi
Introduction   vii
 1 Tractatus Logico-Philosophicus   1
 2 The Rejection of Logical Atomism   33
 3 Meaning and Understanding   51
 4 Intentionality   67
 5 Following a Rule   85
 6 Thinking   109
 7 The Will   127
 8 Private Language and Private Experience   139
 9 Aspect and Image   171
10 The First Person   189
11 The Inner and the Outer   209
12 Necessity   225
13 Scepticism and Certainty   245
14 The Nature of Philosophy   261
15 Ethics, Life and Faith   287
Note on Sources   306
Index   308

Acknowledgements

The editor and publishers wish to thank the following for permission to use copyright material:

Macmillan College Publishing, Inc. for material from Ludwig Wittgenstein, *Philosophical Investigations* Vols 1 & 2, trans. G. E. M. Anscombe. Copyright © 1953, 1981 by Macmillan College Publishing Company, Inc. The MIT Press for material from Ludwig Wittgenstein, *Remarks on the Foundations of Mathematics*, Vols 1 & 2, eds G. H. von Wright, R. Rhees and G. E. M. Anscombe, 1956; Routledge for material from Ludwig Wittgenstein, *Tractatus Logico-Philosophicus*, 1922; University of California Press for material from Ludwig Wittgenstein, *Philosophical Grammar*, trans./ed. R. Rhees, 1969; University of Chicago Press for material from Ludwig Wittgenstein, *Remarks on the Philosophy of Psychology* Vols 1 & 2, eds G. H. von Wright and H. Nyman, trans. C. G. Luchardt and M. A. E. Aue, 1980; and Ludwig Wittgenstein, *Lecture on Ethics*, ed. G. H. von Wright, trans. P. Winch.

Blackwell Publishers on behalf of the Wittgenstein Estate hold the copyright for all Wittgenstein material not cited above.

Introduction

Ludwig Wittgenstein was born in Vienna in 1889. After being educated at Linz and in Berlin he became an engineering research student at Manchester in 1908–11. He then studied philosophy at Trinity College, Cambridge, in 1912–13 where he was a pupil of Bertrand Russell. During the 1914–18 war he served in the Austrian army; while in the field, and later in a prisoner of war camp at Monte Cassino, he composed a masterpiece, the *Tractatus Logico-Philosophicus*, which was the only philosophical work he published in his lifetime. This was published in England in 1922.

For a while he then gave up philosophy and became first a gardener and then a schoolteacher. Later, however, he began to have serious doubts about the soundness of the philosophy ('logical atomism') presented in the *Tractatus* and accordingly he resumed philosophical reflection. He returned to Cambridge in 1929 and became a Fellow of Trinity from 1930 onward. He was appointed Professor of Philosophy in 1939, but served during the war as a medical orderly; he held the chair, in practice, only from 1945–7. Philosophical notebooks and lectures from the pre-war Cambridge period have been published posthumously under the titles *Philosophical Grammar* and *The Blue and Brown Books*.

After his retirement from Cambridge in 1947 Wittgenstein settled for a while in Ireland, where he worked on *Philosophical Investigations*, a work containing the substance of his mature thought which he left for posthumous publication. In 1949 he spent some time in America, returning to England later the same year with an incurable cancer which killed him at Cambridge in 1951. Some of the writings of the last year and a half of his life were published in 1969 under the title *On Certainty*. After his death his literary executors published volumes of selections from his notebooks including *Remarks on the Foundations of*

Mathematics (1956), *Zettel* (1967) and *Culture and Value*. Most recently there have appeared *Remarks on the Philosophy of Psychology* (1982) and other late writings.

The present volume is a selection from the works listed above. The *Tractatus* has a special position in Wittgenstein's oeuvre: not only was it the only philosophical work he published himself, but it also set the agenda for almost everything else he wrote, however far he travelled from his initial theoretical positions. Accordingly, this reader begins with an abridgement of the *Tractatus*. Later readings are grouped thematically, but the ordering of the themes corresponds very roughly to the chronological development of the focus of Wittgenstein's philosophical interest. The works from which the readings have been selected are identified in the note on sources at the end of the book. I am grateful to Dr Peter Hacker for many helpful suggestions of texts to include.

Anthony Kenny

1

Tractatus Logico-Philosophicus

1	The world is everything that is the case.
1.1	The world is the totality of facts, not of things.
1.11	The world is determined by the facts, and by these being *all* the facts.
1.12	For the totality of facts determines both what is the case, and also all that is not the case.
1.13	The facts in logical space are the world.
1.2	The world divides into facts.
1.21	Any one can either be the case or not be the case, and everything else remain the same.
2	What is the case, the fact, is the existence of atomic facts.
2.01	An atomic fact is a combination of objects (entities, things).
2.011	It is essential to a thing that it can be a constituent part of an atomic fact.
2.012	In logic nothing is accidental: if a thing *can* occur in an atomic fact the possibility of that atomic fact must already be prejudged in the thing.
2.013	Everything is, as it were, in a space of possible atomic facts. I can think of this space as empty, but not of the thing without the space.
2.014	Objects contain the possibility of all states of affairs.
2.0141	The possibility of its occurrence in atomic facts is the form of the object.
2.02	The object is simple.
2.0201	Every statement about complexes can be analysed into a statement about their constituent parts, and into those propositions which completely describe the complexes.

2.021   Objects form the substance of the world. Therefore they cannot be compound.

2.022   It is clear that however different from the real one an imagined world may be, it must have something – a form – in common with the real world.

2.023   This fixed form consists of the objects.

2.024   Substance is what exists independently of what is the case.

2.025   It is form and content.

2.0251   Space, time and colour (colouredness) are forms of objects.

2.026   Only if there are objects can there be a fixed form of the world.

2.027   The fixed, the existent and the object are one.

2.03   In the atomic fact objects hang one in another, like the links of a chain.

2.031   In the atomic facts the objects are combined in a definite way.

2.032   The way in which objects hang together in the atomic fact is the structure of the atomic fact.

2.033   The form is the possibility of the structure.

2.034   The structure of the fact consists in the structures of the atomic facts.

2.04   The totality of existent atomic facts is the world.

2.05   The totality of existent atomic facts also determines which atomic facts do not exist.

2.06   The existence and non-existence of atomic facts is the reality.

                (The existence of atomic facts we also call a positive fact, their non-existence a negative fact.)

2.061   Atomic facts are independent of one another.

2.062   From the existence or non-existence of an atomic fact we cannot infer the existence or non-existence of another.

2.063   The total reality is the world.

2.1   We make to ourselves pictures of facts.

2.11   The picture presents the facts in logical space, the existence and non-existence of atomic facts.

2.12   The picture is a model of reality.

2.13	To the objects correspond in the picture the elements of the picture.
2.131	The elements of the picture stand, in the picture, for the objects.
2.14	The picture consists in the fact that its elements are combined with one another in a definite way.
2.141	The picture is a fact.
2.15	That the elements of the picture are combined with one another in a definite way, represents that the things are so combined with one another.

This connexion of the elements of the picture is called its structure, and the possibility of this structure is called the form of representation of the picture.

2.151	The form of representation is the possibility that the things are combined with one another as are the elements of the picture.
2.1511	Thus the picture is linked with reality; it reaches up to it.
2.1512	It is like a scale applied to reality.
2.15121	Only the outermost points of the dividing lines touch the object to be measured.
2.1513	According to this view the representing relation which makes it a picture, also belongs to the picture.
2.1514	The representing relation consists of the co-ordinations of the elements of the picture and the things.
2.1515	These co-ordinations are as it were the feelers of its elements with which the picture touches reality.
2.16	In order to be a picture a fact must have something in common with what it pictures.
2.161	In the picture and pictured there must be something identical in order that the one can be a picture of the other at all.
2.17	What the picture must have in common with reality in order to be able to represent it after its manner – rightly or falsely – is its form of representation.
2.171	The picture can represent every reality whose form it has.

The spatial picture, everything spatial, the coloured, everything coloured, etc.

| 2.172 | The picture, however, cannot represent its form of representation; it shows it forth. |

2.173   The picture represents its object from without (its standpoint is its form of representation), therefore the picture represents its object rightly or falsely.

2.174   But the picture cannot place itself outside of its form of representation.

2.18   What every picture, of whatever form, must have in common with reality in order to be able to represent it at all – rightly or falsely – is the logical form, that is, the form of reality.

2.181   If the form of representation is the logical form, then the picture is called a logical picture.

2.182   Every picture is *also* a logical picture. (On the other hand, for example, not every picture is spatial.)

2.19   The logical picture can depict the world.

2.2   The picture has the logical form of representation in common with what it pictures.

2.201   The picture depicts reality by representing a possibility of the existence and non-existence of atomic facts.

2.202   The picture represents a possible state of affairs in logical space.

2.203   The picture contains the possibility of the state of affairs which it represents.

2.21   The picture agrees with reality or not; it is right or wrong, true or false.

2.22   The picture represents what it represents, independently of its truth or falsehood, through the form of representation.

2.221   What the picture represents is its sense.

2.222   In the agreement or disagreement of its sense with reality, its truth or falsity consists.

2.223   In order to discover whether the picture is true or false we must compare it with reality.

2.224   It cannot be discovered from the picture alone whether it is true or false.

2.225   There is no picture which is *a priori* true.

3   The logical picture of the facts is the thought.

3.01   The totality of true thoughts is a picture of the world.

3.02   The thought contains the possibility of the state of affairs which it thinks.

What is thinkable is also possible.

3.03　　　We cannot think anything unlogical, for otherwise we should have to think unlogically.

3.04　　　An *a priori* true thought would be one whose possibility guaranteed its truth.

3.05　　　We could know *a priori* that a thought was true only if its truth was to be recognized from the thought itself (without an object of comparison).

3.1　　　In the proposition the thought is expressed perceptibly through the senses.

3.11　　　We use the sensibly perceptible sign (sound or written sign, etc.) of the proposition as a projection of the possible state of affairs.

The method of projection is the thinking of the sense of the proposition.

3.12　　　The sign through which we express the thought I call the propositional sign. And the proposition is the propositional sign in its projective relation to the world.

3.13　　　To the proposition belongs everything which belongs to the projection; but not what is projected.

Therefore the possibility of what is projected but not this itself.

In the proposition, therefore, its sense is not yet contained, but the possibility of expressing it.

('The content of the proposition' means the content of the significant proposition.)

In the proposition the form of its sense is contained, but not its content.

3.14　　　The propositional sign consists in the fact that its elements, the words, are combined in it in a definite way.

The propositional sign is a fact.

3.142　　　Only facts can express a sense, a class of names cannot.

3.1432　　We must not say 'The complex sign "aRb" says "a stands in relation R to b" '; but we must say '*That* "a" stands in a certain relation to "b" says *that aRb*'.

3.144　　　States of affairs can be described, but not *named*.

(Names resemble points; propositions resemble arrows, they have sense.)

3.2   In the propositions thoughts can be so expressed that to the objects of the thoughts correspond the elements of the propositional sign.

3.201   These elements I call 'simple signs' and the proposition 'completely analysed'.

3.202   The simple signs employed in propositions are called names.

3.203   The name means the object. The object is its meaning. ('A' is the same sign as 'A'.)

3.21   To the configuration of the simple signs in the propositional sign corresponds the configuration of the objects in the state of affairs.

3.22   In the proposition the name represents the object.

3.221   Objects I can only *name*. Signs represent them. I can only speak *of* them. I cannot *assert them*. A proposition can only say *how* a thing is, not *what* it is.

3.23   The postulate of the possibility of the simple signs is the postulate of the determinateness of the sense.

3.24   A proposition about a complex stands in internal relation to the proposition about its constituent part.

        A complex can only be given by its description, and this will either be right or wrong. The proposition in which there is mention of a complex, if this does not exist, becomes not nonsense but simply false.

        That a propositional element signifies a complex can be seen from an indeterminateness in the proposition in which it occurs. We *know* that everything is not yet determined by this proposition. (The notation for generality *contains* a prototype).

        The combination of the symbols of a complex in a simple symbol can be expressed by a definition.

3.25   There is one and only one complete analysis of the proposition.

3.251   The proposition expresses what it expresses in a definite and clearly specifiable way: the proposition is articulate.

3.26   The name cannot be analysed further by any definition. It is a primitive sign.

3.3   Only the proposition has sense; only in the context of a proposition has a name meaning.

3.31   Every part of a proposition which characterizes its sense I call an expression (a symbol).

(The proposition itself is an expression.)

Expressions are everything – essential for the sense of the proposition – that propositions can have in common with one another.

An expression characterises a form and a content.

3.32   The sign is the part of the symbol perceptible by the senses.

3.321   Two different symbols can therefore have the sign (the written sign or the sound sign) in common – they then signify in different ways.

3.322   It can never indicate the common characteristic of two objects that we symbolise them with the same sign but by different *methods of symbolising*. For the sign is arbitrary. We could therefore equally well choose two different signs and where then would be what was common in the symbolisation?

3.323   In the language of everyday life it very often happens that the same word signifies in two different ways – and therefore belongs to two different symbols – or that two words, which signify in different ways, are apparently applied in the same way in the proposition.

Thus the word 'is' appears as the copula, as the sign of equality, and as the expression of existence; 'to exist' as an intransitive verb like 'to go'; 'identical' as an adjective; we speak of *something* but also of the fact of *something* happening.

(In the proposition 'Green is green' – where the first word is a person's name and the last an adjective – these words have not merely different meanings but they are *different symbols*.)

3.324   Thus there easily arise the most fundamental confusions (of which the whole of philosophy is full).

3.325   In order to avoid these errors, we must employ a symbolism which excludes them, by not applying the same sign in different symbols and by not applying

signs in the same ways which signify in different ways.
A symbolism, that is to say, which obeys the rules of
logical grammar – of logical syntax.

The logical symbolism of Frege and Russell is such
a language which, however, does still not exclude all
errors.

3.326   In order to recognise the symbol in the sign we
must consider the significant use.

3.327   The sign determines a logical form only together
with its logical syntactic application.

3.328   If a sign is *not used* then it is meaningless. That is
the meaning of Occam's razor.

(If everything in the symbolism works as though a
sign had meaning, then it has meaning.)

3.33   In logical syntax the meaning of a sign ought never
to play a role; it must admit of being established
without mention being thereby made of the *meaning*
of a sign; it ought to presuppose *only* the description
of the expressions.

3.34   A proposition possesses essential and accidental
features.

Accidental are the features which are due to a
particular way of producing the propositional sign.
Essential are those which alone enable the proposition to express its sense.

3.341   The essential in a proposition is therefore that
which is common to all propositions which can express the same sense.

And in the same way in general the essential in a
symbol is that which all symbols which can fulfil the
same purpose have in common.

3.342   In our notations there is indeed something arbitrary,
but *this* is not arbitrary, namely that *if* we have determined anything arbitrarily, then something else *must* be
the case. (This results from the *essence* of the notation.)

3.343   Definitions are rules for the translation of one language into another. Every correct symbolism must be
translatable into every other according to such rules.
It is *this* which all have in common.

3.344　　　What signifies in the symbol is what is common to all those symbols by which it can be replaced according to the rules of logical syntax.

3.4　　　The proposition determines a place in logical space: the existence of this logical place is guaranteed by the existence of the constituent parts alone, by the existence of the significant proposition.

3.41　　　The propositional sign and the logical co-ordinates: that is the logical place.

3.411　　　The geometrical and the logical place agree in that each is the possibility of an existence.

3.42　　　Although a proposition may only determine one place in logical space, the whole logical space must already be given by it.

(Otherwise denial, the logical sum, the logical product, etc. would always introduce new elements – in co-ordination.)

(The logical scaffolding round the picture determines the logical space. The proposition reaches through the whole logical space.)

3.5　　　The applied, thought, propositional sign is the thought.

4　　　The thought is the significant proposition.

4.01　　　The proposition is a picture of reality.

The proposition is a model of the reality as we think it is.

4.011　　　At the first glance the proposition – say as it stands printed on paper – does not seem to be a picture of the reality of which it treats. But nor does the musical score appear at first sight to be a picture of a musical piece; nor does our phonetic spelling (letters) seem to be a picture of our spoken language. And yet these symbolisms prove to be pictures – even in the ordinary sense of the word – of what they represent.

4.012　　　It is obvious that we perceive a proposition of the form aRb as a picture. Here the sign is obviously a likeness of the signified.

4.02　　　This we see from the fact that we understand the sense of the propositional sign, without having had it explained to us.

4.021   The proposition is a picture of reality, for I know the state of affairs presented by it, if I understand the proposition. And I understand the proposition without its sense having been explained to me.

4.022   The proposition *shows* its sense.

The proposition *shows* how things stand, *if* it is true. And it *says*, that they do so stand.

4.023   The proposition determines reality to this extent, that one only needs to say 'Yes' or 'No' to it to make it agree with reality.

Reality must therefore be completely described by the proposition.

A proposition is the description of a fact.

As the description of an object describes it by its external properties so propositions describe reality by its internal properties.

The proposition constructs a world with the help of a logical scaffolding, and therefore one can actually see in the proposition all the logical features possessed by reality *if* it is true. One can *draw conclusions* from a false proposition.

4.024   To understand a proposition means to know what is the case if it is true.

(One can therefore understand it without knowing whether it is true or not.)

One understands it if one understands its constituent parts.

4.025   The translation of one language into another is not a process of translating each proposition of the one into a proposition of the other, but only the constituent parts of propositions are translated.

(And the dictionary does not only translate substantives but also adverbs and conjunctions, etc., and it treats them all alike.)

4.026   The meanings of the simple signs (the words) must be explained to us, if we are to understand them.

But propositions are self-explanatory.

4.027   It is essential to propositions, that they can communicate a *new* sense to us.

4.03   A proposition must communicate a new sense with old words.

The proposition communicates to us a state of affairs, therefore it must be *essentially* connected with the state of affairs.

And the connexion is, in fact, that it is its logical picture.

The proposition only asserts something, in so far as it is a picture.

4.031   In the proposition a state of affairs is, as it were, put together for the sake of experiment.

One can say, instead of, 'This proposition has such and such a sense', 'This proposition represents such and such a state of affairs'.

4.0311 One name stands for one thing, and another for another thing, and they are connected together. And so the whole, like a living picture, presents the atomic fact.

4.0312 The possibility of propositions is based upon the principle of the representation of objects by signs.

My fundamental thought is that the 'logical constants' do not represent. That the *logic* of facts cannot be represented.

4.032   The proposition is a picture of its state of affairs, only in so far as it is logically articulated.

(Even the proposition 'ambulo' is composite, for its stem gives a different sense with another termination, or its termination with another stem.)

4.04   In the proposition there must be exactly as many things distinguishable as there are in the state of affairs, which it represents.

They must both possess the same logical (mathematical) multiplicity (cf. Hertz's *Mechanics*, on Dynamic Models).

4.041   This mathematical multiplicity naturally cannot in its turn be represented. One cannot get outside it in the representation.

4.05   Reality is compared with the proposition.

4.06   Propositions can be true or false only by being pictures of the reality.

4.1   A proposition presents the existence and non-existence of atomic facts.

4.11   The totality of true propositions is the total natural science (or the totality of the natural sciences).

4.111   Philosophy is not one of the natural sciences.

(The word 'philosophy' must mean something which stands above or below, but not beside the natural sciences.)

4.112   The object of philosophy is the logical clarification of thoughts.

Philosophy is not a theory but an activity.

A philosophical work consists essentially of elucidations.

The result of philosophy is not a number of 'philosophical propositions', but to make propositions clear.

Philosophy should make clear and delimit sharply the thoughts which otherwise are, as it were, opaque and blurred.

4.113   Philosophy limits the disputable sphere of natural science.

4.114   It should limit the thinkable and thereby the unthinkable.

It should limit the unthinkable from within through the thinkable.

4.115   It will mean the unspeakable by clearly displaying the speakable.

4.116   Everything that can be thought at all can be thought clearly. Everything that can be said can be said clearly.

4.12   Propositions can represent the whole reality, but they cannot represent what they must have in common with reality in order to be able to represent it – the logical form.

To be able to represent the logical form, we should have to be able to put ourselves with the propositions outside logic, that is outside the world.

4.121   Propositions cannot represent the logical form: this mirrors itself in the propositions.

That which mirrors itself in language, language cannot represent.

That which expresses *itself* in language, *we* cannot express by language.

The propositions show the logical form of reality. They exhibit it.

4.2   The sense of a proposition is its agreement and disagreement with the possibilities of the existence and non-existence of the atomic facts.

4.21   The simplest proposition, the elementary proposition, asserts the existence of an atomic fact.

4.211   It is a sign of an elementary proposition, that no elementary proposition can contradict it.

4.22   The elementary proposition consists of names. It is a connexion, a concatenation of names.

4.23   The name occurs in the proposition only in the context of the elementary proposition.

4.24   The names are the simple symbols, I indicate them by single letters (x, y, z).

The elementary proposition I write as function of the names, in the form 'fx' "$\Phi(x, y)$", etc.

Or I indicate it by the letters p, q, r.

4.25   If the elementary proposition is true, the atomic fact exists; if it is false the atomic fact does not exist.

4.26   The specification of all true elementary propositions describes the world completely. The world is completely described by the specification of all elementary propositions, plus the specification which of them are true and which false.

4.27   With regard to the existence of n atomic facts there are $\kappa_n = \sum_{v=0}^{n} \binom{n}{v}$ possibilities.

It is possible for all combinations of atomic facts to exist, and the others not to exist.

4.28   To these combinations correspond the same number of possibilities of the truth – and falsehood – of n elementary propositions.

4.3   The truth-possibilities of the elementary propositions mean the possibilities of the existence and non-existence of the atomic facts.

4.31   The truth-possibilities can be presented by schemata of the following kind ('T' means 'true', 'F' 'false'. The rows of T's and F's under the row of the elementary propositions mean their truth-possibilities in an easily intelligible symbolism).

p	q	r
T	T	T
F	T	T
T	F	T
T	T	F
F	F	T
F	T	F
T	F	F
F	F	F

p	q
T	T
F	T
T	F
F	F

p
T
F

4.4   A proposition is the expression of agreement and disagreement with the truth-possibilities of the elementary propositions.

4.41   The truth-possibilities of the elementary propositions are the conditions of the truth and falsehood of the propositions.

4.411   It seems probable even at first sight that the introduction of the elementary propositions is fundamental for the comprehension of the other kinds of propositions. Indeed the comprehension of the general propositions depends *palpably* on that of the elementary propositions.

4.42   With regard to the agreement and disagreement of a proposition with the truth-possibilities of n elementary propositions there are $\sum_{\kappa=0}^{\kappa_n} \binom{\kappa_n}{\kappa} = L_n$ possibilities.

4.45   For n elementary propositions there are L possible groups of truth-conditions.

The groups of truth-conditions which belong to the truth- possibilities of a number of elementary propositions can be ordered in a series.

4.46   Among the possible groups of truth-conditions there are two extreme cases.

In the one case the proposition is true for all the truth-possibilities of the elementary propositions. We say that the truth-conditions are *tautological.*

In the second case the proposition is false for all the truth-possibilities. The truth-conditions are *self-contradictory.*

In the first case we call the proposition a tautology, in the second case a contradiction.

4.461   The proposition shows what it says, the tautology and the contradiction that they say nothing.

The tautology has no truth-conditions, for it is unconditionally true; and the contradiction is on no condition true.

Tautology and contradiction are without sense.

(Like the point from which two arrows go out in opposite directions.)

(I know, e.g. nothing about the weather, when I know that it rains or does not rain.)

4.5   Now it appears to be possible to give the most general form of proposition; i.e. to give a description of the propositions of some one sign language, so that every possible sense can be expressed by a symbol, which falls under the description, and so that every symbol which falls under the description can express a sense, if the meanings of the names are chosen accordingly.

It is clear that in the description of the most general form of proposition *only* what is essential to it may be described – otherwise it would not be the most general form.

That there is a general form is proved by the fact that there cannot be a proposition whose form could not have been foreseen (i.e. constructed). The general form of proposition is: Such and such is the case.

4.51   Suppose *all* elementary propositions were given me: then we can simply ask: what propositions I can build out of them. And these are *all* propositions, and *so* they are limited.

4.52   The propositions are everything which follows from the totality of all elementary propositions (of course also from the fact that it is the *totality of them all*). (So, in some sense, one could say, that *all* propositions are generalisations of the elementary propositions.)

4.53   The general propositional form is a variable.

5   Propositions are truth-functions of elementary propositions.

(An elementary proposition is a truth-function of itself.)

5.01   The elementary propositions are the truth-arguments of propositions.

5.1   The truth-functions can be ordered in series.

That is the foundation of the theory of probability.

5.101   The truth-functions of every number of elementary propositions can be written in a schema of the following kind:

(T T T T) (p, q) Tautology (if p then p, and if q then q) $[p{\supset}p.\ q{\supset}q]$
(F T T T) (p, q) in words: Not both p and q. $[{\sim}(p.\ q)]$
(T F T T) (p, q) ” ” If q then p. $[q \supset p]$
(T T F T) (p, q) ” ” If p then q. $[p \supset q]$
(T T T F) (p, q) ” ” p or q. $[p \vee q]$
(F F T T) (p, q) ” ” Not q. $[{\sim}q]$
(F T F T) (p, q) ” ” Not p. $[{\sim}p]$
(F T T F) (p, q) ” ” p or q, but not both. $[p.\ {\sim}q : \vee : q.\ {\sim}p]$
(T F F T) (p, q) ” ” If p, then q; and if q, then p. $[p \equiv q]$
(T F T F) (p, q) ” ” p
(T T F F) (p, q) ” ” q
(F F F T) (p, q) ” ” Neither p nor q. $[{\sim}p.\ {\sim}q$ or $p\,/q]$
(F F T F) (p, q) ” ” p and not q. $[p.\ {\sim}q]$
(F T F F) (p, q) ” ” q and not p. $[q.\ {\sim}p]$
(T F F F) (p, q) ” ” p and q. $[p.\ q]$
(F F F F) (p, q) Contradiction (p and not p; and q and not q.) $[p.\ {\sim}p.$ $q.\ {\sim}q]$

Those truth-possibilities of its truth-arguments, which verify the proposition, I shall call its *truth-grounds*.

5.11   If the truth-grounds which are common to a number of propositions are all also truth-grounds of some one proposition, we say that the truth of this proposition follows from the truth of those propositions.

5.12   In particular the truth of a proposition p follows from that of a proposition q, if all the truth-grounds of the second are truth-grounds of the first.

5.121   The truth-grounds of q are contained in those of p; p follows from 'q'.

5.122   If p follows from q, the sense of 'p' is contained in that of 'q'.

5.123   If a god creates a world in which certain propositions are true, he creates thereby also a world in which all propositions consequent on them are true. And similarly he could not create a world in which the proposition '*p*' is true without creating all its objects.

5.124   A proposition asserts every proposition which follows from it.

5.13   That the truth of one proposition follows from the truth of other propositions, we perceive from the structure of the propositions.

5.133   All inference takes place *a priori*.

5.134   From an elementary proposition no other can be inferred.

5.135   In no way can an inference be made from the existence of one state of affairs to the existence of another entirely different from it.

5.136   There is no causal nexus which justifies such an inference.

5.14   If a proposition follows from another, then the latter says more than the former, the former less than the latter.

5.141   If p follows from q and q from p then they are one and the same proposition.

5.142   A tautology follows from all propositions: it says nothing.

5.143   Contradiction is something shared by propositions, which *no* proposition has in common with another. Tautology is that which is shared by all propositions, which have nothing in common with one another.

Contradiction vanishes so to speak outside, tautology inside all propositions.

Contradiction is the external limit of the propositions, tautology their substanceless centre.

5.15   If T_r is the number of the truth-grounds of the proposition '*r*', T_{rs} the number of those truth-grounds of the proposition '*s*' which are at the same time truth-grounds of '*r*', then we call the ratio $T_{rs} : T_r$ the measure of the *probability* which the proposition '*r*' gives to the proposition '*s*'.

5.2   The structures of propositions stand to one another in internal relations.

5.21   We can bring out these internal relations in our

manner of expression, by presenting a proposition as the result of an operation which produces it from other propositions (the bases of the operation).

5.22 The operation is the expression of a relation between the structures of its result and its bases.

5.23 The operation is that which must happen to a proposition in order to make another out of it.

5.24 An operation shows itself in a variable; it shows how we can proceed from one form of proposition to another.

It gives expression to the difference between the forms.

(And that which is common to the bases, and the result of an operation, is the bases themselves.)

5.25 The occurrence of an operation does not characterise the sense of a proposition.

For an operation does not assert anything; only its result does, and this depends on the bases of the operation.

(Operation and function must not be confused with one another.)

5.251 A function cannot be its own argument, but the result of an operation can be its own basis.

5.3 All propositions are results of truth-operations on the elementary propositions.

The truth-operation is the way in which a truth-function arises from elementary propositions.

According to the nature of truth-operations, in the same way as out of elementary propositions arise their truth-functions, from truth-functions arises a new one. Every truth-operation creates from truth-functions of elementary propositions another truth-function of elementary propositions, i.e. a pro- position. The result of every truth-operation on the results of truth-operations on elementary propositions is also the result of *one* truth-operation on elementary propositions.

Every proposition is the result of truth-operations on elementary propositions.

5.31 The Schemata No. 4.31 are also significant, if 'p', 'q', 'r', etc. are not elementary propositions.

And it is easy to see that the propositional sign in No. 4.42 expresses one truth-function of elementary propositions even when '*p*' and '*q*' are truth-functions of elementary propositions.

5.32   All truth-functions are results of the successive application of a finite number of truth-operations to elementary propositions.

5.4   Here it becomes clear that there are no such things as 'logical objects' or 'logical constants' (in the sense of Frege and Russell.)

5.41   For all those results of truth-operations on truth-functions are identical, which are one and the same truth-function of elementary propositions.

5.42   That v, ⊃, etc. are not relations in the sense of right and left, etc., is obvious.

The possibility of crosswise definition of the logical 'primitive signs' of Frege and Russell shows by itself that these are not primitive signs and that they signify no relations.

And it is obvious that the '⊃' which we define by means of ~ and 'v' is identical with that by which we define 'v' with the help of ~, and that this 'v' is the same as the first, and so on.

5.43   That from a fact *p* an infinite number of *others* should follow, namely ~~*p*, ~~~~*p* etc., is indeed hardly to be believed, and it is no less wonderful that the infinite number of propositions of logic (of mathematics) should follow from half a dozen 'primitive propositions'.

But all propositions of logic say the same thing. That is, nothing.

5.46   When we have rightly introduced the logical signs, the sense of all their combinations has been already introduced with them: therefore not only '*pvq*' but also ~(*pv~q*), etc., etc. We should then already have introduced the effect of all possible combinations of brackets; and it would then have become clear that the proper general primitive signs are not '*pvq*', '(∃*x*). *fx*', etc., but the most general form of their combinations.

5.47   It is clear that everything which can be said *beforehand* about the form of *all* propositions at all can be said *no one occasion*.

              For all logical operations are already contained in the elementary proposition. For '*fa*' says the same as '$(\exists x) . fx . x = a$'.

              Where there is composition, there is argument and function, and where these are, all logical constants already are.

              One could say: the one logical constant is that which *all* propositions, according to their nature, have in common with one another.

              That however is the general form of proposition.

5.471   The general form of proposition is the essence of proposition.

5.5   Every truth-function is a result of the successive application of the operation $(------\text{T})$ $(\xi\ldots\ldots)$ to elementary propositions.

              This operation denies all the propositions in the right-hand bracket, and I call it the negation of these propositions.

5.51   If ξ has only one value, then $N(\bar{\xi}) = {\sim}p$ (not p), if it has two values then $N(\bar{\xi}) = {\sim}p{\sim}q$ (neither p nor q).

5.511   How can the all-embracing logic which mirrors the world use such special catches and manipulations? Only because all these are connected into an infinitely fine network, to the great mirror.

5.512   '${\sim}p$' is true if 'p' is false. Therefore in the true proposition '${\sim}p$' 'p' is a false proposition. How then can the stroke '${\sim}$' bring it into agreement with reality?

              That which denies in '${\sim}p$' is however not '${\sim}$', but that which all signs of this notation, which deny p, have in common.

              Hence the common rule according to which '${\sim}p$', '${\sim}{\sim}{\sim}p$', "${\sim}p. {\sim}p$", etc., etc. (to infinity) are constructed. And this which is common to them all mirrors denial.

5.513   We could say: What is common to all symbols, which assert both p and q, is the proposition '$p.q$'. What is common to all symbols, which assert either p or q, is the proposition 'pvq'.

And similarly we can say: Two propositions are opposed to one another when they have nothing in common with one another; and every proposition has only one negative, because there is only one proposition which lies altogether outside it.

5.52   If the values of ξ are the total values of a function fx for all values of x, then $N(\bar{\xi}) = {\sim}(\exists x) \,.\, fx$.

5.521   I separate the concept *all* from the truth-function.

Frege and Russell have introduced generality in connexion with the logical product or the logical sum. Then it would be difficult to understand the propositions '$(\exists x) \,.\, fx$' and '$(x) \,.\, fx$' in which both ideas lie concealed.

5.522   That which is peculiar to the 'symbolism of generality' is firstly, that it refers to a logical prototype, and secondly, that it makes constants prominent.

5.523   The generality symbol occurs as an argument.

5.524   If the objects are given, therewith are *all* objects given.

If the elementary propositions are given, then there with *all* elementary propositions are also given.

5.53   Identity of the object I express by identity of the sign and not by means of a sign of identity. Difference of the objects by difference of the signs.

5.531   I write therefore not '$f(a, b) \,.\, a = b$', but '$f(a, a)$ (or '$f(b.\ b)$. And not '$f(a, b) \,.\, {\sim}a = b$'. but '$f(a, b)$.

5.533   The identity sign is therefore not an essential constituent of logical notation.

5.54   In the general propositional form, propositions occur in a proposition only as bases of the truth-operations.

5.541   At first sight it appears as if there were also a different way in which one proposition could occur in another.

Especially in certain propositional forms of psychology, like 'A thinks, that p is the case', or 'A thinks p', etc.

Here it appears superficially as if the proposition p stood to the object A in a kind of relation.

And in modern epistemology (Russell, Moore, etc.) these propositions have been conceived in this way.

5.542   But it is clear that 'A believes that p', 'A thinks p',
          'A says p', are of the form ' "p" says p': and here we
          have no co-ordination of a fact and an object, but a
          co-ordination of facts by means of a co-ordination of
          their objects.

5.5421   This shows that there is no such thing as the soul –
          the subject, etc. – as it is conceived in contemporary
          superficial psychology.
          A composite soul would not be a soul any longer.

5.5422   The correct explanation of the form of the proposi-
          tion 'A judges p' must show that it is impossible to
          judge a nonsense. (Russell's theory does not satisfy
          this condition.)

5.5423   To perceive a complex means to perceive that its
          constituents are combined in such and such a way.

5.55   We must now answer *a priori* the question as to all
          possible forms of the elementary propositions.
          The elementary proposition consists of names. Since
          we cannot give the number of names with different
          meanings, we cannot give the composition of the
          elementary proposition.

5.551   Our fundamental principle is that every question
          which can be decided at all by logic can be decided
          off-hand.
          (And if we get into a situation where we need to
          answer such a problem by looking at the world, this
          shows that we are on a fundamentally wrong track.)

5.552   The 'experience' which we need to understand logic
          is not that such and such is the case, but that some-
          thing *is*; but that is *no* experience.
          Logic *precedes* every experience – that something is
          so.
          It is before the How, not before the What.

5.6   *The limits of my language* mean the limits of my world.

5.61   Logic fills the world: the limits of the world are also
          its limits.
          We cannot therefore say in logic: This and this
          there is in the world, that there is not.
          For that would apparently presuppose that we ex-
          clude certain possibilities, and this cannot be the case

since otherwise logic must get outside the limits of the world: that is, if it could consider these limits from the other side also.

What we cannot think, that we cannot think: we cannot therefore *say* what we cannot think.

5.62   This remark provides a key to the question, to what extent solipsism is a truth.

In fact what solipsism *means* is quite correct, only it cannot be *said*, but it shows itself.

That the world is *my* world, shows itself in the fact that the limits of that language (*the* language which I understand) mean the limits of *my* world.

5.621   The world and life are one.

5.63   I am my world. (The microcosm.)

5.631   The thinking, presenting subject; there is no such thing.

If I wrote a book 'The world as I found it', I should also have therein to report on my body and say which members obey my will and which do not, etc. This then would be a method of isolating the subject or rather of showing that in an important sense there is no subject: that is to say, of it alone in this book mention could *not* be made.

5.64   Here we see that solipsism strictly carried out coincides with pure realism. The I in solipsism shrinks to an extensionless point and there remains the reality coordinated with it.

5.641   There is therefore really a sense in which in philosophy we can talk of a non-psychological I.

The I occurs in philosophy through the fact that the 'world is my world'.

The philosophical I is not the man, not the human body or the human soul of which psychology treats, but the metaphysical subject, the limit – not a part of the world.

6   The general form of truth-function is: $[\bar{p}\, \bar{\xi}\, N(\bar{\xi})]$.

6.001   This says nothing else than that every proposition is the result of successive applications of the operation $N'\,(\bar{\xi})$ to the elementary propositions.

6.1   The propositions of logic are tautologies.

6.11   The propositions of logic therefore say nothing.
          (They are the analytical propositions.)

6.111   Theories which make a proposition of logic appear
          substantial are always false. One could e.g. believe
          that the words 'true' and 'false' signify two properties
          among other properties, and then it would appear as
          a remarkable fact that every proposition possesses one
          of these properties. This now by no means appears
          self-evident, no more so than the proposition 'All
          roses are either yellow or red' would sound even if it
          were true. Indeed our proposition now gets quite the
          character of a proposition of natural science and this
          is a certain symptom of its being falsely understood.

6.112   The correct explanation of logical propositions
          must give them a peculiar position among all proposi-
          tions

6.113   It is the characteristic mark of logical propositions
          that one can perceive in the symbol alone that they
          are true; and this fact contains in itself the whole
          philosophy of logic. And so also it is one of the most
          important facts that the truth or falsehood of non-
          logical propositions can *not* be recognised from the
          propositions alone.

6.12   The fact that the propositions of logic are tauto-
          logies *shows* the formal – logical – properties of lan-
          guage, of the world.

          That its constituent parts connected together *in this
          way* give a tautology characterises the logic of its
          constituent parts.

          In order that propositions connected together in a
          definite way may give a tautology they must have
          definite properties of structure. That they give a tau-
          tology when *so* connected shows therefore that they
          possess these properties of structure.

6.121   The propositions of logic demonstrate the logical
          properties of propositions, by combining them into
          propositions which say nothing.

          This method could be called a zero-method. In a
          logical proposition propositions are brought into
          equilibrium with one another, and the state of equili-

brium then shows how these propositions must be logically constructed.

6.122   Whence it follows that we can get on without logical propositions, for we can recognise in an adequate notation the formal properties of the propositions by mere inspection.

6.13   Logic is not a theory but a reflexion of the world.
         Logic is transcendental.

6.2   Mathematics is a logical method.
         The propositions of mathematics are equations, and therefore pseudo-propositions.

6.21   Mathematical propositions express no thoughts.

6.211   In life it is never a mathematical proposition which we need, but we use mathematical propositions *only* in order to infer from propositions which do not belong to mathematics to others which equally do not belong to mathematics.
         (In philosophy the question 'Why do we really use that word, that proposition?' constantly leads to valuable results.)

6.22   The logic of the world which the propositions of logic show in tautologies, mathematics shows in equations.

6.23   If two expressions are connected by the sign of equality, this means that they can be substituted for one another. But whether this is the case must show itself in the two expressions themselves.
         It characterises the logical form of two expressions, that they can be substituted for one another.

6.24   The method by which mathematics arrives at its equations is the method of substitution.
         For equations express the substitutability of two expressions, and we proceed from a number of equations to new equations, replacing expressions by others in accordance with the equations.

6.3   Logical research means the investigation of *all regularity*. And outside logic all is accident.

6.31   The so-called law of induction cannot in any case be a logical law, for it is obviously a significant proposition. And therefore it cannot be a law *a priori* either.

6.32   The law of causality is not a law but the form of a law.

6.33   We do not *believe a priori* in a law of conservation, but we *know a priori* the possibility of a logical form.

6.34   All propositions, such as the law of causation, the law of continuity in nature, etc. etc., all these are *a priori* intuitions of possible forms of the propositions of science.

6.36   If there were a law of causality, it might run: 'There are natural laws'.

            But that can clearly not be said: it shows itself.

6.361   In the terminology of Hertz we might say: only *uniform* connexions are *thinkable*.

6.362   What can be described can happen too, and what is excluded by the law of causality cannot be described.

6.363   The process of induction is the process of assuming the *simplest* law that can be made to harmonize with our experience.

6.3631   This process, however, has no logical foundation but only a psychological one.

            It is clear that there are no grounds for believing that the simplest course of events will really happen.

6.36311   That the sun will rise tomorrow, is an hypothesis; and that means that we do not *know* whether it will rise.

6.37   A necessity for one thing to happen because another has happened does not exist. There is only *logical* necessity.

6.371   At the basis of the whole modern view of the world lies the illusion that the so-called laws of nature are the explanations of natural phenomena.

6.372   So people stop short at natural laws as at something unassailable, as did the ancients at God and Fate.

            And they both are right and wrong. But the ancients were clearer, in so far as they recognised one clear terminus, whereas the modern system makes it appear as though *everything* were explained.

6.373   The world is independent of my will.

6.374   Even if everything we wished were to happen, this would only be, so to speak, a favour of fate, for there is no *logical* connexion between will and world, which would guarantee this, and the assumed physical connexion itself we could not again will.

6.375   As there is only a *logical* necessity, so there is only a *logical* impossibility.

6.3751   For two colours, e.g. to be at one place in the visual field, is impossible, logically impossible, for it is excluded by the logical structure of colour.

Let us consider how this contradiction presents itself in physics. Somewhat as follows: That a particle cannot at the same time have two velocities, i.e. that at the same time it cannot be in two places, i.e. that particles in different places at the same time cannot be identical.

(It is clear that the logical product of two elementary propositions can neither be a tautology nor a contradiction. The assertion that a point in the visual field has two different colours at the same time, is a contradiction.)

6.4   All propositions are of equal value.

6.41   The sense of the world must lie outside the world. In the world everything is as it is and happens as it does happen. *In* it there is no value – and if there were, it would be of no value.

If there is a value which is of value, it must lie outside all happening and being-so. For all happening and being-so is accidental.

What makes it non-accidental cannot lie *in* the world, for otherwise this would again be accidental.

It must lie outside the world.

6.42   Hence also there can be no ethical propositions. Propositions cannot express anything higher.

6.421   It is clear that ethics cannot be expressed.

Ethics is transcendental.

(Ethics and aesthetics are one.)

6.423   Of the will as the subject of the ethical we cannot speak. And the will as a phenomenon is only of interest to psychology.

6.43   If good or bad willing changes the world, it can only change the limits of the world, not the facts; not the things that can be expressed in language.

In brief, the world must thereby become quite another. It must so to speak wax or wane as a whole.

The world of the happy is quite another than that of the unhappy.

6.431   As in death, too, the world does not change, but ceases.

6.4311   Death is not an event of life. Death is not lived through.

If by eternity is understood not endless temporal duration but timelessness, then he lives eternally who lives in the present.

Our life is endless in the way that our visual field is without limit.

6.4312   The temporal immortality of the human soul, that is to say, its eternal survival after death, is not only in no way guaranteed, but this assumption in the first place will not do for us what we always tried to make it do. Is a riddle solved by the fact that I survive for ever? Is this eternal life not as enigmatic as our present one? The solution of the riddle of life in space and time lies *outside* space and time.

(It is not problems of natural science which have to be solved).

6.432   *How* the world is, is completely indifferent for what is higher. God does not reveal himself *in* the world.

6.4321   The facts all belong only to the task and not to its performance.

6.44   Not *how* the world is, is the mystical, but *that* it is.

6.45   The contemplation of the world *sub specie aeterni* is its contemplation as a limited whole.

The feeling of the world as a limited whole is the mystical feeling.

6.5   For an answer which cannot be expressed the question too cannot be expressed.

The riddle does not exist.

If a question can be put at all, then it *can* also be answered.

6.51   Scepticism is *not* irrefutable, but palpably senseless, if it would doubt where a question cannot be asked.

For doubt can only exist where there is a question;

a question only where there is an answer, and this only where something *can* be *said*.

6.52   We feel that even if *all possible* scientific questions be answered, then problems of life have still not been touched at all. Of course there is then no question left, and just this is the answer.

6.251   The solution of the problem of life is seen in the vanishing of this problem.

(Is not this the reason why men to whom after long doubting the sense of life became clear, could not then say wherein this sense consisted?)

6.522   There is indeed the inexpressible. This *shows* itself; it is the mystical.

6.53   The right method of philosophy would be this. To say nothing except what can be said, i.e. the propositions of natural science, i.e. something that has nothing to do with philosophy: and then always, when someone else wished to say something metaphysical, to demonstrate to him that he has given no meaning to certain signs in his propositions. This method would be unsatisfying to the other – he would not have the feeling that we were teaching him philosophy – but it would be the only strictly correct method.

6.54   My propositions are elucidatory in this way: he who understands me finally recognises them as senseless, when he has climbed out through them, on them, over them. (He must so to speak throw away the ladder, after he has climbed up on it.)

He must surmount these propositions; then he sees the world rightly.

7   Whereof one cannot speak, thereof one must be silent.

2

The Rejection of Logical Atomism

Concept and Object, Property and Substrate

When Frege and Russell talk of concept and object they really mean property and thing; and here I'm thinking in particular of a spatial body and its colour. Or one can say: concept and object are the same as predicate and subject. The subject-predicate form is one of the forms of expression that occur in human languages. It is the form 'x is y' ('x $\in$ y'): 'My brother is tall', 'The storm is nearby', 'This circle is red', 'Augustus is strong', '2 is a number', 'This thing is a piece of coal'.

The concept of a material point in physics is an abstraction from the material objects of experience; in the same way the subject–predicate form of logic is an abstraction from the subject-predicate form of our languages. The pure subject-predicate form is supposed to be a $\in$ f(x), where 'a' is the name of an object. Now let's look for an application of this schema. The first things that come to mind as 'names of objects' are the names of persons and of other spatial objects (the Koh-i-Noor). Such names are given by ostensive definitions ('that ↗ is called "N" '). Such a definition might be conceived as a rule substituting the word 'N' for a gesture pointing to the object, with the proviso that the gesture can always be used in place of the name. Thus, I may have explained 'this man is called "N" ', and I go on to say ' "N" is a mathematician', 'N is lazy', and in each of these sentences I might have said 'this man' (with the ostensive gesture) instead of 'N'. (In that case, incidentally it would have been better to phrase the ostensive definition 'this man is called "N" '[1] or 'I want to call this man "N" ', because the version above is also the proposition that this man bears this name).

---

[1] There appears to be something wrong with the German text here. Possibly Wittgenstein meant to write 'let this man be called "N" ' and inadvertently wrote a version which is the same as the one he is correcting. (Trs.)

However, this isn't the normal way of using a name; it is an essential feature of the normal use that I can't fall back on to a sign of the gesture language in place of the name. That's to say, in the way in which we use the name 'N', if N goes out of the room and later a man comes into the room it makes sense to ask whether this man is N, whether he is the same man as the one who left the room earlier. And the sentence 'N has come back into the room' only makes sense if I can decide the question. And its sense will vary with the criterion for this being the object that I earlier called 'N'. Different kinds of criteria will make different rules hold for the sign 'N', will make it a 'name' in a different sense of the word. Thus the word 'name' and the corresponding word 'object' are each headings to countless different lists of rules.

If we give names to spatial objects, our use of such names depends on a criterion of identity which presupposes the impenetrability of bodies and the continuity of their movement. So if I could treat two bodies A and B as I can treat their shadows on the wall, making two into one and one into two again, it would be senseless to ask which of the two after the division is A and which is B, unless I go on to introduce a totally new criterion of identity e.g. the direction of their movements. (There is a rule for the name of a river arising from the confluence of two rivers, thus:

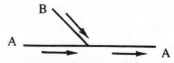

The resulting river takes the name of that source in whose approximate direction it flows onward.)

Think of the possible criteria of identity for things like colour patches in my visual field (or figures on a cinema screen) and of the different kinds of use of names given to such patches or figures.

If we turn to the form of expression '($\exists$x) . fx' it's clear that this is a sublimation of the form of expression in our language: 'There are human beings on this island' 'There are stars that we do not see'. To every proposition of the form '($\exists$x) . fx' there is supposed to correspond a proposition 'fa', and 'a' is supposed to be a name. So one must be able to say '($\exists$x) . fx, namely a and b', ('There are some values of x, which satisfy fx, namely a and b'), or '(∃x) . fx, e.g. a', etc. And this is indeed possible in a case like 'There are human beings on this island, namely Messrs A, B, C, D.' But then is it essential to the sense of the sentence 'There are men on this island' that we should be able to name them, and fix a particular criterion for their identification? That is only so in the case where the proposition '(∃x) . fx' is defined as a disjunction of propositions of the form 'f(x)', if e.g. it is laid down that 'There are men on this island' means 'Either Mr A or Mr B or Mr C or Mr D. or Mr E is on this island' – if, that is, one determines the concept 'man' extensionally (which of course is quite contrary to the normal use of this word.) (On the other hand the concept 'primary colour' really is determined extensionally.)

So it doesn't always make sense when presented with a proposition '(∃x) . fx' to ask '*Which* xs satisfy f?' 'Which red circle a centimetre across is in the middle of this square'? – One mustn't confuse the question 'which object satisfies f?' with the question '*what sort of* object . . . etc.?' The first question would have to be answered by a name, and so the answer would have to be able to take the form 'f(a)'; the question '*what sort of* . . .?' is answered by '(∃x) . fx . φx'. So it may be senseless to ask 'which red spot do you see?' and yet make sense to ask 'what kind of a red spot do you see (a round one, a square one, etc.)?'

I would like to say: the old logic contains more convention and physics than has been realised. If a noun is the name of a *body*, a verb is to denote a movement, and an adjective to denote a property of a body, it is easy to see how much that logic presupposes; and it is reasonable to conjecture that those original presuppositions go still deeper into the application of the words, and the logic of propositions.

(Suppose we were set the task of projecting figures of various shapes on a given plane I into a plane II. We could then fix a method of projection (say orthogonal projection) and carry out the mapping in accordance with it. We could also easily make inferences from the representations on plane II about the figures on plane I. But we could also adopt another procedure: we might decide that the representations in the second plane should all be circles, no matter what the copied figures in the first plane might be. (Perhaps this is the most convenient form of representation for us.) That is, different figures on I are mapped onto

II by different methods of projection. In order in this case to construe the circles in II as representations of the figures in I, I shall have to give the method of projection for each circle; the mere fact that a figure in I is represented as a circle in II[2] by itself tells us nothing about the shape of the figure copied. That an image in II is a circle is just the established norm of our mapping. – Well, the same thing happens when we depict reality in our language in accordance with the subject-predicate form. The subject-predicate form serves as a projection of countless different logical forms.

Frege's 'Concept and Object' is the same as subject and predicate.

If a table is painted brown, then it's easy to think of the wood as bearer of the property brown and you can imagine what remains the same when the colour changes. Even in the case of *one* particular circle which appears now red, now blue. It is thus easy to imagine *what* is red, but difficult to imagine what is circular. What *remains* in this case if form and colour alter? For position is part of the form and it is arbitrary for me to lay down that the centre should stay fixed and the only changes in form be changes in the radius.

We must once more adhere to ordinary language and say that a *patch* is circular.

It is clear that here the phrase 'bearer of a property' in this context conveys a completely wrong – an impossible – picture. If I have a lump of clay, I can consider it as the bearer of a form, and that, roughly, is where this picture comes from.

'The patch changes its form' and 'the lump of clay changes its form' are different forms of propositions.

You can say 'Measure whether *that* is a circle' or 'See whether *that* over there is a hat'. You can also say 'Measure whether that is a circle or an ellipse', but not '. . . whether that is a circle or a hat'; nor 'See whether that is a hat or red'.

If I point to a curve and say 'That is a circle' then someone can object that if it were not a circle it would no longer be *that*. That is to say, what I mean by the word 'that' must be independent of what I assert about it.

[2]   I have here corrected an inadvertent transposition of 'I' and 'II' in Wittgenstein's German. (Trs.)

('Was *that* thunder, or gunfire?' Here you could not ask 'Was that a noise?')

How are two circles of the same size distinguished? This question makes it sound as if they were pretty nearly one circle and only distinguished by a nicety.

In the technique of representation by equations what is common is expressed by the form of the equation, and the difference by the difference in the coordinates of the centres.

So it is as if what corresponds with the objects falling under the concept were here the coordinates of the centres.

Couldn't you then say, instead of 'This is a circle', 'This point is the centre of a circle'? For to be the centre of a circle is an external property of the point.

What is necessary to a description that – say – a book is in a certain position? The internal description of the book, i.e. of the concept, and a description of its place which it would be possible to give by giving the co-ordinates of three points. The proposition 'Such a book is *here*' would mean that it had *these* three co-ordinates. For the specification of the 'here' must not prejudge *what* is here.

But doesn't it come to the same thing whether I say '*This* is a book' or '*Here* is a book'? The proposition would then amount to saying, 'These are three corners of such a book'.

Similarly you can also say 'This circle is the projection of a sphere' or 'This is a man's appearance'.

All that I am saying comes to this, that $\Phi(x)$ must be an *external* description of x.

If in this sense I now say in three-dimensional space 'Here is a circle' and on another occasion 'Here is a sphere' are the two 'here's' of the same type? I want to ask: can one significantly say of the same 'object': it is a circle, and: it is a sphere? Is the subject of each of these predicates of the same type? Both could be the three coordinates of the relevant centre-point. But the position of the circle in three-dimensional space is not fixed by the co-ordinates of its centre.

On the other hand you can of course say 'It's not the noise, but the colour that makes me nervous' and here it might look as if a variable assumed a colour and a noise as values. ('Sounds and colours can be used as vehicles of communication'.) It is clear that this proposition is of the same kind as 'if you hear a shot, or see me wave, run'. For this is the kind of co-ordination on the basis of which a heard or seen language functions.

'Is it conceivable that two things have all their properties in common?' – If it isn't conceivable, then neither is its opposite.

We do indeed talk about a circle, its diameter, etc. etc., as if we were describing a concept in complete abstraction from the objects falling under it. – But in that case 'circle' is not a predicate in the original sense. And in general geometry is the place where concepts from the most different regions get mixed up together.

* * *

Elementary propositions

A

Can a logical product be hidden in a proposition? And if so, how does one tell, and what methods do we have of bringing the hidden element of a proposition to light? If we haven't yet got a method, then we can't speak of something being hidden or possibly hidden. And if we do have a method of discovery then the only way in which something like a logical product can be hidden in a proposition is the way in which a quotient like 753/3 is hidden until the division has been carried out.

The question whether a logical product is hidden in a sentence is a mathematical problem.

So an elementary proposition is a proposition which, in the calculus as I am now using it, is not represented as a truth-function of other sentences.

The idea of constructing elementary propositions (as e.g. Carnap has tried to do) rests on a false notion of logical analysis. It is not the task of that analysis to discover a *theory* of elementary propositions, like discovering principles of mechanics.

My notion in the *Tractatus Logico-Philosophicus* was wrong:

1) because I wasn't clear about the sense of the words 'a logical product is *hidden* in a sentence' (and suchlike), 2) because I too thought that logical analysis had to bring to light what was hidden (as chemical and physical analysis does).

The proposition 'this place is now red' (or 'this circle is now red') can be called an elementary proposition if this means that it is neither a truth-function of other propositions nor defined as such. (Here I am disregarding combinations such as p . : qv ~ q and the like.)

But from 'a is now red' there follows 'a is now not green' and so elementary propositions in this sense aren't independent of each other like the elementary propositions in the calculus I once described – a calculus to which, misled as I was by a false notion of reduction, I thought that the whole use of propositions must be reducible.

B

If you want to use the appellation 'elementary proposition' as I did in the *Tractatus Logico-Philosophicus*, and as Russell used 'atomic proposition', you may call the sentence 'Here there is a red rose' an elementary proposition. That is to say, it doesn't contain a truth-function and it isn't defined by an expression which contains one. But if we're to say that a proposition isn't an elementary proposition unless its complete logical analysis shows that it isn't built out of other propositions by truth-functions, we are presupposing that we have an idea of what such an 'analysis' would be. Formerly, I myself spoke of a 'complete analysis', and I used to believe that philosophy had to give a definitive dissection of propositions so as to set out clearly all their connections and remove all possibilities of misunderstanding. I spoke as if there was a calculus in which such a dissection would be possible. I vaguely had in mind something like the definition that Russell had given for the definite article, and I used to think that in a similar way one would be able to use visual impressions etc. to define the concept say of a sphere, and thus exhibit once for all the connections between the concepts and lay bare the source of all misunderstandings, etc. At the root of all this there was a false and idealized picture of the use of language. Of course, in particular cases one can clarify by definitions the connections between the different types of use of expressions. Such a definition may be useful in the case of the connection between 'visual impression' and 'sphere'. But for this purpose it is not a definition of the concept of a physical sphere that we need; instead we must describe a language game related to our own, or rather a whole series of related language games, and it will be in these that such definitions may occur. Such a contrast destroys grammatical prejudices and makes it possible for us to see the use of a word as it really is, instead of *inventing* the use for the word.

There could perhaps be a calculus for dissecting propositions; it isn't hard to imagine one. Then it becomes a problem of calculation to discover whether a proposition is or is not an elementary proposition.

The question whether e.g. a logical product is hidden in a sentence is a mathematical problem. – What 'hidden' means here is defined by the method of discovery (or, as it might be, by the lack of a method).

.   .   .   .

What gives us the idea that there is a kind of agreement between thought and reality? – Instead of 'agreement' here one might say with a clear conscience 'pictorial character'.

But is this pictorial character an agreement? In the *Tractatus Logico-Philosophicus* I said something like: it is an agreement of form. But that is an error.

First of all, 'picture' here is ambiguous. One wants to say that an order is the picture of the action which was carried out on the order; but also, a picture of the action which *is to be* carried out as an order.

We may say: a blueprint *serves as a picture* of the object which the workman is to make from it.

And here we might call the way in which the workman turns such a drawing into an artefact 'the method of projection'. We might now express ourselves thus: the method of projection mediates between the drawing and the object, it reaches from the drawing to the artefact. Here we are comparing the method of projection with projection lines which go from one figure to another. – But if the method of projection is a bridge, it is a bridge which isn't built until the application is made. – This comparison conceals the fact that the picture *plus* the projection lines leaves open various methods of application; it makes it look as if what is depicted, even if it does not exist in fact, is determined by the picture and the projection lines in an ethereal manner; every bit as determined, that is to say, as if it did exist. (It is 'determined give or take a yes or no.') In that case what we may call 'picture' is the blueprint plus the method of its application. And we now imagine the method as something which is attached to the blueprint whether or not it is used. (One can '*describe*' an application even if it doesn't exist).

Now I would like to ask 'How can the blueprint be used as a representation, unless there is already an agreement with what is to be made?' – But what does that mean? Well, perhaps this: how could I play the notes in the score on the piano if they didn't already have a relationship to particular types of movement of the hand? Of course such a relationship *sometimes* consists in a certain agreement, but sometimes not in any agreement, but merely in our having learnt to apply the signs in a particular way. What the comparison between the method of projection and the projection lines connecting the picture with the object does is to make all these cases alike – because *that* is what attracts us. You may say: I count the projection lines as part of the picture – but not the method of projection.

You may of course also say: I count a *description* of a method of projection as part of the picture.

So I am imagining that the difference between proposition and reality is ironed out by the lines of projection belonging to the picture, the thought, and that no further room is left for a method of application, but only for agreement and disagreement.

Is time essential to propositions? Comparison between time and truth-functions

If we had grammar set out in the form of a book, it wouldn't be a series of chapters side by side, it would have quite a different structure. And it is here, if I am right, that we would have to see the distinction between phenomenological and non-phenomenological. There would be, say, a chapter about colours, setting out the rules for the use of colour-words; but there would be nothing comparable in what the grammar had to say about the words 'not', 'or', etc. (the 'logical constants').

It would, for instance, be a consequence of the rules, that these latter words unlike the colour words were usable in every proposition; and the generality belonging to this 'every' would not be the kind that is discovered by experience, but the generality of a supreme rule of the game admitting of no appeal.

How does the temporal character of facts manifest itself? How does it express itself, if not by certain expressions having to occur in our sentences? That means: how does the temporal character of facts express itself, if not grammatically? 'Temporal character' – that doesn't mean that I come at 5 o'clock, but that I come at some time or other, i.e. that my proposition has the structure it has.

We are inclined to say that negation and disjunction are connected with the nature of the proposition, but that time is connected with its content rather than with its nature.

But if two things are equally universal, how can it show itself in grammar that one of them is connected with the nature of the proposition and the other is not?

Or should I have said that time is not equally universal since mathematical propositions can be negated and occur in disjunctions, without being temporal? There is indeed a connection here, though this form of portraying the matter is misleading.

But that shows what I mean by 'proposition.' or 'nature of the proposition'.

Why – I want to ask – is the temporal character of propositions so universal?

Might one also put the question thus: 'How does it happen that every fact of experience can be brought into a relationship with what is shown by a clock?'

Having two kinds of generality in the way I spoke of would be as strange as if there were two equally exceptionless rules of a game and one of them were pronounced to be more fundamental. As if one could ask whether in chess the king or the chess board was more important; which of the two was more essential, and which more accidental.

There's at least one question that seems in order: suppose I had written up the grammar, and the different chapters on the colour words, etc. etc. were there one after the other, like rules for each of the chess pieces, how would I know that those were *all* the chapters? If there turns out to be a common property in all the chapters so far in existence, we seem to have encountered a logical generality that is not an essential, i.e. *a priori* generality. But we can't say that the fact that chess is played with 16 pieces is any less essential to it than its being played on a chessboard.

Since time and the truth-functions taste so different, and since they manifest their nature only and wholly in grammar, it is grammar that must explain the different taste.
One tastes like content, the other like form of representation.
They taste as different as a plan and a line through a plan.
It appears to me that the present, as it occurs in the proposition 'the sky is blue' (if this proposition isn't meant as a hypothesis), is not a form of time, so that the present in *this* sense is atemporal.

Does time enter into a landscape picture? or into a still life?
Literature consisting of descriptions of landscapes.

It is noteworthy that the time of which I am here speaking is not time in a physical sense. We are not concerned with measuring time. It is fishy that something which is unconnected with measurement is supposed to have a role in propositions like that of physical time in the hypotheses of physics.

Discuss:
The distinction between the logic of the content and the logic of the propositional form in general. The former seems, so to speak, brightly coloured, and the latter plain; the former seems to be concerned with what the picture represents, the latter to be a characteristic of the pictorial form like a frame.

By comparison with the way in which the truth-functions are applicable to all propositions, it seems to us accidental that all propositions contain time in some way or other.
The former seems to be connected with their nature as propositions, the latter with the nature of the reality we encounter.

((Added later in the margins))
A sentence can contain time in very different senses.
You are hurting me.
The weather is marvellous outside.
The Inn flows into the Danube.
Water freezes at 0°.
I often make slips of the pen
Some time ago . . .
I hope he will come.
At 5 o'clock.
This kind of steel is excellent.
The earth was once a ball of gas.

★ ★ ★

If we say thinking is essentially operating with signs, the first
question you might ask is: 'What are signs?' – Instead of giving
any kind of general answer to this question, I shall propose to
you to look closely at particular cases which we should call
'operating with signs'. Let us look at a simple example of operating with words. I give someone the order: 'fetch me six apples
from the grocer', and I will describe a way of making use of such
an order: The words 'six apples' are written on a bit of paper, the
paper is handed to the grocer, the grocer compares the word
'apple' with labels on different shelves. He finds it to agree with
one of the labels, counts from 1 to the number written on the
slip of paper, and for every number counted takes a fruit off the
shelf and puts it in a bag. – And here you have *one* use of words.
I shall in the future again and again draw your attention to what
I shall call language games. These are ways of using signs simpler than those in which we use the signs of our highly complicated everyday language. Language games are the forms of
language with which a child begins to make use of words. The
study of language games is the study of primitive forms of
language or primitive languages. If we want to study the problems of truth and falsehood, of the agreement and disagreement
of propositions with reality, of the nature of assertion, assumption, and question, we shall with great advantage look at primitive forms of language in which these forms of thinking appear
without the confusing background of highly complicated pro-

cesses of thought. When we look at such simple forms of language, the mental mist which seems to enshroud our ordinary use of language disappears. We see activities, reactions, which are clear-cut and transparent. On the other hand we recognize in these simple processes forms of language not separated by a break from our more complicated ones. We see that we can build up the complicated forms from the primitive ones by gradually adding new forms.

Now what makes it difficult for us to take this line of investigation is our craving for generality.

★ ★ ★

But how many kinds of sentence are there? Say assertion, question, and command? – There are *countless* kinds: countless different kinds of use of what we call 'symbols', 'words', 'sentences'. And this multiplicity is not something fixed, given once for all; but new types of language, new language-games, as we may say, come into existence, and others become obsolete and get forgotten. (We can get a *rough picture* of this from the changes in mathematics.)

Here the term 'language-*game*' is meant to bring into prominence the fact that the *speaking* of language is part of an activity, or of a form of life.

Review the multiplicity of language-games in the following e xamples, and in others:

Giving orders, and obeying them –
Describing the appearance of an object, or giving its measurements –
Constructing an object from a description (a drawing) –
Reporting an event –
Speculating about an event –

Imagine a picture representing a boxer in a particular stance. Now, this picture can be used to tell someone how he should stand, should hold himself; or how he should not hold himself; or how a particular man did stand in such-and-such a place; and so on. One might (using the language of chemistry) call this picture a proposition-radical. This will be how Frege thought of the 'assumption'.

Forming and testing a hypothesis –
Presenting the results of an experiment in tables and diagrams –
Making up a story; and reading it –
Play-acting –
Singing catches –
Guessing riddles –
Making a joke; telling it –
Solving a problem in practical arithmetic –
Translating from one language into another –
Asking, thanking, cursing, greeting, praying.

– It is interesting to compare the multiplicity of the tools in language and of the ways they are used, the multiplicity of kinds of word and sentence, with what logicians have said about the structure of language. (Including the author of the *Tractatus Logico-Philosophicus*.)

★ ★ ★

Here we come up against the great question that lies behind all these considerations. – For someone might object against me: 'You take the easy way out! You talk about all sorts of language-games, but have nowhere said what the essence of a language-game, and hence of language, is: what is common to all these activities, and what makes them into language or parts of language. So you let yourself off the very part of the investigation that once gave you yourself most headache, the part about the *general form of propositions* and of language.'

And this is true. – Instead of producing something common to all that we call language, I am saying that these phenomena have no one thing in common which makes us use the same word for all, – but that they are *related* to one another in many different ways. And it is because of this relationship, or these relationships, that we call them all 'language'. I will try to explain this.

Consider for example the proceedings that we call 'games'. I mean board-games, card-games, ball-games, Olympic games, and so on. What is common to them all? – Don't say: 'There *must* be something common, or they would not be called "games" ' – but *look and see* whether there is anything common to all. – For if you look at them you will not see something that is common to *all*, but similarities, relationships, and a whole series of them at that. To repeat: don't think, but look! – Look for example at board-games, with their multifarious relationships. Now pass to card-games; here you find many correspondences with the first group, but many common features drop out, and others appear. When we pass next to ball-games, much that is common is retained, but much is lost. – Are they all 'amusing'? Compare chess with noughts and crosses. Or is there always winning and losing, or competition between players? Think of patience. In ball games there is winning and losing; but when a child throws his ball at the wall and catches it again, this feature has disappeared. Look at the parts played by skill and luck; and at the difference between skill in chess and skill in tennis. Think now of games like ring-a-ring-a-roses; here is the element of amusement, but how many other characteristic features have disappeared! And we can go through the many, many other groups of games in the same way; can see how similarities crop up and disappear.

And the result of this examination is: we see a complicated network of similarities overlapping and criss-crossing: sometimes overall similarities, sometimes similarities of detail.

I can think of no better expression to characterize these similarities than 'family resemblances'; for the various resemblances between members of a family: build, features, colour of eyes, gait, temperament, etc. etc. overlap and criss-cross in the same way. – And I shall say: 'games' form a family.

And for instance the kinds of number form a family in the same way. Why do we call something a 'number'? Well, perhaps because it has a – direct – relationship with several things that have hitherto been called number; and this can be said to give it an indirect relationship to other things we call the same name. And we extend our concept of number as in spinning a thread we twist fibre on fibre. And the strength of the thread does not reside in the fact that some one fibre runs through its whole length, but in the overlapping of many fibres.

But if someone wished to say: 'There is something common to all these constructions – namely the disjunction of all their common properties' – I should reply: Now you are only playing with words. One might as well say: 'Something runs through the whole thread – namely the continuous overlapping of those fibres'.

3

Meaning and Understanding

'Cum ipsi (majores homines) appellabant rem aliquam, et cum secundum eam vocem corpus ad aliquid movebant, videbam, et tenebam hoc ab eis vocari rem illam, quod sonabant, cum eam vellent ostendere. Hoc autem eos velle ex motu corporis aperiebatur: tamquam verbis naturalibus omnium gentium, quae fiunt vultu et nutu oculorum, ceterorumque membrorum actu, et sonitu vocis indicante affectionem animi in petendis, habendis, rejiciendis, fugiendisve rebus. Ita verba in variis sententiis locis suis posita, et crebro audita, quarum rerum signa essent, paulatim colligebam, measque jam voluntates, edomito in eis signis ore, per haec enuntiabam.' (Augustine, *Confessions*, I. 8.)[1]

These words, it seems to me, give us a particular picture of the essence of human language. It is this: the individual words in language name objects – sentences are combinations of such names. — In this picture of language we find the roots of the following idea: Every word has a meaning. This meaning is correlated with the word. It is the object for which the word stands.

Augustine does not speak of there being any difference between kinds of word. If you describe the learning of language in this way you are, I believe, thinking primarily of nouns like 'table', 'chair', 'bread', and of people's names, and only

---

[1] 'When they (my elders) named some object, and accordingly moved towards something, I saw this and I grasped that the thing was called by the sound they uttered when they meant to point it out. Their intention was shewn by their bodily movements, as it were the natural language of all peoples: the expression of the face, the play of the eyes, the movement of other parts of the body, and the tone of voice which expresses our state of mind in seeking, having, rejecting, or avoiding something. Thus, as I heard words repeatedly used in their proper places in various sentences, I gradually learnt to understand what objects they signified; and after I had trained my mouth to form these signs, I used them to express my own desires.'

secondarily of the names of certain actions and properties; and of the remaining kinds of word as something that will take care of itself.

One thinks that learning language consists in giving names to objects. Viz, to human beings, to shapes, to colours, to pains, to moods, to numbers, etc.. To repeat – naming is something like attaching a label to a thing. One can say that this is preparatory to the use of a word. But *what* is it a preparation *for*?

'We name things and then we can talk about them: can refer to them in talk.' – As if what we did next were given with the mere act of naming. As if there were only one thing called 'talking about a thing'. Whereas in fact we do the most various things with our sentences. Think of exclamations alone, with their completely different functions.

> Water!
> Away!
> Ow!
> Help!
> Fine!
> No!

Are you inclined still to call these words 'names of objects'?

One can ostensively define a proper name, the name of a colour, the name of a material, a numeral, the name of a point of the compass and so on. The definition of the number two, 'That is called "two" ' – pointing to two nuts – is perfectly exact. – But how can two be defined like that? The person one gives the definition to doesn't know what one wants to call 'two'; he will suppose that 'two' is the name given to *this* group of nuts! — He *may* suppose this; but perhaps he does not. He might make the opposite mistake; when I want to assign a name to this group of nuts, he might understand it as a numeral. And he might equally well take the name of a person, of which I give an ostensive definition, as that of a colour, of a race, or even of a point of the compass. That is to say: an ostensive definition can be variously interpreted in *every* case.

Perhaps you say: two can only be ostensively defined in *this* way: 'This *number* is called "two" '. For the word 'number' here shews what place in language, in grammar, we assign to the word. But this means that the word 'number' must be explained before the ostensive definition can be understood. – The word 'number' in the definition does indeed shew this place; does shew the post at which we station the word. And we can prevent misunderstandings by saying: 'This *colour* is called so-and-so', 'This *length* is called so-and-so', and so on. That is to say: misunderstandings are sometimes averted in this way. But is there only *one* way of taking the word 'colour' or 'length'? – Well, they just need defining. – Defining, then, by means of other words! And what about the last definition in this chain? (Do not say: 'There isn't a "last" definition'. That is just as if you chose to say: 'There isn't a last house in this road; one can always build an additional one'.)

Whether the word 'number' is necessary in the ostensive definition depends on whether without it the other person takes the definition otherwise than I wish. And that will depend on the circumstances under which it is given, and on the person I give it to.

And how he 'takes' the definition is seen in the use that he makes of the word defined.

So one might say: the ostensive definition explains the use – the meaning – of the word when the overall role of the word in language is clear. Thus if I know that someone means to explain a colour-word to me the ostensive definition. 'That is called "sepia" ' will help me to understand the word. – And you can say this, so long as you do not forget that all sorts of problems attach to the words 'to know' or 'to be clear'.

One has already to know (or be able to do) something in order to be capable of asking a thing's name. But what does one have to know?

When one shews someone the king in chess and says: 'This is the king', this does not tell him the use of this piece – unless he already knows the rules of the game up to this last point: the shape of the king. You could imagine his having learnt the rules of the game without ever having been shewn an actual piece. The shape of the chessman corresponds here to the sound or shape of a word.

One can also imagine someone's having learnt the game without ever learning or formulating rules. He might have learnt

quite simple board-games first, by watching, and have pro-
gressed to more and more complicated ones. He too might be
given the explanation 'This is the king', – if, for instance, he
were being shewn chessmen of a shape he was not used to. This
explanation again only tells him the use of the piece because, as
we might say, the place for it was already prepared. Or even: we
shall only say that it tells him the use, if the place is already
prepared. And in this case it is so, not because the person to
whom we give the explanation already knows rules, but because
in another sense he is already master of a game.

Consider this further case: I am explaining chess to someone;
and I begin by pointing to a chessman and saying: 'This is the
king; it can move like this, . . . and so on.' – In this case we shall
say: the words 'This is the king' (or 'This is called the "king" ')
are a definition only if the learner already 'knows what a piece in
a game is'. That is, if he has already played other games, or has
watched other people playing 'and understood' – *and similar
things*. Further, only under these conditions will he be able to
ask relevantly in the course of learning the game: 'What do you
call this?' – that is, this piece in a game.

We may say: only someone who already knows how to do
something with it can significantly ask a name.

And we can imagine the person who is asked replying: 'Settle
the name yourself' – and now the one who asked would have to
manage everything for himself.

Someone coming into a strange country will sometimes learn
the language of the inhabitants from ostensive definitions that
they give him; and he will often have to *guess* the meaning of these
definitions; and will guess sometimes right, sometimes wrong.

And now, I think, we can say: Augustine describes the learning of human language as if the child came into a strange
country and did not understand the language of the country;
that is, as if it already had a language, only not this one. Or
again: as if the child could already *think*, only not yet speak. And
'think' would here mean something like 'talk to itself'.

★ ★ ★

What is the meaning of a word?

Let us attack this question by asking, first, what is an explanation of the meaning of a word; what does the explanation of a word look like?

The way this question helps us is analogous to the way the question 'how do we measure a length?' helps us to understand the problem 'what is length?'

The questions 'What is length?', 'What is meaning?', 'What is the number one?' etc., produce in us a mental cramp. We feel that we can't point to anything in reply to them and yet ought to point to something. (We are up against one of the great sources of philosophical bewilderment: we try to find a substance for a substantive.)

Asking first 'What's an explanation of meaning?' has two advantages. You in a sense bring the question 'what is meaning?' down to earth. For, surely, to understand the meaning of 'meaning' you ought also to understand the meaning of 'explanation of meaning'. Roughly: 'let's ask what the explanation of meaning is, for whatever that explains will be the meaning.' Studying the grammar of the expression 'explanation of meaning' will teach you something about the grammar of the word 'meaning' and will cure you of the temptation to look about you for something which you might call the 'meaning'.

What one generally calls 'explanations of the meaning of a word' can, *very roughly*, be divided into verbal and ostensive definitions. It will be seen later in what sense this division is only rough and provisional (and that it is, is an important point). The verbal definition, as it takes us from one verbal expression to another, in a sense gets us no further. In the ostensive definition however we seem to make a much more real step towards learning the meaning.

One difficulty which strikes us is that for many words in our language there do not seem to be ostensive definitions; e.g. for such words as 'one', 'number', 'not', etc.

Question: Need the ostensive definition itself be understood? – Can't the ostensive definition be misunderstood?

If the definition explains the meaning of a word, surely it can't be essential that you should have heard the word before. It is the ostensive definition's business to *give* it a meaning. Let us then explain the word 'tove' by pointing to a pencil and saying 'this is tove'. (Instead of 'this is tove' I could here have said 'this is called "tove" '. I point this out to remove, once and for all, the idea that the words of the ostensive definition predicate something of the defined; the confusion between the sentence 'this is red', attributing the colour red to something, and the ostensive definition 'this is called "red" '.) Now the ostensive definition 'this is tove' can be interpreted in all sorts of ways. I will give a few such interpretations and use English words with well established usage. The definition then can be interpreted to mean:

'This is a pencil',
'This is round',
'This is wood',
'This is one',
'This is hard', etc. etc.

One might object to this argument that all these interpretations presuppose another word-language. And this objection is significant if by 'interpretation' we only mean 'translation into a word-language'. – Let me give some hints which might make this clearer. Let us ask ourselves what is our criterion when we say that someone has interpreted the ostensive definition in a particular way. Suppose I give to an Englishman the ostensive definition 'this is what the Germans call "Buch" '. Then, in the great majority of cases, at any rate, the English word 'book' will come into the Englishman's mind. We may say he has interpreted 'Buch' to mean 'book'. The case will be different if e.g. we point to a thing which he has never seen before and say: 'This is a banjo'. Possibly the word 'guitar' will then come into his mind, possibly no word at all but the image of a similar instrument, possibly nothing at all. Supposing then I give him the order 'now pick a banjo from amongst those things.' If he picks what we call a 'banjo' we might say 'he has given the word "banjo" the correct interpretation'; if he picks some other instrument – 'he has interpreted "banjo" to mean "string instrument" '.

We say 'he has given the word "banjo" this or that interpretation', and are inclined to assume a definite act of interpretation besides the act of choosing.

Our problem is analogous to the following:

If I give someone the order 'fetch me a red flower from that meadow', how is he to know what sort of flower to bring, as I have only given him a *word*?

Now the answer one might suggest first is that he went to look for a red flower carrying a red image in his mind, and comparing it with the flowers to see which of them had the colour of the image. Now there is such a way of searching, and it is not at all essential that the image we use should be a mental one. In fact the process may be this: I carry a chart co-ordinating names and coloured squares. When I hear the order 'fetch me etc.' I draw my finger across the chart from the word 'red' to a certain square, and I go and look for a flower which has the same colour as the square. But this is not the only way of searching and it isn't the usual way. We go, look about us, walk up to a flower and pick it, without comparing it to anything. To see that the process of obeying the order can be of this kind, consider the order '*imagine* a red patch'. You are not tempted in this case to think that *before* obeying you must have imagined a red patch to serve you as a pattern for the red patch which you were ordered to imagine.

Now you might ask: do we *interpret* the words before we obey the order? And in some cases you will find that you do something which might be called interpreting before obeying, in some cases not. – It seems that there are *certain definite* mental processes bound up with the working of language, processes through which alone language can function. I mean the processes of understanding and meaning. The signs of our language seem dead without these mental processes; and it might seem that the only function of the signs is to induce such processes, and that these are the things we ought really to be interested in. Thus, if you are asked what is the relation between a name and the thing it names, you will be inclined to answer that the relation is a psychological one, and perhaps when you say this you think in particular of the mechanism of association. – We are tempted to think that the action of language consists of two parts; an inorganic part, the handling of signs, and an organic part, which we may call understanding these signs, meaning them, interpreting them, thinking. These latter activities seem to take place in a queer kind of medium, the mind; and the mechanism of the mind, the nature of which, it seems, we don't quite understand, can bring about effects which no material mechanism could. Thus e.g. a thought (which is such a mental process) can agree or disagree with reality; I am able to think of a man who isn't present; I am able to imagine him, "mean him" in a remark which I make about him, even if he is thousands of miles away or dead. 'What a queer mechanism,' one might say, 'the mechanism of wishing must be if I can wish that which will never happen'.

There is one way of avoiding at least partly the occult appearance of the process of thinking, and it is, to replace in these processes any working of the imagination by acts of looking at real objects. Thus it may seem essential that, at least in certain cases, when I hear the word 'red' with understanding, a red image should be before my mind's eye. But why should I not substitute seeing a red bit of paper for imagining a red patch? The visual image will only be the more vivid. Imagine a man always carrying a sheet of paper in his pocket on which the names of colours are co-ordinated with coloured patches. You may say that it would be a nuisance to carry such a table of samples about with you, and that the mechanism of association is what we always use instead of it. But this is irrelevant; and in many cases it is not even true. If, for instance, you were ordered to paint a particular shade of blue, called 'Prussian Blue', you might have to use a table to lead you from the word 'Prussian Blue' to a sample of the colour, which would serve you as your copy.

We could perfectly well, for our purposes, replace every process of imagining by a process of looking at an object or by painting, drawing or modelling; and every process of speaking to oneself by speaking aloud or by writing.

Frege ridiculed the formalist conception of mathematics by saying that the formalists confused the unimportant thing, the sign, with the important, the meaning. Surely, one wishes to say, mathematics does not treat of dashes on a bit of paper. Frege's idea could be expressed thus: the propositions of mathematics, if they were just complexes of dashes, would be dead and utterly uninteresting, whereas they obviously have a kind of life. And the same, of course, could be said of any proposition: Without a sense, or without the thought, a proposition would be an utterly dead and trivial thing. And further it seems clear that no adding of inorganic signs can make the proposition live. And the conclusion which one draws from this is that what must be added to the dead signs in order to make a live proposition is something immaterial, with properties different from all mere signs.

But if we had to name anything which is the life of the sign, we should have to say that it was its *use*.

If the meaning of the sign (roughly, that which is of import-ance about the sign) is an image built up in our minds when we see or hear the sign, then first let us adopt the method we just described of replacing this mental image by some outward ob-ject seen, e.g. a painted or modelled image. Then why should the written sign plus this painted image be alive if the written sign alone was dead? – In fact, as soon as you think of replacing the mental image by, say, a painted one, and as soon as the image thereby loses its occult character, it ceases to seem to impart any life to the sentence at all. (It was in fact just the occult character of the mental process which you needed for your purposes.)

The mistake we are liable to make could be expressed thus: We are looking for the use of a sign, but we look for it as though it were an object *co-existing* with the sign. (One of the reasons for this mistake is again that we are looking for a 'thing correspond-ing to a substantive.')

The sign (the sentence) gets its significance from the system of signs, from the language to which it belongs. Roughly: under-standing a sentence means understanding a language.

As a part of the system of language, one may say, the sentence has life. But one is tempted to imagine that which gives the sentence life as something in an occult sphere, accompanying the sentence. But whatever accompanied it would for us just be another sign.

It is a prevalent notion that we can only imperfectly *exhibit* our understanding; that we can only point to it from afar or come close to it, but never lay our hands on it, and that the ultimate thing can never be said. We say: 'Understanding is something *different* from the expression of understanding. *Understanding* cannot be exhibited; it is something inward and spiritual.' – Or 'Whatever I do to exhibit understanding, whether I repeat an explanation of a word, or carry out an order to show that I have understood it, these bits of behaviour do not *have* to be taken as proofs of understanding.' Similarly, people also say 'I cannot show anyone else my toothache; I cannot *prove* to anyone else that I have toothache.' But the impossibility spoken of here is supposed to be a logical one. 'Isn't it the case that the expres-sion of understanding is always an incomplete expression?' That means, I suppose, an expression with something missing – but the something missing is essentially *inexpressible*, because otherwise I might find a better expression for it. And 'essentially inexpressible' means that it makes no sense to talk of a more complete expression.

The psychological processes which are found by experience to accompany sentences are of no interest to us. What does interest us is the understanding that is embodied in an explanation of the sense of the sentence.

To understand the grammar of the word 'to mean' we must ask ourselves what is the criterion for an expression's being meant *thus*. What should be regarded as a criterion of the meaning?

An answer to the question 'How is that meant?' exhibits the relationship between two linguistic expressions. So the question too is a question about that relationship.

The process we call the understanding of a sentence or of a description is sometimes a process of translation from one symbolism into another; tracing a picture, copying something, or translating into another mode of representation.

In that case understanding a description means making oneself a picture of what is described. And the process is more or less like making a drawing to match a description.

We also say: 'I understand the picture exactly, I could model it in clay'.

We speak of the understanding of a sentence as a condition of being able to apply it. We say 'I cannot obey an order if I do not understand it' or 'I cannot obey it before I understand it'.

'Must I really understand a sentence to be able to act on it? – Certainly, otherwise you wouldn't know what you had to do.' – But how does this knowing help me? Isn't there in turn a jump from knowing to doing?

'But all the same I must understand an order to be able to act according to it' – here the 'must' is fishy. If it is a logical must, then the sentence is a grammatical remark.

Here it could be asked: How long before obeying it *must* you understand the order? – But of course the proposition 'I must understand the order before I can act on it' makes good sense: but not a metalogical sense. – And "understanding" and "meaning" are not metalogical concepts.

If 'to understand a sentence' means somehow or other to act on it, then understanding cannot be a precondition for our acting on it. But of course experience may show that the specific behaviour of understanding is a precondition for obedience to an order.

'I cannot carry out the order because I don't understand what you mean. – Yes, I understand you now.' – What went on when I suddenly understood him? Here there are *many* possibilities. For example: the order may have been given in a familiar language but with a wrong emphasis, and the right emphasis suddenly occurred to me. In that case perhaps I should say to a third party: 'Now I understand him: he means . . .' and should repeat the order with the right emphasis. And when I grasped the familiar sentence I'd have understood the order, – I mean, I should not first have had to grasp an abstract sense. – Alternatively: I understood the order in *that* sense, so it was a correct English sentence, but it seemed preposterous. In such a case I would say: 'I do not understand you: because you can't mean *that*.' But then a more comprehensible interpretation occurred to me. Before I understand several interpretations, several explanations, may pass through my mind, and then I decide on one of them.

★ ★ ★

'Understanding a word' may mean: *knowing* how it is used; *being able to* apply it.

'Can you lift this ball?' – 'Yes'. Then I try and fail. Then perhaps I say '*I was wrong*, I cannot'. Or perhaps 'I can't now, because I am too tired; but when I said I could, I really could.' Similarly 'I thought I could play chess, but now I have forgotten how', but on the other hand 'When I said "I can play chess" I really could, but now I've lost it.' – But what is the criterion for my being able at that particular time? How did I know that I could? To that question I would answer 'I've always been able to lift that sort of weight', 'I lifted it just a moment before', 'I've played chess quite recently and my memory is good', 'I'd just recited the rules' and so on. What I regard as an answer to that question will show me in what way I use the word 'can'.

Knowing, being able to do something, a capacity is what we

would call a *state*. Let us compare with each other propositions which all in various senses describe states.

'I have had toothache since yesterday.'

'I have been longing for him since yesterday.'

'I have been expecting him since yesterday.'

'I have known since yesterday that he is coming.'

'Since yesterday I can play chess.'

Can one say: 'I have known continuously since yesterday that he is coming?' In which of the above sentences can one sensibly insert the word 'continuously'?

If knowledge is called a 'state' it must be in the sense in which we speak of the state of a body or of a physical model. So it must be in a physiological sense or in the sense used in a psychology that talks about unconscious states of a mind-model. Certainly no one would object to that; but in that case one still has to be clear that we have moved from the grammatical realm of "conscious states" into a different grammatical realm. I can no doubt speak of unconscious toothache, if the sentence 'I have unconscious toothache' means something like 'I have a bad tooth that doesn't ache'. But the expression 'conscious state' (in its old sense) doesn't have the same grammatical relationship to the expression 'unconscious state' as the expression 'a chair which I see' has to 'a chair which I don't see because it's behind me'.

Instead of 'to know something' we might say 'to keep a piece of paper on which it is written'.

If 'to understand the meaning of a word' means to know the grammatically possible ways of applying it, then I can ask 'How can I know what I mean by a word at the moment I utter it? After all, I can't have the whole mode of application of a word in my head all at once.'

I can have the possible ways of applying a word in my head in the same sense as the chess player has all the rules of chess in his head, and the alphabet and the multiplication table. Knowledge is the hypothesized reservoir out of which the visible water flows.

So we mustn't think that when we understand or mean a word what happens is an act of instantaneous, as it were non-discursive, grasp of grammar. As if it could all be swallowed down in a single gulp.

It is as if I get tools in the toolbox of language ready for future use.

'I can use the word "yellow" ' is like 'I know how to move the king in chess'.

In this example of chess we can again observe the ambiguity of the word 'understand'. When a man who knows the game watches a game of chess, the experience he has when a move is made usually differs from that of someone else watching without understanding the game. (It differs too from that of a man who doesn't even know that it's a game.) We can also say that it's the knowledge of the rules of chess which makes the difference between the two spectators, and so too that it's the knowledge of the rules which makes the first spectator have the particular experience he has. But this experience is not the knowledge of the rules. Yet we are inclined to call them both 'understanding'.

The understanding of language, as of a game, seems like a background against which a particular sentence acquires meaning. – But this understanding, the knowledge of the language, isn't a conscious state that accompanies the sentences of the language. Not even if one of its consequences is such a state. It's much more like the understanding or mastery of a calculus, something like the *ability* to multiply.

Suppose it were asked: 'When do you know how to play chess? All the time? Or just while you say that you can? Or just during a move in the game?' – How queer that knowing how to play chess should take such a short time, and a game of chess so much longer!
(Augustine: '*When* do I measure a period of time?')

It can seem as if the rules of grammar are in a certain sense an unpacking of something we experience all at once when we use a word.

In order to get clearer about the grammar of the word 'understand', let's ask: *when* do we understand a sentence? – When we've uttered the whole of it? Or while uttering it? – Is understanding, like the uttering of a sentence, an articulated process and does its articulation correspond exactly to that of the sentence? Or is it non-articulate, something accompanying the sentence in the way a pedal note accompanies a melody?

How long does it take to understand a sentence?

And if we understand a sentence for a whole hour, are we always starting afresh?

Chess is characterized by its rules (by the list of rules). If I define the game (distinguish it from draughts) by its rules, then these rules belong to the grammar of the word 'chess'. Does that mean that if someone uses the word 'chess' intelligently he must have a definition of the word in mind? Certainly not. – He will only give one if he's asked what he means by 'chess'.

Suppose I now ask: 'When you uttered the word, what did you mean by it?' – If he answered 'I meant the game we've played so often, etc. etc.' I would know that this explanation hadn't been in his mind at all when he used the word, and that he wasn't giving an answer to my question in the sense of telling me what 'went on inside him' while he was uttering the word.

When someone interprets, or understands, a sign in one sense or another, what he is doing is taking a step in a calculus (like a calculation). What he *does* is roughly what he does if he gives expression to his interpretation.

'Thought' sometimes means a particular mental process which may accompany the utterance of a sentence and sometimes the sentence itself in the system of language.

'He said those words, but he didn't think any thoughts with them.' – 'Yes, I did think a thought while I said them'. '*What* thought?' 'Just what I said.'

On hearing the assertion 'This sentence makes sense' you cannot really ask 'what sense?' Just as on hearing the assertion 'this combination of words is a sentence' you cannot ask 'what sentence?'

4
Intentionality

'That's *him*' (this picture represents *him*) – that contains the whole problem of representation.

What is the criterion, how is it to be verified, that this picture is the portrait of that object, i.e. that it is *meant* to represent it? It is not similarity that makes the picture a portrait (it might be a striking resemblance of one person, and yet be a portrait of someone else it resembles less).

How can I know that someone means the picture as a portrait of N? – Well, perhaps because he says so, or writes it underneath.

What is the connection between the portrait of N and N himself? Perhaps, that the name written underneath is the name used to address him.

When I remember my friend and see him 'in my mind's eye', what is the connection between the memory image and its subject? The likeness between them?

Well, the image, *qua picture*, can't do more than resemble him.

The image of him is an unpainted portrait.

In the case of the image too, I have to write his name under the picture to make it the image of him.

I have the intention of carrying out a particular task and I make a plan. The plan in my mind is supposed to consist in my seeing myself acting thus and so. But how do I know, that it is myself that I'm seeing? Well, it isn't myself, but a kind of a picture. But why do I call it the picture of *me*?

'How do I know that it's myself?': the question makes sense if it means, for example, 'how do I know that I'm the one I see there'. And the answer mentions characteristics by which I can be recognized.

But it is my own decision that makes my image represent

myself. And I might as well ask 'how do I know that the word "I" stands for myself?' For my shape in the picture was only another word 'I'.

'I can imagine your being about to go out of the door.' We suffer from a strange delusion that in the proposition, the thought, the objects do what the proposition states about them. It's as though the command contained a shadow of the execution. But a shadow of just *this* execution. It is *you* in the command who go to such and such a place. – Otherwise it would be just a *different* command.

This identity is indeed the identity contrasted with the diversity of two different commands.

'I thought Napoleon was crowned in the year 1805.' – What has your thought got to do with Napoleon? – What connection is there between your thought and Napoleon? – It may be, for example, that the word 'Napoleon' occurs in the expression of my thought, plus the connection that word had with its bearer; e.g. that was the way he signed his name, that was how he was spoken to and so on.

'But when you utter the word "Napoleon" you designate that man and no other' – 'How then does this act of designating work, in your view? Is it instantaneous? Or does it take time?' – 'But after all if someone asks you "did you mean the very man who won the battle of Austerlitz" you will say "yes". So you meant that man *when you uttered the sentence*.' – Yes, but only in the kind of way that I then knew also that $6 \times 6 = 36$.

The answer 'I meant the victor of Austerlitz' is a new step in our calculus. The past tense is deceptive, because it looks as if it was giving a description of what went on 'inside me' while I was uttering the sentence.

('But I meant *him*'. A strange process, this meaning! Can you mean in Europe someone who's in America? Even if he no longer exists?)

* * *

I can look for him when he is not there, but not hang him when he is not there.

One might want to say: 'But he must be somewhere there if I

am looking for him.' – Then he must be somewhere there too if I don't find him and even if he doesn't exist at all.

A search for a particular thing (e.g. my stick) is a particular kind of search, and differs from a search for something else because of what one does (says, thinks) while searching, not because of what one finds.

Suppose while I am searching I carry with me a picture or an image – very well. If I say that the picture is a picture of what I am looking for, that merely tells the place of the picture in the process of searching. And if I find it and say 'There it is! *That's* what I was looking for' those words aren't a kind of definition of the name of the object of the search (e.g. of the words 'my stick'), a definition that couldn't have been given until the object had been found.

'You were looking for *him*? You can't even have known if he was there!' (Contrast looking for the trisection of the angle.)

One may say of the bearer of a name that he does not exist; and of course that is not an activity, although one may compare it with one and say: he must be there all the same, if he does not exist. (And this has certainly already been written some time by a philosopher.)

The idea that it takes finding to show what we were looking for, and fulfilment of a wish to show what we wanted, means one is judging the process like the symptoms of expectation or search in someone else. I see him uneasily pacing up and down his room; then someone comes in at the door and he relaxes and gives signs of satisfaction. And I say 'obviously he was expecting this person.'

The symptoms of expectation are not the expression of expectation.

One may have the feeling that in the sentence 'I expect he is coming' one is using the words 'he is coming' in a different sense from the one they have in the assertion 'he is coming'. But if it were so, how could I say that my expectation had been fulfilled? And the words 'he is coming' mean the same in the expression of expectation as in the description of its fulfilment, because if I wanted to explain the words 'he' and 'is coming', say by means of ostensive definitions, the same definitions of these words would go for both sentences.

But it might now be asked: what's it like for him to come? –
The door opens, someone walks in, and so on. – What's it like
for me to expect him to come? – I walk up and down the room,
look at the clock now and then, and so on. But the one set of
events has not the smallest similarity to the other! So how can
one use the same words in describing them? What has become
now of the hollow space and the corresponding solid?

But perhaps I say as I walk up and down: 'I expect he'll come
in.' Now there is a similarity somewhere. But of what kind?!

But of course I might walk up and down in my room and
look at the clock and so on without expecting him to come. I
wouldn't describe doing that by saying 'I expect he is coming'.
So what made it e.g. the expectation precisely of *him*?

I may indeed say: to walk restlessly up and down in my room,
to look at the door, to listen for a noise is: to expect N. – That is
simply a definition of the expression 'to expect N'. Of course it
isn't a definition of the word 'expect', because it doesn't explain
what e.g. 'to expect M' means. Well, we can take care of that; we
say something like: to expect X means to act as described and to
utter the name 'X' while doing so. On this definition the person
expected is the person whose name is uttered. Or I may give as
a definition: to expect a person X is to do what I described in the
second example, and to make a drawing of a person. In that
case, the person expected is the bearer of the name X, the person
who corresponds to the drawing. – That of course wouldn't
explain what 'to expect N to *go*' means, and I would have to give
either an independent definition of that, or a general definition
including going and coming. And even that wouldn't explain say
what 'to expect a storm' means; etc. etc.

What characterizes all these cases is, that the definition can be
used to read off the object of the expectation from the expectant
behaviour. It isn't a later experience that decides *what* we are
expecting.

And I may say: it is in language that expectation and its
fulfilment make contact.

So *in this case* the behaviour of the expectant person is behaviour which can be translated in accordance with given rules
into the proposition 'He is expecting it to happen that p'. And
so the simplest typical example to illustrate this use of the word

'expect' is that the expectation of its happening that p should consist in the expectant person *saying* 'I expect it to happen that p'. Hence in so many cases it clarifies the grammatical situation to say: let us put the expression of expectation in place of the expectation, the expression of the thought in place of the thought.

★ ★ ★

When I expect someone, – what happens? I perhaps look at my calendar and see his name against today's date and the note '5 p.m.' I say to someone else 'I can't come to see you today, because I'm expecting N'. I make preparations to receive a guest. I wonder 'Does N smoke?', I remember having seen him smoke and put out cigarettes. Towards 5 p.m. I say to myself 'Now he'll come soon', and as I do so I imagine a man looking like N; then I imagine him coming into the room and my greeting him and calling him by his name. This and many other more or less *similar* trains of events are called 'expecting N to come'.

But perhaps I'm also prepared to say 'I have been expecting N' in a case where the only thing that connects him with my expectant activity is for instance that on a particular day I prepare a meal for myself and one other person, and that N. has announced his intention of taking that meal with me.

What does the process or state of wanting an apple consist in? Perhaps I experience hunger or thirst or both, and meanwhile imagine an apple, or remember that I enjoyed one yesterday; perhaps I say 'I would like to eat an apple'; perhaps I go and look in a cupboard where apples are normally kept. Perhaps all these states and activities are combined among themselves and with others.

The same sort of thing must be said of intention. If a mechanism is *meant* to act as a brake, but for some reason does not slow down the motion of the machine, then the purpose of the mechanism cannot be found out *immediately* from it and from its effect. If you were to say 'that is a brake, but it doesn't work' you would be talking about intention. But now suppose that whenever the mechanism didn't work as a brake a particular person became angry. Wouldn't the intention of the mechanism now be expressed in its effect? No, for now it could be said that the lever sometimes triggers the brake and sometimes triggers the anger. For how does it come out that the man is angry *because* the lever doesn't operate the brake? 'Being annoyed that the apparatus does not function' is itself something like 'wishing that it did function in that way'. – Here we have the old problem, which we would like to express in the following way: 'the thought that p is the case doesn't presuppose that it is the case; yet on the other hand there must be something in the fact that is a presupposition even of having the thought (I can't think that something is red, if the colour red does not exist)'. It is the problem of the harmony between world and thought. – To this it may be replied that thoughts are in the same space as the things that admit of doubt; they are laid against them in the same way as a ruler is laid against what is to be measured.

What I really want to say is this: the wish that he should come is the wish that really *he* should really *come*. If a further explanation of this assurance is wanted, I would go on to say 'and by "he" I mean that man there, and by "come" I mean doing this . . .' But these are just grammatical explanations, explanations which *create* language.

It is *in language* that it's all done.

'I couldn't think that something is red if red didn't exist.' What that proposition really means is the image of something red, or the existence of a red sample *as part of our language*. But of course one can't say that our language *has to* contain such a sample; if it didn't contain it, it would just be another, a different language. But one can say, and emphasize, that it does contain it.

It's beginning to look somehow as if intention could never be recognized as *intention* from outside; as if one must be doing the meaning of it oneself in order to understand it as meaning. That would amount to considering it not as a phenomenon or fact but as something intentional which has a direction given to it. What this direction is, we do not know; it is something which is absent from the phenomenon as such.

Here, of course, our earlier problem returns, because the point is that one has to read off from a thought that it is the thought that such and such is the case. If one can't read it off (as one can't read off the cause of a stomach-ache) then it is of no logical interest.

My idea seems nonsensical if it is expressed like *this*. It's supposed to be possible to see what someone is thinking of by opening up his head. But how is that possible? The objects he's thinking about are certainly not in his head – any more than in his thoughts!

If we consider them "from outside" we have to understand thoughts as thoughts, intentions as intentions and so on, *without* getting any information about something's meaning. For it is with the phenomenon of thinking that meaning belongs.

If a thought is observed there can be no further question of an understanding; for if the thought is seen it must be recognized as a thought with a certain content; it doesn't need to be interpreted! – That really is how it is; when we are thinking, there isn't any interpretation going on.

★ ★ ★

By 'intention' I mean here what uses a sign in a thought. The intention seems to interpret, to give the final interpretation; which is not a further sign or picture, but something else, the thing that cannot be further interpreted. But what we have reached is a psychological, not a logical terminus.

Think of a sign language, an "abstract" one, I mean one that is strange to us, in which we do not feel at home, in which, as we should say, we do not *think* (we used a similar example once before), and let us imagine this language interpreted by a translation into – as we should like to say – an unambiguous picture-language, a language consisting of pictures painted in perspective. It is quite clear that it is much easier to imagine different *interpretations* of the written language than of a picture painted in the usual way depicting say a room with normal furniture. Here we shall also be inclined to think that there is no further possibility of interpretation.

Here we might also say we didn't enter into the sign-language, but did enter into the painted picture.

(This is connected with the fact that what we call a "picture by similarity" is not a picture in accordance with some established method of projection. In this case the 'likeness' between two objects means something like the possibility of mistaking one for the other.)

'Only the intended picture reaches up to reality like a yard-stick. Looked at from outside, there it is, lifeless and isolated.' – It is as if at first we looked at a picture so as to enter into it and the objects in it surrounded us like real ones; and then we stepped back, and were now outside it; we saw the frame, and the picture was a painted surface. In this way, when we intend, we are surrounded by our intention's pictures and we are inside them. But when we step outside intention, they are mere patches on a canvas, without life and of no interest to us. When we intend, we exist among the pictures (shadows) of intention, as well as with real things. Let us imagine we are sitting in a darkened cinema and entering into the happenings in the film. Now the lights are turned on, though the film continues on the screen. But suddenly we see it 'from outside' as movements of light and dark patches on a screen.

(In dreams it sometimes happens that we first read a story and then are ourselves participants in it. And after waking up after a dream it is sometimes as if we had stepped back out of the dream and now see it before us as an alien picture.) And it also means something to speak of 'living in the pages of a book'. That is connected with the fact that our body is not at all essential for the occurrence of our experience. (Cf. eye and visual field.)

(Compare also the remark: if we understand a sentence, it has a certain depth for us.)

What happens is not that this symbol cannot be further interpreted, but: I do no interpreting. I do not interpret because I feel natural in the present picture. When I interpret, I step from one level of my thought to another.

If I see the thought symbol 'from outside', I become conscious that it *could* be interpreted thus or thus; if it is a step in the course of my thoughts, then it is a stopping-place that is natural to me, and its further interpretability does not occupy (or trouble) me. As I have a railway time-table and use it without being concerned with the fact that a table can be interpreted in various ways.

When I said that my image wouldn't be a portrait unless it bore the name of its subject, I didn't mean that I have to imagine it and his name at the same time. Suppose I say something like: 'What I see in my mind isn't just a picture which is like N (and perhaps like others too). No, I know that it is him, that he is the person it portrays.' I might then ask: *when* do I know that and what does knowing it amount to? There's no need for anything to take place during the imagining that could be called 'knowing' in this way. Something of that sort may happen after the imagining; I may go on from the picture to the name, or perhaps say that I imagined N, even though at the time of the imagining there wasn't anything, except a kind of similarity, to characterize the image as N's. Or again there might be something preceding the image that made the connection with N. And so the interpretation isn't something that accompanies the image; what gives the image its interpretation is the *path* on which it lies.

That all becomes clearer if one imagines images replaced by drawings, if one imagines people who go in for drawing instead of imagining.

If I try to describe the process of intention, I feel first and foremost that it can do what it is supposed to only by containing an extremely faithful picture of what it intends. But further, that that too does not go far enough, because a picture, whatever it may be, can be variously interpreted; hence this picture too in its turn stands isolated. When one has the picture in view by itself it is suddenly dead, and it is as if something had been taken away from it, which had given it life before. It is not a thought, not an intention; whatever accompaniments we imagine for it, articulate or inarticulate processes, or any feeling whatsoever, it remains isolated, it does not point outside itself to a reality beyond.

Now one says: 'Of course it is not the picture that intends, but we who use it to intend.' But if this intending, this meaning, is something that is done with the picture, then I cannot see why that has to involve a human being. The process of digestion can also be studied as a chemical process, independently of whether it takes place in a living being. We want to say 'Meaning is surely essentially a mental process, a process of consciousness and life, not of dead matter.' But what will give such a thing the specific character of what goes on? – so long as we speak of it as a process. And now it seems to us as if intending could not be any process at all, of any kind whatever. – For what we are dissatisfied with here is the grammar of *process*, not the specific kind of process. – It could be said: we should call any process 'dead' in this sense.

Let's say the wish for this table to be a little higher is the act of my holding my hand above the table at the height I wish it to be. Now comes the objection: 'The hand above the table can't be the wish: it doesn't express that the table is to be higher; it is where it is and the table is where it is. And *whatever other* gesture I made it wouldn't make any difference.'

(It might almost be said: 'Meaning *moves*, whereas a process stands still.')

However, if I imagine the expression of a wish as the act of wishing, the problem appears solved, because the system of language seems to provide me with a medium in which the proposition is no longer dead.

If we imagine the expression of a wish as the wish, it is rather as if we were led by a train of thought to imagine something like a network of lines spread over the earth, and living beings who moved only along the lines.

But now someone will say: even if the *expression* of the wish is the wish, still the whole language isn't present during this expression, yet surely the wish is!

So how does language help? Well, it just isn't necessary that anything should be *present* except the expression.

* * *

A great many philosophical difficulties are connected with that sense of the expressions 'to wish', 'to think', etc., which we are now considering. These can all be summed up in the question: 'How can one think what is not the case?'

This is a beautiful example of a philosophical question. It asks 'How can one . . . ?' and while this puzzles us we must admit that nothing is easier than to think what is not the case. I mean, this shows us again that the difficulty which we are in does not arise through our inability to imagine how thinking something is done; just as the philosophical difficulty about the measurement of time did not arise through our inability to imagine how time was actually measured. I say this because sometimes it almost seems as though our difficulty were one of remembering exactly what happened when we thought something, a difficulty of introspection, or something of the sort; whereas in fact it arises when we look at the facts through the medium of a misleading form of expression.

'How can one think what is not the case? If I think that King's College is on fire when it is not on fire, the fact of its being on fire does not exist. Then how can I think it? How can we hang a thief who doesn't exist?' Our answer could be put in this form: 'I can't hang him when he doesn't exist; but I can look for him when he doesn't exist'.

We are here misled by the substantives 'object of thought' and 'fact', and by the different meanings of the word 'exist'.

* * *

Let us revert to our question: 'What is the object of a thought?' (e.g. when we say, 'I think that King's College is on fire').

The question as we put it is already the expression of several confusions. This is shown by the mere fact that it almost sounds like a question of physics; like asking: 'What are the ultimate constituents of matter?' (It is a typically metaphysical question; the characteristic of a metaphysical question being that we express an unclarity about the grammar of words in the *form* of a scientific question.)

One of the origins of our question is the two-fold use of the propositional function 'I think x'. We say, 'I think that so-and-so will happen' or 'that so-and-so is the case', and also 'I think just the same *thing* as he'; and we say 'I expect him', and also 'I expect that he will come'. Compare 'I expect him' and 'I shoot him'. We can't shoot him if he isn't there. This is how the question arises: 'How can we expect something that is not the case?', 'How can we expect a fact which does not exist?'

The way out of this difficulty seems to be: what we expect is not the fact, but a shadow of the fact; as it were, the next thing to the fact. We have said that this is only pushing the question one step further back. There are several origins to this idea of a shadow. One of them is this: we say 'Surely two sentences of different languages can have the same sense'; and we argue, 'therefore the sense is not the same as the sentence', and ask the question 'What is the sense?' And we make of 'it' a shadowy being, one of the many which we create when we wish to give meaning to substantives to which no material objects correspond.

Another source of the idea of a shadow being the object of our thought is this: We imagine the shadow to be a picture the intention of which *cannot be questioned*, that is, a picture which we don't interpret in order to understand it, but which we understand without interpreting it. Now there are pictures of which we should say that we interpret them, that is, translate them into a different kind of picture, in order to understand them; and pictures of which we should say that we understand them immediately, without any further interpretation. If you see a telegram written in cipher, and you know the key to this cipher, you will, in general, not say that you understand the telegram before you have translated it into ordinary language. Of course you have only replaced one kind of symbols by another; and yet if now you read the telegram in your language no further process of interpretation will take place. – Or rather, you may now, in certain cases, again translate this telegram, say into a picture; but then too you have only replaced one set of symbols by another.

The shadow, as we think of it, is some sort of a picture; in fact, something very much like an image which comes before our mind's eye; and this again is something not unlike a painted representation in the ordinary sense. A source of the idea of the shadow certainly is the fact that in some cases saying, hearing, or reading a sentence brings images before our mind's eye, images which more or less strictly correspond to the sentence, and which are therefore, in a sense, translations of this sentence into a pictorial language. – But it is absolutely essential for the picture which we imagine the shadow to be that it is what I shall call a 'picture by similarity'. I don't mean by this that it is a picture similar to what it is intended to represent, but that it is a picture which is correct only when it is similar to what it represents. One might use for this kind of picture the word 'copy'. Roughly speaking, copies are good pictures when they can easily be mistaken for what they represent.

A plane projection of one hemisphere of our terrestrial globe is not a picture by similarity or a copy in this sense. It would be conceivable that I portrayed some one's face by projecting it in some queer way, though correctly according to the adopted rule of projection, on a piece of paper, in such a way that no one would normally call the projection 'a good portrait of so-and-so' because it would not look a bit like him.

If we keep in mind the possibility of a picture which, though correct, has no similarity with its object, the interpolation of a shadow between the sentence and reality loses all point. For now the sentence itself can serve as such a shadow. The sentence is just such a picture, which hasn't the slightest similarity with what it represents. If we were doubtful about how the sentence 'King's College is on fire' can be a picture of King's College on fire, we need only ask ourselves: 'How should we explain what the sentence means?' Such an explanation might consist of ostensive definitions. We should say, e.g., 'this is King's College' (pointing to the building), 'this is a fire' (pointing to a fire). This shews you the way in which words and things may be connected.

The idea that that which we wish to happen must be present as a shadow in our wish is deeply rooted in our forms of expression. But, in fact, we might say that it is only the next best absurdity to the one which we should really like to say. If it weren't too absurd we should say that the fact which we wish for must be present in our wish. For how can we wish *just this* to happen if just this isn't present in our wish? It is quite true to say: The mere shadow won't do; for it stops short before the object; and we want the wish to contain the object itself. – We want that the wish that Mr Smith should come into this room should wish that just *Mr Smith*, and no substitute, should do the *coming*, and no substitute for that, *into my room*, and no substitute for that. But this is exactly what we said.

Our confusion could be described in this way: Quite in accordance with our usual form of expression we think of the fact which we wish for as a thing which is not yet here, and to which, therefore, we cannot point. Now in order to understand the grammar of our expression 'object of our wish' let's just consider the answer which we give to the question: 'What is the object of your wish?' The answer to this question of course is 'I wish that so-and-so should happen'. Now what would the answer be if we went on asking: 'And what is the object of this wish?' It could only consist in a repetition of our previous expression of the wish, or else in a translation into some other form of expression. We might, e.g., state what we wished in other words or illustrate it by a picture, etc., etc. Now when we are under the impression that what we call the object of our wish is, as it were, a man who has not yet entered our room, and therefore can't yet be seen, we imagine that any explanation of what it is we wish is only the next best thing to the explanation which would show *the actual fact* – which, we are afraid, can't yet be shown as it has not yet entered. – It is as though I said to some one 'I am expecting Mr Smith', and he asked me 'Who is Mr Smith?', and I answered, 'I can't show him to you now, as he isn't there. All I can show you is a picture of him'. It then seems as though I could never entirely explain what I wished until it had actually happened. But of course this is a delusion. The truth is that I needn't be able to give a better explanation of what I wished after the wish was fulfilled than before; for I might perfectly well have shown Mr Smith to my friend, and have shown him what 'coming in' means, and have shown him what my room is, before Mr Smith came into my room.

Our difficulty could be put this way: We think about things, – but how do these things enter into our thoughts? We think about Mr Smith; but Mr Smith need not be present. A picture of him won't do; for how are we to know whom it represents? In fact no substitute for him will do. Then how can he himself be an object of our thoughts? (I am here using the expression 'object of our thought' in a way different from that in which I have used it before. I mean now a thing I am thinking *about*, not 'that which I am thinking'.)

We said the connection between our thinking, or speaking, about a man and the man himself was made when, in order to explain the meaning of the word 'Mr Smith' we pointed to him, saying 'this is Mr Smith'. And there is nothing mysterious about this connection. I mean, there is no queer mental act which somehow conjures up Mr Smith in our minds when he really isn't here. What makes it difficult to see that this is the connection is a peculiar form of expression of ordinary language, which makes it appear that the connection between our thought (or the expression of our thought) and the thing we think about must have subsisted *during* the act of thinking.

'Isn't it queer that in Europe we should be able to mean

someone who is in America?' – If someone had said 'Napoleon was crowned in 1804', and we asked him 'Did you mean the man who won the battle of Austerlitz?' he might say 'Yes, I meant him'. And the use of the past tense 'meant' might make it appear as though the idea of Napoleon having won the battle of Austerlitz must have been present in the man's mind when he said that Napoleon was crowned in 1804.

Someone says, 'Mr N. will come to see me this afternoon'; I ask 'Do you mean him?' pointing to someone present, and he answers 'Yes'. In this conversation a connection was established between the word 'Mr N.' and Mr N. But we are tempted to think that while my friend said, 'Mr N. will come to see me', and meant what he said, his mind must have made the connection.

This is partly what makes us think of meaning or thinking as a peculiar *mental activity*; the word 'mental' indicating that we mustn't expect to understand how these things work.

What we said of thinking can also be applied to imagining. Someone says, he imagines King's College on fire. We ask him: 'How do you know that it's *King's College* you imagine on fire? Couldn't it be a different building, very much like it? In fact, is your imagination so absolutely exact that there might not be a dozen buildings whose representation your image could be?' – And still you say: 'There's no doubt I imagine King's College and no other building'. But can't saying this be making the very connection we want? For saying it is like writing the words 'Portrait of Mr So-and-so' under a picture. It might have been that *while* you imagined King's College on fire you said the words 'King's College is on fire'. But in very many cases you certainly don't speak explanatory words in your mind while you have the image. And consider, even if you do, you are not going the whole way from your image to King's College, but only to the words 'King's College'. The connection between these words and King's College was, perhaps, made at another time.

The fault which in all our reasoning about these matters we are inclined to make is to think that images and experiences of all sorts, which are in some sense closely connected with each other, must be present in our mind at the same time.

5

Following a Rule

Let us now examine the following kind of language-game: when A gives an order B has to write down series of signs according to a certain formation rule.

The first of these series is meant to be that of the natural numbers in decimal notation. – How does he get to understand this notation? – First of all series of numbers will be written down for him and he will be required to copy them. (Do not balk at the expression 'series of numbers'; it is not being used wrongly here.) And here already there is a normal and an abnormal learner's reaction. – At first perhaps we guide his hand in writing out the series 0 to 9; but then the *possibility of getting him to understand* will depend on his going on to write it down independently. – And here we can imagine, e.g., that he does copy the figures independently, but not in the right order: he writes sometimes one sometimes another at random. And then communication stops at *that* point. – Or again, he makes '*mistakes*' in the order. – The difference between this and the first case will of course be one of frequency. – Or he makes a *systematic* mistake; for example, he copies every other number, or he copies the series 0, 1, 2, 3, 4, 5, . . . like this: 1, 0, 3, 2, 5, 4, . . . Here we shall almost be tempted to say that he has understood *wrong*.

Notice, however, that there is no sharp distinction between a random mistake and a systematic one. That is, between what you are inclined to call 'random' and what 'systematic'.

Perhaps it is possible to wean him from the systematic mistake (as from a bad habit). Or perhaps one accepts his way of copying and tries to teach him ours as an offshoot, a variant of his. – And here too our pupil's capacity to learn may come to an end.

★ ★ ★

Suppose the pupil now writes the series 0 to 9 to our satisfaction. – And this will only be the case when he is often successful, not if he does it right once in a hundred attempts. Now I continue the series and draw his attention to the recurrence of the first series in the units; and then to its recurrence in the tens. (Which only means that I use particular emphases, underline figures, write them one under another in such-and-such ways, and similar things.) – And now at some point he continues the series independently – or he does not. – But why do you say that? *so* much is obvious! – Of course; I only wished to say: the effect of any further *explanation* depends on his *reaction*.

Now, however, let us suppose that after some efforts on the teacher's part he continues the series correctly, that is, as we do it. So now we can say he has mastered the system. – But how far need he continue the series for us to have the right to say that? Clearly you cannot state a limit here.

Suppose I now ask: 'Has he understood the system when he continues the series to the hundredth place?' Or – if I should not speak of 'understanding' in connection with our primitive language-game: Has he got the system, if he continues the series correctly so far? – Perhaps you will say here: to have got the system (or, again, to understand it) can't consist in continuing the series up to *this* or *that* number: *that* is only applying one's understanding. The understanding itself is a state which is the *source* of the correct use.

What is one really thinking of here? Isn't one thinking of the derivation of a series from its algebraic formula? Or at least of something analogous? – But this is where we were before. The point is, we can think of more than *one* application of an algebraic formula; and every type of application can in turn be formulated algebraically; but naturally this does not get us any further. – The application is still a criterion of understanding.

'But how can it be? When *I* say I understand the rule of a series, I am surely not saying so because I have *found out* that up to now I have applied the algebraic formula in such-and-such a way! In my own case at all events I surely know that I mean such-and-such a series; it doesn't matter how far I have actually developed it.' –

Your idea, then, is that you know the application of the rule of the series quite apart from remembering actual applications to particular numbers. And you will perhaps say: 'Of course! For the series is infinite and the bit of it that I can have developed finite.'

But what does this knowledge consist in? Let me ask: *When* do you know that application? Always? day and night? or only when you are actually thinking of the rule? do you know it, that is, in the same way as you know the alphabet and the multiplication table? Or is what you call 'knowledge' a state of consciousness or a process – say a thought of something, or the like?

If one says that knowing the ABC is a state of the mind, one is thinking of a state of a mental apparatus (perhaps of the brain) by means of which we explain the *manifestations* of that knowledge. Such a state is called a disposition. But there are objections to speaking of a state of the mind here, inasmuch as there ought to be two different criteria for such a state: a knowledge of the construction of the apparatus, quite apart from what it does. (Nothing would be more confusing here than to use the words 'conscious' and 'unconscious' for the contrast between states of consciousness and dispositions. For this pair of terms covers up a grammatical difference.)

The grammar of the word 'knows' is evidently closely related to that of 'can', 'is able to'. But also closely related to that of 'understands'. ('Mastery' of a technique,)

But there is also *this* use of the word 'to know': we say 'Now I know!' – and similarly 'Now I can do it!' and 'Now I understand!'

Let us imagine the following example: A writes series of numbers down; B watches him and tries to find a law for the sequence of numbers. If he succeeds he exclaims: 'Now I can go on!' — So this capacity, this understanding, is something that makes its appearance in a moment. So let us try and see what it is that makes its appearance here. – A has written down the numbers 1, 5, 11, 19, 29; at this point B says he knows how to go on. What happened here? Various things may have happened; for example, while A was slowly putting one number after another, B was occupied with trying various algebraic formulae on the numbers which had been written down. After A had written the number 19 B tried the formula $a_n = n^2 + n - 1$; and the next number confirmed his hypothesis.

Or again, B does not think of formulae. He watches A writing his numbers down with a certain feeling of tension, and all sorts of vague thoughts go through his head. Finally he asks himself: 'What is the series of differences?' He finds the series 4, 6, 8, 10 and says: Now I can go on.

Or he watches and says 'Yes, I know *that* series' – and continues it, just as he would have done if A had written down the series 1, 3, 5, 7, 9. – Or he says nothing at all and simply continues the series. Perhaps he had what may be called the sensation 'that's easy!'. (Such a sensation is, for example, that of a light quick intake of breath, as when one is slightly startled.)

But are the processes which I have described here *understanding*?

'B understands the principle of the series' surely doesn't mean simply: the formula '$a_n = \dots$' occurs to B. For it is perfectly imaginable that the formula should occur to him and that he should nevertheless not understand. 'He understands' must have more in it than: the formula occurs to him. And equally, more than any of those more or less characteristic *accompaniments* or manifestations of understanding.

We are trying to get hold of the mental process of understanding which seems to be hidden behind those coarser and therefore more readily visible accompaniments. But we do not succeed; or, rather, it does not get as far as a real attempt. For even supposing I had found something that happened in all those cases of understanding, – why should *it* be the understanding? And how can the process of understanding have been hidden, when I said 'Now I understand' *because* I understood?! And if I say it is hidden – then how do I know what I have to look for? I am in a muddle.

But wait – if 'Now I understand the principle' does not mean the same as 'The formula . . . occurs to me' (or 'I say the formula', 'I write it down', etc.) – does it follow from this that I employ the sentence 'Now I understand . . .' or 'Now I can go on' as a description of a process occurring behind or side by side with that of saying the formula?

If there has to be anything 'behind the utterance of the formula' it is *particular circumstances*, which justify me in saying I can go on – when the formula occurs to me.

Try not to think of understanding as a 'mental process' at all. – For *that* is the expression which confuses you. But ask yourself: in what sort of case, in what kind of circumstances, do we say, 'Now I know how to go on,' when, that is, the formula *has* occurred to me? –

In the sense in which there are processes (including mental processes) which are characteristic of understanding, understanding is not a mental process.

(A pain's growing more and less; the hearing of a tune or a sentence: these are mental processes.)

Thus what I wanted to say was: when he suddenly knew how to go on, when he understood the principle, then possibly he had a special experience – and if he is asked: 'What was it? What took place when you suddenly grasped the principle?' perhaps he will describe it much as we described it above — but for us it is *the circumstances* under which he had such an experience that justify him in saying in such a case that he understands, that he knows how to go on.

Let us return to our case (151). It is clear that we should not say B had the right to say the words 'Now I know how to go on', just because he thought of the formula – unless experience shewed that there was a connexion between thinking of the formula – saying it, writing it down – and actually continuing the series. And obviously such a connexion does exist. – And now one might think that the sentence 'I can go on' meant 'I have an experience which I know empirically to lead to the continuation of the series.' But does B mean that when he says he can go on? Does that sentence come to his mind, or is he ready to produce it in explanation of what he meant?

No. The words 'Now I know how to go on' were correctly used when he thought of the formula: that is, given such circumstances as that he had learnt algebra, had used such formula before. – But that does not mean that his statement is only short for a description of all the circumstances which constitute the scene for our language-game. – Think how we learn to use the expressions 'Now I know how to go on', 'Now I can go on' and others; in what family of language-games we learn their use.

We can also imagine the case where nothing at all occurred in B's mind except that he suddenly said 'Now I know how to go on' – perhaps with a feeling of relief; and that he did in fact go on working out the series without using the formula. And in this case too we should say – in certain circumstances – that he did know how to go on.

This is how these words are used. It would be quite misleading, in this last case, for instance, to call the words a 'description of a mental state'. – One might rather call them a 'signal'; and we judge whether it was rightly employed by what he goes on to do.

In order to understand this, we need also to consider the following: suppose B says he knows how to go on – but when he wants to go on he hesitates and can't do it: are we to say that he was wrong when he said he could go on, or rather that he was able to go on then, only now is not? – Clearly we shall say different things in different cases. (Consider both kinds of case.)

The grammar of 'to fit', 'to be able', and 'to understand'. (Exercises: (1) When is a cylinder C said to fit into a hollow cylinder H? Only while C is stuck into H? (2) Sometimes we say that C ceased to fit into H at such-and-such a time. What criteria are used in such a case for its having happened at that time? (3) What does one regard as criteria for a body's having changed its weight at a particular time if it was not actually on the balance at that time? (4) Yesterday I knew the poem by heart; today I no longer know it. In what kind of case does it make sense to ask: 'When did I stop knowing it?' (5) Someone asks me 'Can you lift this weight?' I answer 'Yes'. Now he says 'Do it!' – and I can't. In what kind of circumstances would it count as a justification to say 'When I answered 'yes' I *could* do it, only now I can't'?

The criteria which we accept for 'fitting', 'being able to', 'understanding', are much more complicated than might appear at first sight. That is, the game with these words, their employment in the linguistic intercourse that is carried on by their means, is more involved – the role of these words in our language other – than we are tempted to think.

(This role is what we need to understand in order to resolve philosophical paradoxes. And hence definitions usually fail to resolve them; and so, *a fortiori* does the assertion that a word is 'indefinable'.)

But did 'Now I can go on' mean the same as 'Now the formula has occurred to me' or something different? We may say that, in those circumstances, the two sentences have the same sense, achieve the same thing. But also that *in general* these two sentences do not have the same sense. We do say: 'Now I can go on, I mean I know the formula', as we say 'I can walk, I mean I have time'; but also 'I can walk, I mean I am already strong enough'; or: 'I can walk, as far as the state of my legs is concerned', that is, when we are contrasting *this* condition for walking with others. But here we must be on our guard against thinking that there is some *totality* of conditions corresponding to the nature of each case (e.g. for a person's walking) so that, as it were, he *could not but* walk if they were all fulfilled.

I want to remember a tune and it escapes me; suddenly I say 'Now I know it' and I sing it. What was it like to suddenly know it? Surely it can't have occurred to me *in its entirety* in that moment! – Perhaps you will say: 'It's a particular feeling, as if it were *there*' – but *is* it there? Suppose I now begin to sing it and get stuck? — But may I not have been *certain* at that moment that I knew it? So in some sense or other it was *there* after all! — But in what sense? You would say that the tune was there, if, say, someone sang it through, or heard it mentally from beginning to end. I am not, of course, denying that the statement that the tune is there can also be given a quite different meaning – for example, that I have a bit of paper on which it is written. – And what does his being 'certain', his knowing it, consist in? – Of course we can say: if someone says with conviction that now he knows the tune, then it is (somehow) present to his mind in its entirety at that moment — and this is a definition of the expression 'the tune is present to his mind in its entirety'.

Let us return to our example. Now – judged by the usual criteria – the pupil has mastered the series of natural numbers. Next we teach him to write down other series of cardinal numbers and get him to the point of writing down series of the form

$$0, n, 2n, 3n, \text{etc}$$

at an order of the form '+ n'; so at the order '+ 1' he writes down the series of natural numbers. – Let us suppose we have done exercises and given him tests up to 1000.

Now we get the pupil to continue a series (say + 2) beyond
1000 – and he writes 1000, 1004, 1008, 1012.

We say to him: 'Look what you've done!' – He doesn't understand. We say: 'You were meant to add *two*: look how you began
the series!' – He answers: 'Yes, isn't it right? I thought that was
how I was *meant* to do it.' — Or suppose he pointed to the series
and said: 'But I went on in the same way.' – It would now be no
use to say: 'But can't you see . . . . ?' – and repeat the old
examples and explanations. – In such a case we might say,
perhaps: It comes natural to this person to understand our order
with our explanations as *we* should understand the order: 'Add
2 up to 1000, 4 up to 2000, 6 up to 3000 and so on.'

Such a case would present similarities with one in which a
person naturally reacted to the gesture of pointing with the hand
by looking in the direction of the line from finger-tip to wrist,
not from wrist to finger-tip.

'What you are saying, then, comes to this: a new insight –
intuition – is needed at every step to carry out the order "+ n"
correctly.' – To carry it out correctly! How is it decided what is
the right step to take at any particular stage? – 'The right step is
the one that accords with the order – as it was *meant*.' – So when
you gave the order + 2 you meant that he was to write 1002 after
1000 – and did you also mean that he should write 1868 after
1866, and 100036 after 100034, and so on – an infinite number
of such propositions? – 'No: what I meant was, that he should
write the next but one number after *every* number that he wrote;
and from this all those propositions follow in turn.' – But that is
just what is in question: what, at any stage, does follow from that
sentence. Or, again, what, at any stage we are to call 'being in
accord' with that sentence (and with the *mean*-ing you then put
into the sentence – whatever that may have consisted in). It
would almost be more correct to say, not that an intuition was
needed at every stage, but that a new decision was needed at
every stage.

'But I already knew, at the time when I gave the order, that he
ought to write 1002 after 1000.' – Certainly; and you can also
say you *meant* it then; only you should not let yourself be misled
by the grammar of the words 'know' and 'mean'. For you don't
want to say that you thought of the step from 1000 to 1002 at
that time – and even if you did think of this step, still you did not

think of other ones. When you said 'I already knew at the time
. . .' that meant something like: 'If I had then been asked what
number should be written after 1000, I should have replied
"1002".' And that I don't doubt. This assumption is rather of
the same kind as: 'If he had fallen into the water then, I should
have jumped in after him'. – Now, what was wrong with your
idea?

Here I should first of all like to say: your idea was that that act
of meaning the order had in its own way already traversed all
those steps: that when you meant it your mind as it were flew
ahead and took all the steps before you physically arrived at this
or that one.

Thus you were inclined to use such expressions as: 'The steps
are *really* already taken, even before I take them in writing or
orally or in thought.' And it seemed as if they were in some
unique way pre-determined, anticipated – as only the act of
meaning can anticipate reality.

'But *are* the steps then *not* determined by the algebraic formula?'
– The question contains a mistake.

We use the expression: 'The steps are determined by the
formula . . .'. *How* is it used? – We may perhaps refer to the fact
that people are brought by their education (training) so to use
the formula $y = x^2$, that they all work out the same value for y
when they substitute the same number for x. Or we may say:
'These people are so trained that they all take the same step at
the same point when they receive the order "add 3" '. We might
express this by saying: for these people the order 'add 3' completely determines every step from one number to the next. (In
contrast with other people who do not know what they are to do
on receiving this order, or who react to it with perfect certainty,
but each one in a different way.)

On the other hand we can contrast different kinds of formula,
and the different kinds of use (different kinds of training) appropriate to them. Then we *call* formulae of a particular kind (with
the appropriate methods of use) 'formulae which determine a
number y for a given value of x', and formulae of another kind,
ones which 'do not determine the number y for a given value of
x'. ($y = x^2$ would be of the first kind, $y \neq x^2$ of the second.) The
proposition 'The formula . . . determines a number y' will then
be a statement about the form of the formula – and now we must

distinguish such a proposition as 'The formula which I have written down determines y', or 'Here is a formula which determines y', from one of the following kind: 'The formula $y = x^2$ determines the number y for a given value of x'. The question 'Is the formula written down there one that determines y?' will then mean the same as 'Is what is there a formula of this kind or that?' – but it is not clear off-hand what we are to make of the question 'Is $y = x^2$ a formula which determines y for a given value of x?' One might address this question to a pupil in order to test whether he understands the use of the word 'to determine'; or it might be a mathematical problem to prove in a particular system that x has only one square.

It may now be said: 'The way the formula is meant determines which steps are to be taken'. What is the criterion for the way the formula is meant? It is, for example, the kind of way we always use it, the way we are taught to use it.

We say, for instance, to someone who uses a sign unknown to us: 'If by '$x!2$' you mean x^2, then you get *this* value for y, if you mean 2x, *that* one.' – Now ask yourself: how does one *mean* the one thing or the other by '$x!2$'?

That will be how meaning it can determine the steps in advance.

'It is as if we could grasp the whole use of the word in a flash.' Like *what* e.g.? – Can't the use – in a certain sense – be grasped in a flash? And in *what* sense can it not? – The point is, that it is as if we could 'grasp it in a flash' in yet another and much more direct sense than that. – But have you a model for this? No. It is just that this expression suggests itself to us. As the result of the crossing of different pictures.

You have no model of this superlative fact, but you are seduced into using a super-expression. (It might be called a philosophical superlative.)

* * *

'But I don't mean that what I do now (in grasping a sense) determines the future use *causally* and as a matter of experience, but that in a *queer* way, the use itself is in some sense present.' – But of course it is, 'in *some* sense'! Really the only thing wrong with what you say is the expression 'in a queer way'. The rest is all right; and the sentence only seems queer when one imagines a different language-game for it from the one in which we actually use it. (Someone once told me that as a child he had been surprised that a tailor could 'sew a dress' – he thought this meant that a dress was produced by sewing alone, by sewing one thread on to another.)

In our failure to understand the use of a word we take it as the expression of a queer *process*. (As we think of time as a queer medium, of the mind as a queer kind of being.)

'It's as if we could grasp the whole use of a word in a flash.' – And that is just what we say we do. That is to say: we sometimes describe what we do in these words. But there is nothing astonishing, nothing queer, about what happens. It becomes queer when we are led to think that the future development must in some way already be present in the act of grasping the use and yet isn't present. – For we say that there isn't any doubt that we understand the word, and on the other hand its meaning lies in its use. There is no doubt that I now want to play chess, but chess is the game it is in virtue of all its rules (and so on). Don't I know, then, which game I want to play until I *have* played it? or are all the rules contained in my act of intending? Is it experience that tells me that this sort of game is the usual consequence of such an act of intending? so is it impossible for me to be certain what I am intending to do? And if that is nonsense – what kind of super-strong connexion exists between the act of intending and the thing intended? — Where is the connexion effected between the sense of the expression 'Let's play a game of chess' and all the rules of the game? – Well, in the list of rules of the game, in the teaching of it, in the day-to-day practice of playing.

'But how can a rule shew me what I have to do at *this* point? Whatever I do is, on some interpretation, in accord with the rule.' – That is not what we ought to say, but rather: any interpretation still hangs in the air along with what it interprets, and cannot give it any support. Interpretations by themselves do not determine meaning.

'Then can whatever I do be brought into accord with the rule?' – Let me ask this: what has the expression of a rule – say a sign-post – got to do with my actions? What sort of connexion is there here? – Well, perhaps this one: I have been trained to react to this sign in a particular way, and now I do so react to it.

But that is only to give a causal connexion; to tell how it has come about that we now go by the sign-post; not what this going-by-the-sign really consists in. On the contrary; I have further indicated that a person goes by a sign-post only in so far as there exists a regular use of sign-posts, a custom.

Is what we call 'obeying a rule' something that it would be possible for only *one* man to do, and to do only *once* in his life? – This is of course a note on the grammar of the expression 'to obey a rule'.

It is not possible that there should have been only one occasion on which someone obeyed a rule. It is not possible that there should have been only one occasion on which a report was made, an order given or understood; and so on. – To obey a rule, to make a report, to give an order, to play a game of chess, are *customs* (uses, institutions).   ·

To understand a sentence means to understand a language. To understand a language means to be master of a technique.

It is, of course, imaginable that two people belonging to a tribe unacquainted with games should sit at a chess-board and go through the moves of a game of chess; and even with all the appropriate mental accompaniments. And if *we* were to see it we should say they were playing chess. But now imagine a game of chess translated according to certain rules into a series of actions which we do not ordinarily associate with a *game* – say into yells and stamping of feet. And now suppose those two people to yell and stamp instead of playing the form of chess that we are used to; and this in such a way that their procedure is translatable by suitable rules into a game of chess. Should we still be inclined to say they were playing a game? What right would one have to say so?

This was our paradox: no course of action could be determined by a rule, because every course of action can be made out to accord with the rule. The answer was: if everything can be made out to accord with the rule, then it can also be made out to conflict with it. And so there would be neither accord nor conflict here.

It can be seen that there is a misunderstanding here from the mere fact that in the course of our argument we give one interpretation after another; as if each one contented us at least for a moment, until we thought of yet another standing behind it. What this shews is that there is a way of grasping a rule which is *not* an *interpretation*, but which is exhibited in what we call 'obeying the rule' and 'going against it' in actual cases.

Hence there is an inclination to say: every action according to the rule is an interpretation. But we ought to restrict the term 'interpretation' to the substitution of one expression of the rule for another.

And hence also 'obeying a rule' is a practice. And to *think* one is obeying a rule is not to obey a rule. Hence it is not possible to obey a rule 'privately': otherwise thinking one was obeying a rule would be the same thing as obeying it.

Language is a labyrinth of paths. You approach from *one* side and know your way about; you approach the same place from another side and no longer know your way about.

As things are I can, for example, invent a game that is never played by anyone. – But would the following be possible too: mankind has never played any games; once, however, someone invented a game – which no one ever played?

'But it is just the queer thing about *intention*, about the mental process, that the existence of a custom, of a technique, is not necessary to it. That, for example, it is imaginable that two people should play chess in a world in which otherwise no games existed; and even that they should begin a game of chess – and then be interrupted.'

But isn't chess defined by its rules? And how are these rules present in the mind of the person who is intending to play chess?

Following a rule is analogous to obeying an order. We are trained to do so; we react to an order in a particular way. But what if one person reacts in one way and another in another to the order and the training? Which one is right?

Suppose you came as an explorer into an unknown country with a language quite strange to you. In what circumstances would you say that the people there gave orders, understood them, obeyed them, rebelled against them, and so on?

The common behaviour of mankind is the system of reference by means of which we interpret an unknown language.

Let us imagine that the people in that country carried on the usual human activities and in the course of them employed, apparently, an articulate language. If we watch their behaviour we find it intelligible, it seems 'logical'. But when we try to learn their language we find it impossible to do so. For there is no regular connexion between what they say, the sounds they make, and their actions; but still these sounds are not superfluous, for if we gag one of the people, it has the same consequences as with us; without the sounds their actions fall into confusion – as I feel like putting it.

Are we to say that these people have a language: orders, reports, and the rest?

There is not enough regularity for us to call it 'language'.

Then am I defining 'order' and 'rule' by means of 'regularity'? – How do I explain the meaning of 'regular', 'uniform', 'same' to anyone? – I shall explain these words to someone who, say, only speaks French by means of the corresponding French words. But if a person has not yet got the *concepts*, I shall teach him to use the words by means of *examples* and by *practice*. – And when I do this I do not communicate less to him than I know myself.

In the course of this teaching I shall shew him the same colours, the same lengths, the same shapes, I shall make him find them and produce them, and so on. I shall, for instance, get him to continue an ornamental pattern uniformly when told to do so. – And also to continue progressions. And so, for example, when given: . . . . . . to go on: . . . .

I do it, he does it after me; and I influence him by expressions of agreement, rejection, expectation, encouragement. I let him go his way, or hold him back; and so on.

Imagine witnessing such teaching. None of the words would be explained by means of itself; there would be no logical circle.

The expressions 'and so on', 'and so on ad infinitum' are also explained in this teaching. A gesture, among other things, might serve this purpose. The gesture that means 'go on like this', or 'and so on' has a function comparable to that of pointing to an object or a place.

We should distinguish between the 'and so on' which is, and the 'and so on' which is not, an abbreviated notation. 'And so on ad inf.' is *not* such an abbreviation. The fact that we cannot write down all the digits of π is not a human shortcoming, as mathematicians sometimes think.

Teaching which is not meant to apply to anything but the examples given is different from that which '*points beyond*' them.

'But then doesn't our understanding reach beyond all the examples?' – A very queer expression, and a quite natural one! – But is that *all*? Isn't there a deeper explanation; or mustn't at least the *understanding* of the explanation be deeper? – Well, have I myself a deeper understanding? Have I *got* more than I give in the explanation? – But then, whence the feeling that I have got more?

Is it like the case where I interpret what is not limited as a length that reaches beyond every length?

'But do you really explain to the other person what you yourself understand? Don't you get him to *guess* the essential thing? You give him examples, – but he has to guess their drift, to guess your intention.' – Every explanation which I can give myself I give to him too. – 'He guesses what I intend' would mean: various interpretations of my explanation come to his mind, and he lights on one of them. So in this case he could ask; and I could and should answer him.

How can he *know* how he is to continue a pattern by himself – whatever instruction you give him? – Well, how do I know? — If that means 'Have I reasons?' the answer is: my reasons will soon give out. And then I shall act, without reasons.

When someone whom I am afraid of orders me to continue the series, I act quickly, with perfect certainty, and the lack of reasons does not trouble me.

'But this initial segment of a series obviously admitted of various interpretations (e.g. by means of algebraic expressions) and so you must first have chosen *one* such interpretation.' – Not at all. A doubt was possible in certain circumstances. But that is not to say that I did doubt, or even could doubt. (There is something to be said, which is connected with this, about the psychological 'atmosphere' of a process.)

So it must have been intuition that removed this doubt? – If intuition is an inner voice – how do I know *how* I am to obey it? And how do I know that it doesn't mislead me? For if it can guide me right, it can also guide me wrong.

((Intuition an unnecessary shuffle.))

If you have to have an intuition in order to develop the series 1 2 3 4 . . . you must also have one in order to develop the series 2 2 2 2 . . .

But isn't *the same* at least the same?

We seem to have an infallible paradigm of identity in the identity of a thing with itself. I feel like saying: 'Here at any rate there can't be a variety of interpretations. If you are seeing a thing you are seeing identity too.'

Then are two things the same when they are what *one* thing is? And how am I to apply what the *one* thing shews me to the case of two things?

'A thing is identical with itself.' – There is no finer example of a useless proposition, which yet is connected with a certain play of the imagination. It is as if in imagination we put a thing into its own shape and saw that it fitted.

We might also say: 'Every thing fits into itself.' Or again: 'Every thing fits into its own shape.' At the same time we look at a thing and imagine that there was a blank left for it, and that now it fits into it exactly.

Does this spot *'fit'* into its white surrounding? – *But that is just how it would look* if there had at first been a hole in its place and it then fitted into the hole. But when we say 'it fits' we are not simply describing this appearance; not simply this *situation*.

'Every coloured patch fits exactly into its surrounding' is a rather specialized form of the law of identity.

'How am I able to obey a rule?' – if this is not a question about causes, then it is about the justification for my following the rule in the way I do.

If I have exhausted the justifications I have reached bedrock, and my spade is turned. Then I am inclined to say: 'This is simply what I do.'

(Remember that we sometimes demand definitions for the sake not of their content, but of their form. Our requirement is an architectural one; the definition a kind of ornamental coping that supports nothing.)

Whence comes the idea that the beginning of a series is a visible section of rails invisibly laid to infinity? Well, we might imagine rails instead of a rule. And infinitely long rails correspond to the unlimited application of a rule.

'All the steps are really already taken' means: I no longer have any choice. The rule, once stamped with a particular meaning, traces the lines along which it is to be followed through the whole of space. — But if something of this sort really were the case, how would it help?

No; my description only made sense if it was to be understood symbolically. – I should have said: *This is how it strikes me.*

When I obey a rule, I do not choose.

I obey the rule *blindly*.

★ ★ ★

What does it mean to say: a straight line can be arbitrarily produced? Is there not an 'and so on ad inf.' here which is quite different from that of mathematical induction? According to the foregoing there would exist the expression for the possibility of producing the line, in the sense of the description of the produced part, or of its production. Here at first sight there does not seem to be any question of numbers. I can imagine the pencil that draws the line continuing its movement and keeping on going the same way. But is it also conceivable that there should be no possibility of accompanying this process with some countable process? I believe not.

When do we say: 'The line intimates this to me *like a rule* – always the same'? And on the other hand: 'It keeps on intimating to me what I have to do – it is not a rule'?

In the first case the thought is: I have no further court of appeal for what I have to do. The rule does it all by itself: I only have to obey it – (and obeying is *one* thing!). I do not feel, for example: it is queer that the line always tells me something. – The other proposition says: I do not know what I am going to do: the line will tell me.

One might imagine someone multiplying, correctly multiplying, with such feelings as these; he keeps on saying 'I don't know – now the rule suddenly intimates *this* to me!' – and we answer 'Of course; you are going on quite in accord with the rule.'

★ ★ ★

I give the rules of a game. The other party makes a move, perfectly in accord with the rules, whose possibility I had not foreseen, and which spoils the game, that is, as I had wanted it to be. I now have to say: 'I gave bad rules; I must change or perhaps add to my rules.'

So in this way have I a picture of the game in advance? In a sense: Yes.

It was surely possible, for example, for me not to have foreseen that a quadratic equation need have no real root.

Thus the rule leads me to something of which I say: 'I did not expect this pattern: I imagined a solution always like *this* . . .'

In one case we make a move in an existent game, in the other we establish a rule of the game. Moving a piece could be conceived in these two ways: as a paradigm for future moves, or as a move in an actual game.

You must remember that there may be such a language-game as 'continuing a series of digits' in which no rule, no expression of a rule is ever given, but learning happens *only* through examples. So that the idea that every step should be justified by a something – a sort of pattern – in our mind, would be quite alien to these people.

How queer: It looks as if a physical (mechanical) form of guidance could misfire and let in something unforeseen, but not a rule! As if a rule were, so to speak, the only reliable form of guidance. But what does guidance not allowing a movement, and a rule's not allowing it, consist in? – How does one know the one and how the other?

'How do I manage always to use a word correctly – i.e. significantly; do I keep on consulting a grammar? No; the fact that I mean something – the thing I mean, prevents me from talking nonsense.' – 'I mean something by the words' here means: I *know* that I can apply them.

I may however believe I can apply them, when it turns out that I was wrong.

From this it does not follow that understanding is the activity by which we shew that we understand. It is misleading to ask whether it is this activity. The question ought not to be conceived as: 'Is understanding *this* activity then, isn't it a different

one instead?' – But rather as: 'Is "understanding" used to designate this activity – isn't its use *different?*'

We say: 'If you really follow the rule in multiplying, it *must*
come out the same.' Now, when this is merely the slightly
hysterical style of university talk, we have no need to be particularly interested. It is however the expression of an attitude
towards the technique of multiplying, which comes out every-
where in our lives. The emphasis of the 'must' corresponds only
to the inexorability of this attitude, not merely towards the
technique of calculating, but also towards innumerable related
practices.

With the words '*This* number is the right continuation of this
series' I may bring it about that for the future someone calls
such-and-such the 'right continuation'. What 'such-and-such' is
I can only show in examples. That is, I teach him to continue a
series (basic series), without using any expression of the 'law of
the series'; rather, I am forming a substratum for the meaning of
algebraic rules or what is like them.

He must go on like this *without a reason*. Not, however, because he cannot yet grasp the reason but because – in *this* system
– there is no reason. ('The chain of reasons comes to an end.')
And the *like this* (in 'go on like this') is signified by a number,
a value. For at *this* level the expression of the rule is explained by
the value, not the value by the rule.

For just where one says 'But don't you *see* . . . ?' the rule is no
use, it is what is explained, not what does the explaining.

'He grasps the rule intuitively.' – But why the rule? Why not
how he is to continue?

'Once he has seen the right thing, seen the one of infinitely
many references which I am trying to push him towards – once
he has got hold of it, he will continue the series right without
further ado. I grant that he can only guess (intuitively guess) the
reference that I mean – but once he has managed that the
game is won.' But this 'right thing' that I mean does not exist.
The comparison is wrong. There is no such thing here as, so to
say, a wheel that he is to catch hold of, the right machine which,
once chosen, will carry him on automatically. It could be that

something of the sort happens in our brain but that is not our concern.

'Do the same.' But in saying this I must point to the rule. So its *application* must already have been learnt. For otherwise what meaning will its expression have for him?

To guess the meaning of a rule, to grasp it intuitively, could surely mean nothing but: to guess its *application*. And that can't now mean: to guess the kind of application; the rule for it. Nor does guessing come in here.

I might e.g. guess what continuation will give the other pleasure (by his expression, perhaps). The application of a rule can be guessed only when there is already a choice between different applications.

We might in that case also imagine that, instead of 'guessing the application of the rule,' he *invents* it. Well, what would that look like? Ought he perhaps to say 'Following the rule + 1 may mean writing 1, 1 + 1, 1 + 1 + 1, and so on'? But what does he mean by that? For the 'and so on' presupposes that one has already mastered a technique.

Instead of 'and so on' he might also have said: 'Now you know what I mean.' And his explanation would simply be a *definition* of the expression 'following the rule + 1'. *This* would have been his discovery.

We copy the numerals from 1 to 100, say, and this is the way we *infer, think.*

I might put it this way: If I copy the numerals from 1 to 100 – how do I know that I shall get a series of numerals that is right when I count them? And here *what* is a check on *what*? Or how am I to describe the important empirical fact here? Am I to say experience teaches that I always count the same way? Or that none of the numerals gets lost in copying? Or that the numerals remain on the paper as they are, even when I don't watch them? Or *all* these facts? Or am I to say that we simply don't get into difficulties? Or that almost always everything seems all right to us?

This is how we think. *This* is how we act. *This* is how we talk about it.

Imagine you had to describe how humans learn to count (in

the decimal system, for example). You describe what the teacher says and does and how the pupil reacts to it. What the teacher says and does will include e.g. words and gestures which are supposed to encourage the pupil to continue a sequence; and also expressions such as 'Now he can count'. Now should the description which I give of the process of teaching and learning include, in addition to the teacher's words, my own judgment: the pupil can count now, or: now the pupil has understood the numeral system? If I do not include such a judgment in the description – is it incomplete? And if I do include it, am I going beyond pure description? – Can I refrain from that judgment, giving as my ground: '*That is all that happens*'?

Must I not rather ask: 'What does the description do anyway? What purpose does it serve?' – In another context, indeed, we know what is a complete and what an incomplete description. Ask yourself: How do we use the expressions 'complete' and 'incomplete description'?

Giving a complete (or incomplete) report of a speech. Is it part of this to report the tone of voice, the play of expression, the genuineness or falsity of feeling, the intentions of the speaker, the strain of speaking? Whether this or that belongs to a complete description will depend on the purpose of the description, on what the recipient does with the description.

The expression 'that is all that *happens*' sets limits to what we call 'happening'.

Here the temptation is overwhelming to say something further, when everything has already been described. – Whence this pressure? What analogy, what wrong interpretation produces it?

Here we come up against a remarkable and characteristic phenomenon in philosophical investigation: the difficulty – I might say – is not that of finding the solution but rather that of recognizing as the solution something that looks as if it were only a preliminary to it. 'We have already said everything. – Not anything that follows from this, no, *this* itself is the solution!'

This is connected, I believe, with our wrongly expecting an explanation, whereas the solution of the difficulty is a description, if we give it the right place in our considerations. If we dwell upon it, and do not try to get beyond it.

The difficulty here is: to stop.

6
Thinking

In order to get clear about the meaning of the word 'think' we watch ourselves while we think; what we observe will be what the word means! – But this concept is not used like that. (It would be as if without knowing how to play chess, I were to try and make out what the word 'mate' meant by close observation of the last move of some game of chess.)

Misleading parallels: the expression of pain is a cry – the expression of thought, a proposition.

As if the purpose of the proposition were to convey to one person how it is with another: only, so to speak, in his thinking part and not in his stomach.

Suppose we think while we talk or write – I mean, as we normally do – we shall not in general say that we think quicker than we talk, but the thought seems *not to be separate* from the expression. On the other hand, however, one does speak of the speed of thought; of how a thought goes through one's head like lightning; how problems become clear to us in a flash, and so on. So it is natural to ask if the same thing happens in lightning-like thought – only extremely accelerated – as when we talk and 'think while we talk.' So that in the first case the clockwork runs down all at once, but in the second bit by bit, braked by the words.

I can see or understand a whole thought in a flash in exactly the sense in which I can make a note of it in a few words or a few pencilled dashes.

What makes these notes into an epitome of this thought?

The lightning-like thought may be connected with the spoken thought as the algebraic formula is with the sequence of numbers which I work out from it.

When, for example, I am given an algebraic function, I am

CERTAIN that I shall be able to work out its values for the arguments 1, 2, 3, . . . up to 10. This certainty will be called 'well-founded', for I have learned to compute such functions, and so on. In other cases no reasons will be given for it – but it will be justified by success.

'What happens when a man suddenly understands?' – The question is badly framed. If it is a question about the meaning of the expression 'sudden understanding', the answer is not to point to a process that we give this name to. – The question might mean: what are the tokens of sudden understanding; what are its characteristic psychical accompaniments?

(There is no ground for assuming that a man feels the facial movements that go with his expression, for example, or the alterations in his breathing that are characteristic of some emotion. Even if he feels them as soon as his attention is directed towards them.) ((Posture.))

The question what the expression means is not answered by such a description; and this misleads us into concluding that understanding is a specific indefinable experience. But we forget that what should interest us is the question: how do we *compare* these experiences; what criterion of identity *do we fix* for their occurrence?

'Now I know how to go on!' is an exclamation; it corresponds to an instinctive sound, a glad start. Of course it does not follow from my feeling that I shall not find I am stuck when I do try to go on. – Here there are cases in which I should say: 'When I said I knew how to go on, I *did* know.' One will say that if, for example, an unforeseen interruption occurs. But what is unforeseen must not simply be that I get stuck.

We could also imagine a case in which light was always seeming to dawn on someone – he exclaims 'Now I have it!' and then can never justify himself in practice. – It might seem to him as if in the twinkling of an eye he forgot again the meaning of the picture that occurred to him.

Would it be correct to say that it is a matter of induction, and that I am as certain that I shall be able to continue the series, as I am that this book will drop on the ground when I let it go; and that I should be no less astonished if I suddenly and for no obvious reason got stuck in working out the series, than I should be if the book remained hanging in the air instead of falling? – To that I will reply that we don't need any grounds for *this* certainty either. What could justify the certainty *better* than success?

'The certainty that I shall be able to go on after I have had this experience – seen the formula, for instance, – is simply based on induction.' What does this mean? – 'The certainty that the fire will burn me is based on induction.' Does that mean that I argue to myself: 'Fire has always burned me, so it will happen now too?' Or is the previous experience the *cause* of my certainty, not its ground? Whether the earlier experience is the cause of the certainty depends on the system of hypotheses, of natural laws, in which we are looking at the phenomenon of certainty.

Is our confidence justified? – What people accept as a justification – is shewn by how they think and live.

We expect *this*, and are surprised at *that*. But the chain of reasons has an end.

'Can one think without speaking?' – And what is *thinking*? – Well, don't you ever think? Can't you observe yourself and see what is going on? It should be quite simple. You do not have to wait for it as for an astronomical event and then perhaps make your observation in a hurry.

Well, what does one include in 'thinking'? What has one learnt to use this word for? – If I say I have thought – need I always be right? – What *kind* of mistake is there room for here? Are there circumstances in which one would ask: 'Was what I was doing then really thinking; am I not making a mistake?' Suppose someone takes a measurement in the middle of a train of thought: has he interrupted the thought if he says nothing to himself during the measuring?

When I think in language, there aren't "meanings" going through my mind in addition to the verbal expressions: the language is itself the vehicle of thought.

Is thinking a kind of speaking? One would like to say it is what distinguishes speech with thought from talking without thinking. – And so it seems to be an accompaniment of speech. A process, which may accompany something else, or can go on by itself.

Say: 'Yes, this pen is blunt. Oh well, it'll do.' First, thinking it; then without thought; then just think the thought without the words. – Well, while doing some writing I might test the point of my pen, make a face – and then go on with a gesture of resignation. – I might also act in such a way while taking various measurements that an onlooker would say I had – without words – thought: If two magnitudes are equal to a third, they are equal to one another. – But what constitutes thought here is not some process which has to accompany the words if they are not to be spoken without thought.

Imagine people who could only think aloud. (As there are people who can only read aloud.)

While we sometimes call it 'thinking' to accompany a sentence by a mental process, that accompaniment is not what we mean by a 'thought'. — Say a sentence and think it; say it with understanding. – And now do not say it, and just do what you accompanied it with when you said it with understanding! – (Sing this tune with expression. And now don't sing it, but repeat its expression! – And here one actually might repeat something. For example, motions of the body, slower and faster breathing, and so on.)

'Only someone who is *convinced* can say that.' – How does the conviction help him when he says it? – Is it somewhere at hand by the side of the spoken expression? (Or is it masked by it, as a soft sound by a loud one, so that it can, as it were, no longer be heard when one expresses it out loud?) What if someone were to say 'In order to be able to sing a tune from memory one has to hear it in one's mind and sing from that'?

'So you really wanted to say . . .' – We use this phrase in order to lead someone from one form of expression to another. One is tempted to use the following picture: what he really "wanted to say", what he "meant" was already *present somewhere* in his mind even before we gave it expression. Various kinds of thing may persuade us to give up one expression and to adopt another in its place. To understand this, it is useful to consider the relation in which the solutions of mathematical problems stand to the context and ground of their formulation. The concept "trisection of the angle with ruler and compass", when people are trying to do it, and, on the other hand, when it has been proved that there is no such thing.

What happens when we make an effort – say in writing a letter – to find the right expression for our thoughts? – This phrase compares the process with a translation or description: the thoughts are already there (perhaps were there in advance) and we merely look for their expression. This picture is more or less appropriate in different cases. – But can't all sorts of things happen here? – I surrender to a mood and the expression *comes*. Or a picture occurs to me and I try to describe it. Or an English expression occurs to me and I try to hit on the corresponding German one. Or I make a gesture, and ask myself: What words correspond to this gesture? And so on.

Now if it were asked: 'Do you have the thought before finding the expression?' what would one have to reply? And what, to the question: 'What did the thought consist in, as it existed before its expression?'

This case is similar to the one in which someone imagines that one could not think a sentence with the remarkable word order of German or Latin just as it stands. One first has to think it, and then one arranges the words in that queer order. (A French politician once wrote that it was a characteristic of the French language that in it words occur in the order in which one thinks them.)

But didn't I already intend the whole construction of the sentence (for example) at its beginning? So surely it already existed in my mind before I said it out loud! – If it was in my mind, still it would not normally be there in some different word order. But here we are constructing a misleading picture of "intending", that is, of the use of this word. An intention is embedded in its situation, in human customs and institutions. If the technique of the game of chess did not exist, I could not intend to play a game of chess. In so far as I do intend the construction of a sentence in advance, that is made possible by the fact that I can speak the language in question.

After all, one can only say something if one has learned to talk. Therefore in order to *want* to say something one must also have mastered a language; and yet it is clear that one can want to speak without speaking. Just as one can want to dance without dancing.

And when we think about this, we grasp at the *image* of dancing, speaking, etc..

Thinking is not an incorporeal process which lends life and sense to speaking, and which it would be possible to detach from speaking, rather as the Devil took the shadow of Schlemiehl from the ground. — But how 'not an incorporeal process'? Am I acquainted with incorporeal processes, then, only thinking is not one of them? No; I called the expression 'an incorporeal process' to my aid in my embarrassment when I was trying to explain the meaning of the word 'thinking' in a primitive way.

One might say 'Thinking is an incorporeal process', however, if one were using this to distinguish the grammar of the word 'think' from that of, say, the word 'eat'. Only that makes the difference between the meanings look *too slight*. (It is like saying: numerals are actual, and numbers non-actual, objects.) An unsuitable type of expression is a sure means of remaining in a state of confusion. It as it were bars the way out.

One cannot guess how a word functions. One has to *look at* its use and learn from that.

But the difficulty is to remove the prejudice which stands in the way of doing this. It is not a *stupid* prejudice.

Speech with and without thought is to be compared with the playing of a piece of music with and without thought.

William James, in order to shew that thought is possible without speech, quotes the recollection of a deaf-mute, Mr Ballard, who wrote that in his early youth, even before he could speak, he had had thoughts about God and the world. – What can he have meant? – Ballard writes: 'It was during those delightful rides, some two or three years before my initiation into the rudiments of written language, that I began to ask myself the question: how came the world into being?' – Are you sure – one would like to ask – that this is the correct translation of your wordless thought into words? And why does this question – which otherwise seems not to exist – raise its head here? Do I want to say that the writer's memory deceives him? – I don't even know if I should say *that*. These recollections are a queer memory phenomenon, – and I do not know what conclusions one can draw from them about the past of the man who recounts them.

The words with which I express my memory are my memory-reaction.

Would it be imaginable that people should never speak an audible language, but should still say things to themselves in the imagination?

'If people always said things only to themselves, then they would merely be doing *always* what as it is they do *sometimes*.' – So it is quite easy to imagine this: one need only make the easy transition from some to all. (Like: 'An infinitely long row of trees is simply one that does *not* come to an end.') Our criterion for someone's saying something to himself is what he tells us and the rest of his behaviour; and we only say that someone speaks to himself if, in the ordinary sense of the words, he *can speak*. And we do not say it of a parrot; nor of a gramophone.

'What sometimes happens might always happen.' – What kind of proposition is that? It is like the following: If '$F(a)$' makes sense '$(x).F(x)$' makes sense.

'If it is possible for someone to make a false move in some game, then it might be possible for everybody to make nothing but false moves in every game.' – Thus we are under a temptation to misunderstand the logic of our expressions here, to give an incorrect account of the use of our words.

Orders are sometimes not obeyed. But how would it look if no orders were *ever* obeyed? The concept 'order' would have lost its purpose.

But couldn't we imagine God's suddenly giving a parrot understanding, and its now saying things to itself? – But here it is an important fact that I imagined a deity in order to imagine this.

'But at least I know from my own case what it means "to say things to oneself". And if I were deprived of the organs of speech, I could still talk to myself.'

If I know it only from my own case, then I know only what *I* call that, not what anyone else does.

'These deaf-mutes have learned only a gesture-language, but each of them talks to himself inwardly in a vocal language.' –

Now, don't you understand that? – But how do I know whether I understand it?! – What can I do with this information (if it is such)? The whole idea of understanding smells fishy here. I do not know whether I am to say I understand it or don't understand it. I might answer 'It's an English sentence; *apparently* quite in order – that is, until one wants to do something with it; it has a connexion with other sentences which makes it difficult for us to say that nobody really knows what it tells us; but everyone who has not become calloused by doing philosophy notices that there is something wrong here.'

'But this supposition surely makes good sense!' – Yes; in ordinary circumstances these words and this picture have an application with which we are familiar. – But if we suppose a case in which this application is absent we become as it were conscious for the first time of the nakedness of the words and the picture.

* * *

Let us introduce two antithetical terms in order to avoid certain elementary confusions: To the question 'How do you know that so-and-so is the case?', we sometimes answer by giving "*criteria*" and sometimes by giving "*symptoms*". If medical science calls angina an inflammation caused by a particular bacillus, and we ask in a particular case 'why do you say this man has got angina?' then the answer 'I have found the bacillus so-and-so in his blood' gives us the criterion, or what we may call the defining criterion of angina. If on the other hand the answer was, 'His throat is inflamed', this might give us a symptom of angina. I call 'symptom' a phenomenon of which experience has taught us that it coincided, in some way or other, with the phenomenon which is our defining criterion. Then to say 'A man has angina if this bacillus is found in him' is a tautology or it is a loose way of stating the definition of 'angina'. But to say, 'A man has angina whenever he has an inflamed throat' is to make a hypothesis.

In practice, if you were asked which phenomenon is the defining criterion and which is a symptom, you would in most cases be unable to answer this question except by making an arbitrary decision *ad hoc*. It may be practical to define a word by taking one phenomenon as the defining criterion, but we shall easily be persuaded to define the word by means of what, according to our first use, was a symptom. Doctors will use names of diseases without ever deciding which phenomena are to be taken as criteria and which as symptoms; and this need not be a deplorable lack of clarity. For remember that in general we don't use language according to strict rules – it hasn't been taught us by means of strict rules, either. *We*, in our discussions on the other hand, constantly compare language with a calculus proceeding according to exact rules.

This is a very one-sided way of looking at language. In practice we very rarely use language as such a calculus. For not only do we not think of the rules of usage – of definitions, etc. – while using language, but when we are asked to give such rules, in most cases we aren't able to do so. We are unable clearly to circumscribe the concepts we use; not because we don't know their real definition, but because there is no real 'definition' to them. To suppose that there *must* be would be like supposing that whenever children play with a ball they play a game according to strict rules.

When we talk of language as a symbolism used in an exact calculus, that which is in our mind can be found in the sciences and in mathematics. Our ordinary use of language conforms to this standard of exactness only in rare cases.

* * *

The fluctuation in grammar between criteria and symptoms makes it look as if there were nothing at all but symptoms. We say, for example: 'Experience teaches that there is rain when the barometer falls, but it also teaches that there is rain when we have certain sensations of wet and cold, or such-and-such visual impressions.' In defence of this one says that these sense-impressions can deceive us. But here one fails to reflect that the fact that the false appearance is precisely one of rain is founded on a definition.

The point here is not that our sense-impressions can lie, but that we understand their language. (And this language like any other is founded on convention.)

One is inclined to say: 'Either it is raining, or it isn't – how I know, how the information has reached me, is another matter.'

But then let us put the question like this: What do I call 'information that it is raining'? (Or have I only information of this information too?) And what gives this 'information' the character of information about something? Doesn't the form of our expression mislead us here? For isn't it a misleading metaphor to say: 'My eyes give me the information that there is a chair over there'?

We do not say that *possibly* a dog talks to itself. Is that because we are so minutely acquainted with its soul? Well, one might say this: If one sees the behaviour of a living thing, one sees its soul. – But do I also say in my own case that I am saying something to myself, because I am behaving in such-and-such a way? – I do *not* say it from observation of my behaviour. But it only makes sense because I do behave in this way. – Then it is not because I *mean* it that it makes sense?

But isn't it our *meaning* it that gives sense to the sentence? (And here, of course, belongs the fact that one cannot mean a senseless series of words.) And 'meaning it' is something in the sphere of the mind. But it is also something private! It is the intangible *something*; only comparable to consciousness itself.

How could this seem ludicrous? It is, as it were, a dream of our language.

Could a machine think? — Could it be in pain? – Well, is the human body to be called such a machine? It surely comes as close as possible to being such a machine.

But a machine surely cannot think! – Is that an empirical statement? No. We only say of a human being and what is like one that it thinks. We also say it of dolls and no doubt of spirits too. Look at the word 'to think' as a tool.

The chair is thinking to itself: . . .
WHERE? In one of its parts? Or outside its body; in the air around it? Or not *anywhere* at all? But then what is the difference between this chair's saying something to itself and another one's doing so, next to it? – But then how is it with man: where does *he* say things to himself? How does it come about that this question seems senseless; and that no specification of a place is necessary except just that this man is saying something to himself? Whereas the question *where* the chair talks to itself seems

to demand an answer. – The reason is: we want to know *how* the chair is supposed to be like a human being; whether, for instance, the head is at the top of the back and so on.

What is it like to say something to oneself; what happens here? – How am I to explain it? Well, only as you might teach someone the meaning of the expression 'to say something to oneself'. And certainly we learn the meaning of that as children. – Only no one is going to say that the person who teaches it to us tells us 'what takes place'.

Rather it seems to us as though in this case the instructor *imparted* the meaning to the pupil – without telling him it directly; but in the end the pupil is brought to the point of giving himself the correct ostensive definition. And this is where our illusion is.

★ ★ ★

Let us imagine someone doing work that involves comparison, trial, choice. Say he is constructing an appliance out of various bits of stuff with a given set of tools. Every now and then there is the problem 'Should I use *this* bit?' – The bit is rejected, another is tried. Bits are tentatively put together, then dismantled; he looks for one that fits etc., etc.. I now imagine that this whole procedure is filmed. The worker perhaps also produces sound-effects like 'him' or 'ha!' As it were sounds of hesitation, sudden finding, decision, satisfaction, dissatisfaction. But he does not utter a single word. Those sound-effects may be included in the film. I have the film shewn me, and now I invent a soliloquy for the worker, things that fit his manner of work, its rhythm, his play of expression, his gestures and spontaneous noises; they correspond to all this. So I sometimes make him say 'No, that bit is too long, perhaps another'll fit better.' – Or 'What am I to do now?' – 'Got it!' – Or 'That's not bad' etc.

If the worker can talk – would it be a falsification of what actually goes on if he were to describe that precisely and were to say e.g. 'Then I thought: no, that won't do, I must try it another way' and so on – although he had neither spoken during the work nor imagined these words?

I want to say: May he not later give his wordless thoughts in words? And in such a fashion that we, who might see the work

in progress, could accept this account? – And all the more, if we
had often watched the man working, not just once?

Of course we cannot separate his 'thinking' from his activity.
For the thinking is not an accompaniment of the work, any more
than of thoughtful speech.

Were we to see creatures at work whose *rhythm* of work, play
of expression etc. was like our own, but for their not *speaking*,
perhaps in that case we should say that they thought, con-
sidered, made decisions. For there would be a *great deal* there
corresponding to the action of ordinary humans. And there is no
deciding *how* close the correspondence must be to give us the
right to use the concept 'thinking' in their case too.

And anyhow what should we come to this decision for?

We shall be making an important distinction between creatures that can learn to do work, even complicated work, in a
'mechanical' way, and those that make trials and comparisons as
they work. – But what should be called 'making trials' and
'comparisons' can in turn be explained only by giving examples,
and these examples will be taken from our life or from a life that
is like ours.

If he has made some combination in play or by accident and
he now uses it as a method of doing this and that, we shall say
he thinks. – In considering he would mentally review ways and
means. But to do this he must already have some in stock.
Thinking gives him the possibility of *perfecting* his methods. Or
rather: He 'thinks' when, in a definite kind of way, he perfects a
method he has. [*Marginal note*: What does the search look like?]

It could also be said that a man thinks when he *learns* in a
particular way.

And this too could be said: Someone who *thinks* as he works
will intersperse his work with *auxiliary activities*. The word
'thinking' does not now mean these auxiliary activities, just as
thinking is not talking either. Although the concept 'thinking' is
formed on the model of a kind of imaginary auxiliary activity.
(Just as we might say that the concept of the differential quotient is formed on the model of a kind of ideal quotient.)

These auxiliary activities are not the thinking; but one imagines thinking as the stream which must be flowing under the surface of these expedients, if they are not after all to be mere mechanical procedures.

Suppose it were a question of buying and selling creatures (anthropoid brutes) which we use as slaves. They cannot learn to talk, but the cleverer among them can be taught to do quite complicated work; and some of these creatures work 'thinkingly', others quite mechanically. For a thinking one we pay more than for one that is merely mechanically clever.

If there were only quite few people who could get the answer to a sum without speaking or writing, they could not be adduced as testimony to the fact that calculating can be done without signs. The reason is that it would not be clear that these people were 'calculating' at all. Equally Ballard's testimony (in James) cannot convince one that it is possible to think without a language.

Indeed, where no language is used, why should one speak of 'thinking'? If this is done, it shows something about the *concept* of thinking.

'Thinking', a widely ramified concept. A concept that comprises many manifestations of life. The *phenomena* of thinking are widely scattered.

We are not at all *prepared* for the task of describing the use of e.g. The word 'to think' (And why should we be? What is such a description useful for?)

And the naïve idea that one forms of it does not correspond to reality at all. We expect a smooth contour and what we get to see is ragged. Here it might really be said that we have constructed a false picture.

It is not to be expected of this word that it should have a unified employment; we should rather expect the opposite.

Where do we get the concept 'thinking' from which we want to consider here? From everyday language. What first fixes the direction of our attention is the word 'thinking'. But the use of this word is confused. Nor can we expect anything else. And that can of course be said of all psychological verbs. Their employment is not so clear or so easy to get a synoptic view of, as that of terms in mechanics, for example.

One learns the word 'think', i.e. its use, under certain circumstances, which, however, one does not learn to describe.

But I *can teach* a person the use of the word! For a description of those circumstances is not needed for that.

I just teach him the word *under particular circumstances*.

We learn to say it perhaps only of human beings; we learn to assert or deny it of them. The question 'Do fishes think?' does not exist among our applications of language, *it is not raised*. (What can be more natural than such a set-up, such a use of language?)

'No one thought of *that* case' – we may say. Indeed, I cannot enumerate the conditions under which the word 'to think' is to be used – but if a circumstance makes the use doubtful, I can say so, and also say *how* the situation is deviant from the usual ones.

If I have learned to carry out a particular activity in a particular room (putting the room in order, say) and am master of this technique, it does not follow that I must be ready to describe the arrangement of the room; even if I should at once notice, and could also describe, any alteration in it.

'This law was not given with such cases in view.' Does that mean it is senseless?

It could very well be imagined that someone knows his way around a city perfectly, i.e. would confidently find the shortest way from any place in it to any other, – and yet would be quite incompetent to draw a map of the city. That, as soon as he tries, he produces nothing that is not *completely wrong*. (Our concept of 'instinct'.)

Remember that our language might possess a variety of different words: one for 'thinking out loud'; one for thinking as one talks to oneself in the imagination; one for a pause during which something or other floats before the mind, after which, however, we are able to give a confident answer.

One word for a thought expressed in a sentence; one for the lightning thought which I may later 'clothe in words'; one for wordless thinking as one works.

'Thinking is a mental activity' – Thinking is *not* a bodily activity.

Is thinking an activity? Well, one may tell someone: 'Think it over'. But if someone in obeying this order talks to himself or even to someone else, does he then carry out *two* activities?

Concern with what we say has its own specific signs. It also has its own specific consequences and preconditions. Concern is something experienced; we attribute it to ourselves, not on grounds of observation. It is not an accompaniment of what we say. What would make an accompaniment of a sentence into concern about the content of that sentence? (Logical condition.)

Compare the phenomenon of thinking with the phenomenon of burning. May not burning, flame, seem mysterious to us? And why flame more than furniture? – And how do you clear up the mystery?
And how is the riddle of thinking to be solved? – Like that of flame?

Isn't flame mysterious because it is impalpable? All right – but why does that make it mysterious? Why should something impalpable be more mysterious than something palpable? Unless it's because we *want* to catch hold of it. –

The soul is said to *leave* the body. Then, in order to exclude any similarity to the body, any sort of idea that some gaseous thing is meant, the soul is said to be incorporeal, non-spatial; but with that word 'leave' one has already said it all. Shew me how you use the word 'spiritual' and I shall see whether the soul is non-corporeal and what you understand by 'spirit'.

I am inclined to speak of a lifeless thing as lacking something. I see life definitely as a plus, as something added to a lifeless thing. (Psychological atmosphere.)

We don't say of a table and a chair: 'Now they are thinking,' nor 'Now they are not thinking,' nor yet 'They never think'; nor do we say it of plants either, nor of fishes; hardly of dogs; only of human beings. And not even of all human beings.
'A table doesn't think' is not assimilable to an expression like 'a table doesn't grow'. (I shouldn't know 'what it would be like if' a table were to think.) And here there is obviously a gradual transition to the case of human beings.

We only speak of 'thinking' in quite particular circumstances.

7
The Will

It makes sense to ask: 'Do I really love her, or am I only pretending to myself?' and the process of introspection is the calling up of memories; of imagined possible situations, and of the feelings that one would have if . . .

'I am revolving the decision to go away to-morrow.' (This may be called a description of a state of mind.) — 'Your arguments don't convince me; now as before it is my intention to go away to-morrow.' Here one is tempted to call the intention a feeling. The feeling is one of a certain rigidity; of unalterable determination. (But there are many different characteristic feelings and attitudes here.) — I am asked: 'How long are you staying here?' I reply: 'To-morrow I am going away; it's the end of my holidays.' – But over against this: I say at the end of a quarrel 'All right! Then I leave to-morrow!'; I make a decision.

'In my heart I have determined on it.' And one is even inclined to point to one's breast as one says it. Psychologically this way of speaking should be taken seriously. Why should it be taken less seriously than the assertion that belief is a state of mind? (Luther: 'Faith is under the left nipple.')

Someone might learn to understand the meaning of the expression 'seriously *meaning* what one says' by means of a gesture of pointing at the heart. But now we must ask: 'How does it come out that he has learnt it?'

Am I to say that any one who has an intention has an experience of tending towards something? That there are particular experiences of 'tending'? – Remember this case: if one urgently wants to make some remark, some objection, in a discussion, it often happens that one opens one's mouth, draws a breath and holds it; if one then decides to let the objection go, one lets the breath out. The experience of this process is evidently the experience of veering towards saying something. Anyone who observes me will know that I wanted to say something and then thought better of it. In *this* situation, that is. – In a different one he would not so interpret my behaviour, however characteristic of the intention to speak it may be in the present situation. And is there any reason for assuming that this same experience could not occur in some quite different situation – in which it has nothing to do with any 'tending'?

'But when you say "I intend to go away", you surely mean it! Here again it just is the mental act of meaning that gives the sentence life. If you merely repeat the sentence after someone else, say in order to mock his way of speaking, then you say it without this act of meaning.' – When we are doing philosophy it can sometimes look like that. But let us really think out various *different* situations and conversations, and the ways in which that sentence will be uttered in them. – 'I always discover a mental undertone; perhaps not always the *same* one.' And was there no undertone there when you repeated the sentence after someone else? And how is the 'undertone' to be separated from the rest of the experience of speaking?

A main cause of philosophical disease – a one-sided diet: one nourishes one's thinking with only one kind of example.

'But the words, significantly uttered, have after all not only a surface, but also the dimension of depth!' After all, it just is the case that something different takes place when they are uttered significantly from when they are merely uttered. – How I express this is not the point. Whether I say that in the first case they have depth; or that something goes on in me, inside my mind, as I utter them; or that they have an atmosphere – it always comes to the same thing.
'Well, if we all agree about it, won't it be true?'
(I cannot accept someone else's testimony, because it is not *testimony*. It only tells me what he is *inclined* to say.)

'Willing too is merely an experience,' one would like to say (the "will" too only "idea"). It comes when it comes, and I cannot bring it about.
Not bring it about? – Like *what?* What can I bring about, then? What am I comparing willing with when I say this?

I should not say of the movement of my arm, for example: it comes when it comes, etc.. And this is the region in which we say significantly that a thing doesn't simply happen to us, but that we *do* it. 'I don't need to wait for my arm to go up – I can raise it.' And here I am making a contrast between the movement of my arm and, say, the fact that the violent thudding of my heart will subside.

In the sense in which I can ever bring anything about (such as stomach-ache through over-eating), I can also bring about an act of willing. In this sense I bring about the act of willing to swim by jumping into the water. Doubtless I was trying to say: I can't will willing; that is, it makes no sense to speak of willing willing. 'Willing' is not the name of an action; and so not the name of any voluntary action either. And my use of a wrong expression came from our wanting to think of willing as an immediate non-causal bringing-about. A misleading analogy lies at the root of this idea; the causal nexus seems to be established by a mechanism connecting two parts of a machine. The connexion may be broken if the mechanism is disturbed. (We think only of the disturbances to which a mechanism is normally subject, not, say, of cog-wheels suddenly going soft, or passing through one another, and so on.)

When I raise my arm "voluntarily" I do not use any instrument to bring the movement about. My wish is not such an instrument either.

'Willing, if it is not to be a sort of wishing, must be the action itself. It cannot be allowed to stop anywhere short of the action.' If it is the action, then it is so in the ordinary sense of the word; so it is speaking, writing, walking, lifting a thing, imagining something. But it is also trying, attempting, making an effort, – to speak, to write, to lift a thing, to imagine something etc.

When I raise my arm, I have *not* wished it might go up. The voluntary action excludes this wish. It is indeed possible to say: 'I hope I shall draw the circle faultlessly'. And that is to express a wish that one's hand should move in such-and-such a way.

If we cross our fingers in a certain special way we are sometimes unable to move a particular finger when someone tells us to do so, if he only *points* to the finger – merely shews it to the eye. If on the other hand he touches it, we can move it. One would like to describe this experience as follows: we are unable to *will* to move the finger. The case is quite different from that in which we are not able to move the finger because someone is, say, holding it. One now feels inclined to describe the former case by saying: one can't find any point of application for the will till the finger is touched. Only when one feels the finger can the will know where it is to catch hold. – But this kind of expression is misleading. One would like to say: 'How am I to know where I am to catch hold with the will, if feeling does not shew the place?' But then how is it known to what point I am to direct the will when the feeling is there?

That in this case the finger is as it were paralysed until we feel a touch on it is shewn by experience; it could not have been seen *a priori*.

One imagines the willing subject here as something without any mass (without any inertia); as a motor which has no inertia in itself to overcome. And so it is only mover, not moved. That is: One can say 'I will, but my body does not obey me' – but not: 'My will does not obey me.' (Augustine.)

But in the sense in which I cannot fail to will, I cannot try to will either.

And one might say: 'I can always will only inasmuch as I can never try to will.'

Doing itself seems not to have any volume of experience. It seems like an extensionless point, the point of a needle. This point seems to be the real agent. And the phenomenal happenings only to be consequences of this acting. 'I *do* . . .' seems to have a definite sense, separate from all experience.

Let us not forget this: when 'I raise my arm', my arm goes up. And the problem arises: what is left over if I subtract the fact that my arm goes up from the fact that I raise my arm?

((Are the kinaesthetic sensations my willing?))

When I raise my arm I do not usually *try* to raise it.

'At all costs I will get to that house.' – But if there is no difficulty about it – *can* I try at all costs to get to the house?

In the laboratory, when subjected to an electric current, for example, someone says with his eyes shut 'I am moving my arm up and down' – though his arm is not moving. 'So,' we say, 'he has the special feeling of making that movement.' – Move your arm to and fro with your eyes shut. And now try, while you do so, to tell yourself that your arm is staying still and that you are only having certain queer feelings in your muscles and joints!

'How do you know that you have raised your arm?' – 'I feel it.' So what you recognize is the feeling? And are you certain that you recognize it right? – You are certain that you have raised your arm; isn't this the criterion, the measure, of the recognition?

'When I touch this object with a stick I have the sensation of touching in the tip of the stick, not in the hand that holds it.' When someone says 'The pain isn't here in my hand, but in my wrist', this has the consequence that the doctor examines the wrist. But what difference does it make if I say that I feel the hardness of the object in the tip of the stick or in my hand? Does what I say mean 'It is as if I had nerve-endings in the tip of the stick?' *In what sense* is it like that? – Well, I am at any rate inclined to say 'I feel the hardness etc. in the tip of the stick.' What goes with this is that when I touch the object I look not at my hand but at the tip of the stick; that I describe what I feel by saying 'I feel something hard and round there' – not 'I feel a pressure against the tips of my thumb, middle finger, and index finger . . .' If, for example, someone asks me 'What are you now feeling in the fingers that hold the probe?' I might reply: 'I don't know — I feel something hard and rough *over there*.'

Examine the following description of a voluntary action: 'I form the decision to pull the bell at 5 o'clock, and when it strikes 5, my arm makes this movement.' – Is that the correct description, and not *this* one: ' . . . and when it strikes 5, I raise my arm'? — One would like to supplement the first description: 'and see! my arm goes up when it strikes 5.' And this 'and see!' is precisely what doesn't belong here. I do *not* say 'See, my arm is going up!' when I raise it.

So one might say: voluntary movement is marked by the absence of surprise. And now I do not mean you to ask 'But *why* isn't one surprised here?'

When people talk about the possibility of foreknowledge of the future they always forget the fact of the prediction of one's own voluntary movements.

* * *

When a child stamps its feet and howls with rage, who would say it was doing this involuntarily? And why? Why is it assumed to be doing this not involuntarily? What are the *tokens* of voluntary action? Are there such tokens? – What, then, are the tokens of involuntary movement? They don't happen in obedience to orders, like voluntary actions. There is 'Come here!' 'Go over there!' 'Make this movement with your arm,' but not 'Have your heart beat faster'.

There is a peculiar combined play of movements, words, facial expressions etc., as of expressions of reluctance, or of readiness, which characterize the voluntary movements of the normal human being. When one calls the child, it doesn't come automatically: there is, for example, the gesture 'I don't want to!' There is coming gladly, the decision to come, running away with signs of fright, the effects of being addressed, all the reactions of play, the signs of consideration and its effects.

A tune went through my head. Was it voluntary, or involuntary? It would be an answer to say: I could also *not* have had it being sung to me inwardly. And how do I know that? Well, because I can ordinarily interrupt myself if I want to.

How could I prove to myself that I can move my arm voluntarily? Say by telling myself 'Now I'm going to move it' and now it moves? Or shall I say: 'Simply by moving it'? But how do I know that I did it, and it didn't move just by accident? Do I in the end feel it after all? And what if my memory of earlier feelings deceived me, and these weren't at all the right feelings to decide the matter?! (And which are the right ones?) And then how does someone else know whether I moved my arm voluntarily? Perhaps I'll tell him: 'Tell me to make whatever movement you like, and I'll do it in order to convince you.' – And what *do* you feel in your arm? 'Well the usual feelings.' There is nothing unusual about the feelings, the arm is not e.g. without feeling (as if it had 'gone to sleep').

A movement of my body, of which I don't know that it is taking place or has taken place, will be called involuntary. – But how is it when I merely *try* to lift a weight, and so there isn't a movement? What would it be like if someone involuntarily strained to lift a weight? Under what circumstances would *this* behaviour be called 'involuntary'?

Can't rest be just as voluntary as motion? Can't abstention from movement be voluntary? What better argument against a feeling of innervation?

'That glance was not intended' sometimes means: 'I didn't know that I gave such a look' or 'I didn't mean anything by it'.

It ought not to strike us as so much a matter of course that memory shews us the past inner, as well as the past outer, process.

Imagination is voluntary, memory involuntary, but calling something to mind is voluntary.

What a remarkable concept "trying", "attempting", is; how much one can "try to do"! (To remember, to lift a weight, to notice, to think of nothing.) But then one might also say: What a remarkable concept "doing" is! What are the kinship-relations between "talking" and "thinking", between "talking" and "talking to oneself"? (Compare the kinship-relations between the kinds of number.)

One makes quite different inferences from involuntary movements and from voluntary ones: this *characterizes* voluntary movement.

But how do I know that this movement is voluntary? I don't know it, I manifest it.

'I am tugging as hard as I can.' How do I know that? Do my muscular sensations tell me so? The words are a signal; and they have a *function*.

But am I *experiencing* nothing, then? Don't I experience something? something specific? A specific feeling of effort and of inability to do more, of reaching the limit? Of course, but these expressions say no more than 'I'm tugging as hard as I can'.

★ ★ ★

If only *one* person had, *once*, made a bodily movement – could the question exist, whether it was voluntary or involuntary?

'When I make an effort, I surely *do* something, I surely don't merely have a sensation.' And it is so too; for one tells someone 'Make an effort!', and he may express the intention: 'Now I'm going to make an effort' And when he says 'I can't go on!' that does not mean: 'I can't endure the feeling – the pain, for example – in my limbs any longer.' – On the other hand one *suffers* with effort, as with pain. 'I am utterly exhausted' – if someone said that, but moved as briskly as ever, one would not understand him.

An aspect is subject to the will. If something appears blue to me, I cannot see it red, and it makes no sense to say 'See it red'; whereas it does make sense to say 'See it as . . .'. And that the aspect is voluntary (at least to a certain extent) seems to be essential to it, as it is essential to imaging that *it* is voluntary. I mean: voluntariness seems to me (but why?) not to be a mere addition; as if one were to say: 'This movement can, as a matter of experience, also be brought about in *this* way.' That is to say: It is essential that one can say 'Now see it like *this*' and 'Form an image of . . .'. For this hangs together with the aspect's not "teaching us something about the external world". One may teach the words 'red' and 'blue' by saying 'This is red and not blue'; but one can't teach someone the meaning of 'figure' and 'ground' by pointing to an ambiguous figure.

We do not first become acquainted with images and only later learn to bend them to our will. And of course it is anyway quite wrong to think that we have been directing them, so to speak, with our will. As if the will governed them, as orders may govern men. As if, that is, the will were an influence, a force, or again: a primary *action*, which then is the cause of the outward perceptible action.

Is it right to say: what makes an action voluntary is the psychical phenomena in which it is embedded? (The psychological surrounding.)

Are, e.g., my normal movements in walking 'voluntary' in a *non-potential* sense?

A child stamps its feet with rage: isn't that voluntary? And do I know anything about its sensations of movement, when it is doing this? *Stamping with rage is voluntary.* Coming when one is called, in the normal surroundings, is voluntary. Involuntary walking, going for a walk, eating, speaking, singing, would be walking, eating, speaking etc. in an abnormal surrounding. E.g. when one is *unconscious*: if for the rest one is behaving like someone in narcosis; or when the movement goes on and one doesn't know anything about it as soon as one shuts one's eyes; or if one can't adjust the movement however much one wants to; etc.

8

Private Language and Private Experience

A human being can encourage himself, give himself orders, obey, blame and punish himself; he can ask himself a question and answer it. We could even imagine human beings who spoke only in monologue; who accompanied their activities by talking to themselves. – An explorer who watched them and listened to their talk might succeed in translating their language into ours. (This would enable him to predict these people's actions correctly, for he also hears them making resolutions and decisions.)

But could we also imagine a language in which a person could write down or give vocal expression to his inner experiences – his feelings, moods, and the rest – for his private use? – Well, can't we do so in our ordinary language? – But that is not what I mean. The individual words of this language are to refer to what can only be known to the person speaking; to his immediate private sensations. So another person cannot understand the language.

How do words *refer* to sensations? – There doesn't seem to be any problem here; don't we talk about sensations every day, and give them names? But how is the connexion between the name and the thing named set up? This question is the same as: how does a human being learn the meaning of the names of sensations? – of the word 'pain' for example. Here is one possibility: words are connected with the primitive, the natural, expressions of the sensation and used in their place. A child has hurt himself and he cries; and then adults talk to him and teach him exclamations and, later, sentences. They teach the child new pain-behaviour.

'So you are saying that the word "pain" really means crying?' – On the contrary: the verbal expression of pain replaces crying and does not describe it.

For how can I go so far as to try to use language to get between pain and its expression?

In what sense are my sensations *private*? – Well, only I can know whether I am really in pain; another person can only surmise it. – In one way this is wrong, and in another nonsense. If we are using the word 'to know' as it is normally used (and how else are we to use it?), then other people very often know when I am in pain. – Yes, but all the same not with the certainty with which I know it myself! – It can't be said of me at all (except perhaps as a joke) that I *know* I am in pain. What is it supposed to mean – except perhaps that I *am* in pain?

Other people cannot be said to learn of my sensations *only* from my behaviour, – for *I* cannot be said to learn of them. I *have* them.

The truth is: it makes sense to say about other people that they doubt whether I am in pain; but not to say it about myself.

'Only you can know if you had that intention.' One might tell someone this when one was explaining the meaning of the word 'intention' to him. For then it means: *that* is how we use it.

(And here 'know' means that the expression of uncertainty is senseless.)

The proposition 'Sensations are private' is comparable to: 'One plays patience by oneself'.

Are we perhaps over-hasty in our assumption that the smile of an unweaned infant is not a pretence? – And on what experience is our assumption based?

(Lying is a language-game that needs to be learned like any other one.)

Why can't a dog simulate pain? Is he too honest? Could one teach a dog to simulate pain? Perhaps it is possible to teach him to howl on particular occasions as if he were in pain, even when he is not. But the surroundings which are necessary for this behaviour to be real simulation are missing.

What does it mean when we say: 'I can't imagine the opposite of this' or 'What would it be like, if it were otherwise?' – For example, when someone has said that my images are private, or that only I myself can know whether I am feeling pain, and similar things.

Of course, here 'I can't imagine the opposite' doesn't mean: my powers of imagination are unequal to the task. These words are a defence against something whose form makes it look like an empirical proposition, but which is really a grammatical one.

But why do we say: 'I can't imagine the opposite'? Why not: 'I can't imagine the thing itself'?

Example: 'Every rod has a length.' That means something like: we call something (or *this*) 'the length of a rod' – but nothing 'the length of a sphere.' Now can I imagine 'every rod having a length'? Well, I simply imagine a rod. Only this picture, in connexion with this proposition, has a quite different role from one used in connexion with the proposition. 'This table has the same length as the one over there'. For here I understand what it means to have a picture of the opposite (nor need it be a mental picture).

But the picture attaching to the grammatical proposition could only shew, say, what is called 'the length of a rod'. And what should the opposite picture be?

((Remark about the negation of an *a priori* proposition.))

'This body has extension.' To this we might reply: 'Non-sense!' – but are inclined to reply 'Of course!' – Why is this?

'Another person can't have my pains.' – Which are *my* pains? What counts as a criterion of identity here? Consider what makes it possible in the case of physical objects to speak of 'two exactly the same', for example, to say 'This chair is not the one you saw here yesterday, but is exactly the same as it'.

In so far as it makes *sense* to say that my pain is the same as his, it is also possible for us both to have the same pain. (And it would also be imaginable for two people to feel pain in the same – not just the corresponding – place. That might be the case with Siamese twins, for instance.)

I have seen a person in a discussion on this subject strike himself on the breast and say: 'But surely another person can't have THIS pain!' – The answer to this is that one does not define a criterion of identity by emphatic stressing of the word 'this'. Rather, what the emphasis does is to suggest the case in which we are conversant with such a criterion of identity, but have to be reminded of it.

The substitution of 'identical' for 'the same' (for instance) is another typical expedient in philosophy. As if we were talking about shades of meaning and all that were in question were to find words to hit on the correct nuance. That is in question in philosophy only where we have to give a psychologically exact account of the temptation to use a particular kind of expression. What we 'are tempted to say' in such a case is, of course, not philosophy; but it is its raw material. Thus, for example, what a mathematician is inclined to say about the objectivity and reality of mathematical facts, is not a philosophy of mathematics, but something for philosophical *treatment*.

The philosopher's treatment of a question is like the treatment of an illness.

Now, what about the language which describes my inner experiences and which only I myself can understand? *How* do I use words to stand for my sensations? – As we ordinarily do? Then are my words for sensations tied up with my natural expressions of sensation? In that case my language is not a 'private' one. Someone else might understand it as well as I. – But suppose I didn't have any natural expression for the sensation, but only had the sensation? And now I simply *associate* names with sensations and use these names in descriptions. –

'What would it be like if human beings shewed no outward signs of pain (did not groan, grimace, etc.)? Then it would be impossible to teach a child the use of the word "tooth-ache".' – Well, let's assume the child is a genius and itself invents a name for the sensation! – But then, of course, he couldn't make himself understood when he used the word. – So does he understand the name, without being able to explain its meaning to anyone? – But what does it mean to say that he has 'named his pain'? – How has he done this naming of pain?! And whatever he did, what was its purpose? – When one says 'He gave a name to his sensation' one forgets that a great deal of stage-setting in the language is presupposed if the mere act of naming is to make sense. And when we speak of someone's having given a name to pain, what is presupposed is the existence of the grammar of the word 'pain'; it shews the post where the new word is stationed.

Let us imagine the following case. I want to keep a diary about the recurrence of a certain sensation. To this end I associate it with the sign 'S' and write this sign in a calendar for every day on which I have the sensation. — I will remark first of all that a definition of the sign cannot be formulated. – But still I can give myself a kind of ostensive definition. – How? Can I point to the sensation? Not in the ordinary sense. But I speak, or write the sign down, and at the same time I concentrate my attention on the sensation – and so, as it were, point to it inwardly. – But what is this ceremony for? for that is all it seems to be! A definition surely serves to establish the meaning of a sign. – Well, that is done precisely by the concentrating of my attention; for in this way I impress on myself the connexion between the sign and the sensation. – But 'I impress it on myself' can only mean: this process brings it about that I remember the connexion *right* in the future. But in the present case I have no criterion of correctness. One would like to say: whatever is going to seem right to me is right. And that only means that here we can't talk about 'right'.

Are the rules of the private language *impressions* of rules? – The balance on which impressions are weighed is not the *impression* of a balance.

'Well, I *believe* that this is the sensation S again.' – Perhaps you *believe* that you believe it!

Then did the man who made the entry in the calendar make a note of *nothing whatever*? – Don't consider it a matter of course that a person is making a note of something when he makes a mark – say in a calendar. For a note has a function, and this 'S' so far has none.

(One can talk to oneself. – If a person speaks when no one else is present, does that mean he is speaking to himself?)

What reason have we for calling 'S' the sign for a *sensation*? For 'sensation' is a word of our common language, not of one intelligible to me alone. So the use of this word stands in need of a justification which everybody understands. – And it would not help either to say that it need not be a *sensation*; that when he writes 'S', he has *something* – and that is all that can be said. 'Has' and 'something' also belong to our common language. – So in the end when one is doing philosophy one gets to the point where one would like just to emit an inarticulate sound. – But such a sound is an expression only as it occurs in a particular language-game, which should now be described.

It might be said: if you have given yourself a private definition of a word, then you must inwardly *undertake* to use the word in such-and-such a way. And how do you undertake that? Is it to be assumed that you invent the technique of using the word; or that you found it ready-made?

'But I can (inwardly) undertake to call THIS "pain" in the future.' – 'But is it certain that you have undertaken it? Are you sure that it was enough for this purpose to concentrate your attention on your feeling?' – A queer question. –

'Once you know *what* the word stands for, you understand it, you know its whole use.'

Let us imagine a table (something like a dictionary) that exists only in our imagination. A dictionary can be used to justify the translation of a word X by a word Y. But are we also to call it a justification if such a table is to be looked up only in the imagination? – 'Well, yes; then it is a subjective justification.' – But justification consists in appealing to something independent. – 'But surely I can appeal from one memory to another. For example, I don't know if I have remembered the time of departure of a train right and to check it I call to mind how a page of the time-table looked. Isn't it the same here?' – No; for this process has got to produce a memory which is actually *correct*. If the mental image of the time-table could not itself be *tested* for correctness, how could it confirm the correctness of the first memory? (As if someone were to buy several copies of the morning paper to assure himself that what it said was true.)

Looking up a table in the imagination is no more looking up a table than the image of the result of an imagined experiment is the result of an experiment.

I can look at the clock to see what time it is: but I can also look at the dial of a clock in order to *guess* what time it is; or for the same purpose move the hand of a clock till its position strikes me as right. So the look of a clock may serve to determine the time in more than one way. (Looking at the clock in imagination.)

Suppose I wanted to justify the choice of dimensions for a bridge which I imagine to be building, by making loading tests on the material of the bridge in my imagination. This would, of course, be to imagine what is called justifying the choice of dimensions for a bridge. But should we also call it justifying an imagined choice of dimensions?

Why can't my right hand give my left hand money? – My right hand can put it into my left hand. My right hand can write a deed of gift and my left hand a receipt. – But the further practical consequences would not be those of a gift. When the left hand has taken the money from the right, etc., we shall ask: 'Well, and what of it?' And the same could be asked if a person had given himself a private definition of a word; I mean, if he has said the word to himself and at the same time has directed his attention to a sensation.

Let us remember that there are certain criteria in a man's behaviour for the fact that he does not understand a word: that it means nothing to him, that he can do nothing with it. And criteria for his 'thinking he understands', attaching some meaning to the word, but not the right one. And, lastly, criteria for his understanding the word right. In the second case one might speak of a subjective understanding. And sounds which no one else understands but which I '*appear to understand*' might be called a 'private language'.

Let us now imagine a use for the entry of the sign 'S' in my diary. I discover that whenever I have a particular sensation a manometer shews that my blood-pressure rises. So I shall be able to say that my blood-pressure is rising without using any apparatus. This is a useful result. And now it seems quite indifferent whether I have recognized the sensation *right* or not. Let us suppose I regularly identify it wrong, it does not matter in the least. And that alone shews that the hypothesis that I make a mistake is mere show. (We as it were turned a knob which looked as if it could be used to turn on some part of the machine; but it was a mere ornament, not connected with the mechanism at all.)

And what is our reason for calling 'S' the name of a sensation here? Perhaps the kind of way this sign is employed in this language-game. – And why a 'particular sensation,' that is, the same one every time? Well, aren't we supposing that we write 'S' every time?

'Imagine a person whose memory could not retain *what* the word "pain" meant – so that he constantly called different things by that name – but nevertheless used the word in a way fitting in with the usual symptoms and presuppositions of pain' – in short he uses it as we all do. Here I should like to say: a wheel that can be turned though nothing else moves with it, is not part of the mechanism.

The essential thing about private experience is really not that each person possesses his own exemplar, but that nobody knows whether other people also have *this* or something else. The assumption would thus be possible – though unverifiable – that one section of mankind had one sensation of red and another section another.

What am I to say about the word 'red'? – that it means something 'confronting us all' and that everyone should really have another word, besides this one, to mean his *own* sensation of red? Or is it like this: the word 'red' means something known to everyone; and in addition, for each person, it means something known only to him? (Or perhaps rather: it *refers* to something known only to him.)

Of course, saying that the word 'red' 'refers to' instead of 'means' something private does not help us in the least to grasp its function; but it is the more psychologically apt expression for a particular experience in doing philosophy. It is as if when I uttered the word I cast a sidelong glance at the private sensation, as it were in order to say to myself: I know all right what I mean by it.

Look at the blue of the sky and say to yourself 'How blue the sky is!' – When you do it spontaneously – without philosophical intentions – the idea never crosses your mind that this impression of colour belongs only to *you*. And you have no hesitation in exclaiming that to someone else. And if you point at anything as you say the words you point at the sky. I am saying: you have not the feeling of pointing-into-yourself, which often accompanies 'naming the sensation' when one is thinking about 'private language'. Nor do you think that really you ought not to point to the colour with your hand, but with your attention. (Consider what it means 'to point to something with the attention'.)

But don't we at least *mean* something quite definite when we look at a colour and name our colour-impression? It is as if we detached the colour-*impression* from the object, like a membrane. (This ought to arouse our suspicions.)

But how is even possible for us to be tempted to think that we use a word to *mean* at one time the colour known to everyone – and at another the 'visual impression' which *I* am getting *now?* How can there be so much as a temptation here? — I don't turn the same kind of attention on the colour in the two cases. When I mean the colour impression that (as I should like to say) belongs to me alone I immerse myself in the colour – rather like when I 'cannot get my fill of a colour'. Hence it is easier to produce this experience when one is looking at a bright colour, or at an impressive colour-scheme.

'I know how the colour green looks to *me*' – surely that makes sense! – Certainly: what use of the proposition are you thinking of?

Imagine someone saying: 'But I know how tall I am!' and laying his hand on top of his head to prove it.

Someone paints a picture in order to shew how he imagines a theatre scene. And now I say: 'This picture has a double func-tion: it informs others, as pictures or words inform – but for the one who gives the information it is a representation (or piece of information?) of another kind: for him it is the picture of his image, as it can't be for anyone else. To him his private impres-sion of the picture means what he has imagined, in a sense in which the picture cannot mean this to others.' – And what right have I to speak in this second case of a representation or piece of information – if these words were rightly used in the *first* case?

'But doesn't what you say come to this: that there is no pain, for example, without *pain-behaviour?*' – It comes to this: only of a living human being and what resembles (behaves like) a living human being can one say: it has sensations; it sees; is blind; hears; is deaf; is conscious or unconscious.

'But in a fairy tale the pot too can see and hear!' (Certainly; but it *can* also talk.)
'But the fairy tale only invents what is not the case: it does not talk *nonsense*.' – It is not as simple as that. Is it false or nonsens-ical to say that a pot talks? Have we a clear picture of the circumstances in which we should say of a pot that it talked? (Even a nonsense-poem is not nonsense in the same way as the babbling of a child.)

We do indeed say of an inanimate thing that it is in pain: when playing with dolls for example. But this use of the concept of pain is a secondary one. Imagine a case in which people ascribed pain *only* to inanimate things; pitied *only* dolls! (When children play at trains their game is connected with their knowledge of trains. It would nevertheless be possible for the children of a tribe unacquainted with trains to learn this game from others, and to play it without knowing that it was copied from anything. One might say that the game did not make the same *sense* to them as to us.)

What gives us *so much as the idea* that living beings, things, can feel?

Is it that my education has led me to it by drawing my attention to feelings in myself, and now I transfer the idea to objects outside myself? That I recognize that there is something there (in me) which I can call 'pain' without getting into conflict with the way other people use this word? – I do not transfer my idea to stones, plants, etc.

Couldn't I imagine having frightful pains and turning to stone while they lasted? Well, how do I know, if I shut my eyes, whether I have not turned into a stone? And if that has happened, in what sense will *the stone* have the pains? In what sense will they be ascribable to the stone? And why need the pain have a bearer at all here?!

And can one say of the stone that it has a soul and *that* is what has the pain? What has a soul, or pain, to do with a stone?

Only of what behaves like a human being can one say that is *has* pains.

For one has to say it of a body, or, if you like of a soul which some body *has*. And how can a body *have* a soul?

Look at a stone and imagine it having sensations. – One says to oneself: How could one so much as get the idea of ascribing a *sensation* to a *thing*? One might as well ascribe it to a number! – And now look at a wriggling fly and at once these difficulties vanish and pain seems able to get a foothold here, where before everything was, so to speak, too smooth for it.

And so, too, a corpse seems to us quite inaccessible to pain. – Our attitude to what is alive and to what is dead, is not the same. All our reactions are different. – If anyone says: 'That cannot simply come from the fact that a living thing moves about in such-and-such a way and a dead one not', then I want to intimate to him that this is a case of the transition 'from quantity to quality'.

Think of the recognition of *facial expressions*. Or of the description of facial expressions – which does not consist in giving the measurements of the face! Think, too, how one can imitate a man's face without seeing one's own in a mirror.

But isn't it absurd to say of a *body* that it has pain? — And why does one feel an absurdity in that? In what sense is it true that my hand does not feel pain, but I in my hand?

What sort of issue is: Is it the *body* that feels pain? – How is it to be decided? What makes it plausible to say that it is *not* the body? – Well, something like this: if someone has a pain in his hand, then the hand does not say so (unless it writes it) and one does not comfort the hand, but the sufferer: one looks into his face.

How am I filled with pity *for this man*? How does it come out what the object of my pity is? (Pity, one may say, is a form of conviction that someone else is in pain.)

I turn to stone and my pain goes on. – Suppose I were in error and it was no longer *pain*? — But I can't be in error here; it means nothing to doubt whether I am in pain! – That means: if anyone said 'I do not know if what I have got is a pain or something else', we should think something like, he does not know what the English word 'pain' means; and we should explain it to him. – How? Perhaps by means of gestures, or by pricking him with a pin and saying: 'See, that's what pain is!' This explanation, like any other, he might understand right, wrong, or not at all. And he will shew which he does by his use of the word, in this as in other cases.

If he now said, for example: 'Oh, I know what 'pain' means; what I don't know is whether *this*, that I have now, is pain' – we should merely shake our heads and be forced to regard his words as a queer reaction which we have no idea what to do with. (It would be rather as if we heard someone say seriously: 'I distinctly remember that some time before I was born I believed . . . '.)

That expression of doubt has no place in the language-game; but if we cut out human behaviour, which is the expression of sensation, it looks as if I might *legitimately* begin to doubt afresh.

My temptation to say that one might take a sensation for something other than what it is arises from this: if I assume the abrogation of the normal language-game with the expression of a sensation, I need a criterion of identity for the sensation; and then the possibility of error also exists.

'When I say 'I am in pain' I am at any rate justified *before myself*.' – What does that mean? Does it mean: 'If someone else could know what I am calling 'pain', he would admit that I was using the word correctly'?

To use a word without a justification does not mean to use it without right.

What I do is not, of course, to identify my sensation by criteria: but to repeat an expression. But this is not the *end* of the language-game: it is the beginning.

But isn't the beginning the sensation – which I describe? – Perhaps this word 'describe' tricks us here. I say 'I describe my state of mind' and 'I describe my room'. You need to call to mind the differences between the language-games.

What we call '*descriptions*' are instruments for particular uses. Think of a machine-drawing, a cross-section, an elevation with measurements, which an engineer has before him. Thinking of a description as a word-picture of the facts has something misleading about it: one tends to think only of such pictures as hang on our walls: which seem simply to portray how a thing looks, what it is like. (These pictures are as it were idle.)

Don't always think that you read off what you say from the facts; that you portray these in words according to rules. For even so you would have to apply the rule in the particular case without guidance.

If I say of myself that it is only from my own case that I know what the word 'pain' means – must I not say the same of other people too? And how can I generalize the *one* case so irresponsibly?

Now someone tells me that *he* knows what pain is only from his own case! – Suppose everyone had a box with something in it: we call it a 'beetle'. No one can look into anyone else's box, and everyone says he knows what a beetle is only by looking at *his* beetle. – Here it would be quite possible for everyone to have something different in his box. One might even imagine such a thing constantly changing. – But suppose the word 'beetle' had a use in these people's language? – If so it would not be used as the name of a thing. The thing in the box has no place in the language-game at all; not even as a *something*: for the box might even be empty. – No, one can 'divide through' by the thing in the box; it cancels out, whatever it is.

That is to say: if we construe the grammar of the expression of sensation on the model of 'object and designation' the object drops out of consideration as irrelevant.

If you say he sees a private picture before him, which he is describing, you have still made an assumption about what he has before him. And that means that you can describe it or do describe it more closely. If you admit that you haven't any notion what kind of thing it might be that he has before him – then what leads you into saying, in spite of that, that he has something before him? Isn't it as if I were to say of someone: 'He *has* something. But I don't know whether it is money, or debts, or an empty till.'

'I know . . . only from my *own* case' – what kind of proposition is this meant to be at all? An experiential one? No. – A grammatical one?

Suppose everyone does say about himself that he knows what pain is only from his own pain. – Not that people really say that, or are even prepared to say it. But *if* everybody said it — it might be a kind of exclamation. And even if it gives no information, still it is a picture, and why should we not want to call up such a picture? Imagine an allegorical painting take the place of those words.

When we look into ourselves as we do philosophy, we often get to see just such a picture. A full-blown pictorial representation of our grammar. Not facts; but as it were illustrated turns of speech.

'Yes, but there is *something* there all the same accompanying my cry of pain. And it is on account of that that I utter it. And this something is what is important – and frightful.' – Only whom are we informing of this? And on what occasion?

Of course, if water boils in a pot, steam comes out of the pot and also pictured steam comes out of the pictured pot. But what if one insisted on saying that there must also be something boiling in the picture of the pot?

The very fact that we should so much like to say: '*This* is the important thing' – while we point privately to the sensation – is enough to shew how much we are inclined to say something which gives no information.

Being unable – when we surrender ourselves to philosophical thought – to help saying such-and-such; being irresistibly inclined to say it – does not mean being forced into an *assumption*, or having an immediate perception or knowledge of a state of affairs.

It is – we should like to say – not merely the picture of the behaviour that plays a part in the language-game with the words 'he is in pain', but also the picture of the pain. Or, not merely the paradigm of the behaviour, but also that of the pain. – It is a misunderstanding to say 'The picture of pain enters into the language-game with the word "pain".' The image of pain is not a picture and *this* image is not replaceable in the language-game by anything that we should call a picture. – The image of pain certainly enters into the language game in a sense; only not as a picture.

An image is not a picture, but a picture can correspond to it.

If one has to imagine someone else's pain on the model of one's own, this is none too easy a thing to do: for I have to imagine pain which I *do not feel* on the model of the pain which I *do feel*. That is, what I have to do is not simply to make a transition in imagination from one place of pain to another. As, from pain in the hand to pain in the arm. For I am not to imagine that I feel pain in some region of his body. (Which would also be possible.)

Pain-behaviour can point to a painful place – but the subject of pain is the person who gives it expression.

'I can only *believe* that someone else is in pain, but I *know* it if I am.' – Yes: one can make the decision to say 'I believe he is in pain' instead of 'He is in pain'. But that is all. — What looks like an explanation here, or like a statement about a mental process, is in truth an exchange of one expression for another which, while we are doing philosophy, seems the more appropriate one.

Just try – in a real case – to doubt someone else's fear or pain.

'But you will surely admit that there is a difference between pain-behaviour accompanied by pain and pain-behaviour without any pain?' – Admit it? What greater difference could there be? – 'And yet you again and again reach the conclusion that the sensation itself is a *nothing*.' – Not at all. It is not a *something*, but not a *nothing* either! The conclusion was only that a nothing would serve just as well as a something about which nothing could be said. We have only rejected the grammar which tries to force itself on us here.

The paradox disappears only if we make a radical break with the idea that language always functions in one way, always serves the same purpose: to convey thoughts – which may be about houses, pains, good and evil, or anything else you please.

'But you surely cannot deny that, for example, in remembering, an inner process takes place.' – What gives the impression that we want to deny anything? When one says 'Still, an inner process does take place here' – one wants to go on: 'After all, you *see* it.' And it is this inner process that one means by the word 'remembering'. – The impression that we wanted to deny something arises from our setting our faces against the picture of the 'inner process'. What we deny is that the picture of the inner process gives us the correct idea of the use of the word 'to remember'. We say that this picture with its ramifications stands in the way of our seeing the use of the word as it is.

Why should I deny that there is a mental process? But 'There has just taken place in me the mental process of remembering . . .' means nothing more than: 'I have just remembered . . .'. To deny the mental process would mean to deny the remembering; to deny that anyone ever remembers anything.

'Are you not really a behaviourist in disguise? Aren't you at bottom really saying that everything except human behaviour is a fiction?' – If I do speak of a fiction, then it is of a *grammatical* fiction.

How does the philosophical problem about mental processes and states and about behaviourism arise? — The first step is the one that altogether escapes notice. We talk of processes and states and leave their nature undecided. Sometime perhaps we shall know more about them – we think. But that is just what commits us to a particular way of looking at the matter. For we have a definite concept of what it means to learn to know a process better. (The decisive movement in the conjuring trick has been made, and it was the very one that we thought quite innocent.) – And now the analogy which was to make us understand our thoughts falls to pieces. So we have to deny the yet uncomprehended process in the yet unexplored medium. And now it looks as if we had denied mental processes. And naturally we don't want to deny them.

What is your aim in philosophy? – To shew the fly the way out of the fly-bottle.

I tell someone I am in pain. His attitude to me will then be that of belief; disbelief; suspicion; and so on.
Let us assume he says: 'It's not so bad.' – Doesn't that prove that he believes in something behind the outward expression of pain? — His attitude is a proof of his attitude. Imagine not merely the words 'I am in pain' but also the answer 'It's not so bad' replaced by instinctive noises and gestures.

'What difference could be greater?' – In the case of pain I believe that I can give myself a private exhibition of the difference. But I can give anyone an exhibition of the difference between a broken and an unbroken tooth. – But for the private exhibition you don't have to give yourself actual pain; it is enough to *imagine* it – for instance, you screw up your face a bit. And do you know that what you are giving yourself this exhibition of is pain and not, for example, a facial expression? And how do you know what you are to give yourself an exhibition of before you do it? This *private* exhibition is an illusion.

But again, *aren't* the cases of the tooth and the pain similar? For the visual sensation in the one corresponds to the sensation of pain in the other. I can exhibit the visual sensation to myself as little or as well as the sensation of pain.
Let us imagine the following: The surfaces of the things around us (stones, plants, etc.) have patches and regions which produce pain in our skin when we touch them. (Perhaps through the chemical composition of these surfaces. But we need not know that.) In this case we should speak of pain-patches on the leaf of a particular plant just as at present we speak of red

patches. I am supposing that it is useful to us to notice these patches and their shapes; that we can infer important properties of the objects from them.

I can exhibit pain, as I exhibit red, and as I exhibit straight and crooked and trees and stones. – *That* is what we *call* 'exhibiting'.

It shews a fundamental misunderstanding, if I am inclined to study the headache I have now in order to get clear about the philosophical problem of sensation.

★ ★ ★

Should we say that the person who has not learned the language knows that he sees red but can't express it? – Or should we say: 'He knows what he sees but can't express it'? – So, besides seeing it, he also knows what he sees?

Now suppose I asked: 'How do I know that I see, and that I see red? I.e., how do I know that I do what you call seeing and seeing red?' For we use the words 'seeing' and 'red' in a game we play with one another.

Use of: 'He knows what color he sees,' 'I know what color I saw,' etc.

How do we know what color a person sees? By the sample he points to? And how do we know what relation the sample is meant to have to the original? Now are we to say 'We never know . . .'? Or had we better cut these 'We never know' out of our language and consider how as a matter of fact we are wont to use the word 'to know'?

What if someone asked: 'How do I know that what I call seeing red isn't an *entirely* different experience every time? and that I am not deluded into thinking that it is the same or nearly the same?' Here again the answer 'I can't know' and the subsequent removal of the question.

'He's in a better position to say what he sees than we are.' – That depends.

If we say 'he'll tell us what he saw,' it is as though he would make use of language which we had never taught him.

It is as if now we have got an *insight* into something which before we had only seen from the outside.

Inside and outside!

'Our teaching connects the word "red" (or is meant to connect it) with a particular impression of his (a private impression, an impression in him). He then communicates this impression – indirectly, of course – through the medium of speech.'

As long as you use the picture direct-indirect you can't trust yourself about the grammatical situation otherwise [in other ways].

Is telling what one sees something like turning one's inside out? And learning to say what one sees learning to let others see inside us?

'We teach him to make us see what he sees.' He seems in an indirect way to show us *the object* which he sees, the object which is before his mind's eye. 'We can't look at it, it is in him.'

The idea of the private *object* of vision. Appearance, sense datum.

Whence the idea of the privacy of sense data?

'But do you really wish to say that they are not private? That one person can see the picture before the other person's eye?'

Surely you wouldn't think that *telling* someone what one sees could be a more direct way of communicating than by pointing to a sample!

If I say what it is I see, how do I compare what I say with what I see in order to know whether I say the truth?

Lying about what I see, you might say, is knowing what I see and saying something else. Supposing I said it just consists of saying to myself "this is red" and aloud "this is green."

Compare lying and telling the truth in the case of telling what color you see, with the case of describing a picture which you saw, or telling the right number of things you had to count.

Collating what you say and what you see.

Is there always a collating?

Or could one call it giving a picture of the color I see if I say the word red? Unless it be a picture by its connections with a sample.

But isn't it giving a picture if I point to a sample?

'What I show *reveals* what I see' – in what sense does it do that? The idea is that now you can so to speak look inside me. Whereas I only reveal to you what I see in a game of revealing and hiding which is entirely played with signs of one category. 'Direct-indirect.'

We are thinking of a game in which there is an inside in the normal sense.

We must get clear about how the metaphor of revealing (outside and inside) is actually applied by us; otherwise we shall be tempted to look for an inside behind that which in our metaphor is the inside.

'If he had learned to show me (or tell me) what he sees, he could now show me.' Certainly – but what is it like to show me what he sees? It is pointing to something under particular circumstances. Or is it something else (don't be misled by the idea of indirectness)?

You compare it with such a statement as: 'If he had learned to open up, I could now see what's inside.' I say yes, but remember what opening up in this case is like.

But what about the criterion whether there is anything inside or not? Here we say 'I know there's something inside in *my* case. This is how I know about an inside and am led to suppose it in the other person too.'

Further, we are not inclined to say that only hitherto we have not known the inside of another person, but that the idea of this knowledge is bound up with the idea of myself.

'So if I say "he has toothache" I am supposing that he has what I have when I have toothache.' Suppose I said: 'If I say "I *suppose* he has toothache" I am supposing that he has what I have if I have toothache' – this would be like saying 'If I say "this cushion is red" I mean that it has the same color which the sofa has if it is red.' But this isn't what I intended to say with the first sentence. I wished to say that talking about his toothache at all was based upon a supposition, a supposition which by its very essence could not be verified.

But if you look closer you will see that this is an entire misrepresentation of the use of the word "toothache."

★ ★ ★

Consider this case: someone says 'I can't understand it, I see everything red blue today and vice versa.' We answer 'it must look queer!' He says it does and, e.g., goes on to say how cold the glowing coal looks and how warm the clear (blue) sky. I think we should under these or similar circumstances be inclined to say that he saw red what we saw blue. And again we should say that we know that he means by the words "blue" and "red" what we do as he has always used them as we do.

On the other hand: Someone tells us today that yesterday he always saw everything red blue, and so on. We say: But you called the glowing coal red, you know, and the sky blue. He answers: That was because I had also changed the names. We say: But didn't it feel very queer? and he says: No, it seemed all perfectly natural. Would we in this case too say: ... ?

The case of contradictory memory images: tomorrow he remembers this, the day after tomorrow something else.

The whole trend, to show that the expression 'letting one look into his soul,' is often misleading.

Now I ask what are our criteria for there being or having been a personal experience besides the expression? And the answer seems to be that for the other man the criteria are indeed mere outside expressions, but that I myself know whether I have an experience or not; in particular, whether I see red or not.

But let me ask: what is knowing that I see red like? I mean: look at something red, 'know that it is red,' and ask yourself what you are doing. Don't you mean seeing red and impressing it on your mind that you are doing so? But there are, I suppose, several things that you are doing: You probably *say* to yourself the word "red" or "this is red" or something of the sort, or perhaps glance from the red object to another red one which you're taking to be the paradigm of red, and suchlike. On the other hand you just silently stare at the red thing.

In part of their uses the expression 'visual image' and 'picture' run parallel; but where they don't, the analogy which does exist tends to delude us.

(Tautology.)

The grammar of "seeing red" is connected to the expression of seeing red closer than one thinks.

We may say a blind man doesn't see anything. But not only do we say so but he too says that he does not see. I don't mean 'he agrees with us that he does not see – he doesn't dispute it,' but rather: he too describes the facts in this way, having learned the same language as we have. Now whom shall we call blind? What is our criterion for blindness? A certain kind of behavior. And if the person behaves in that particular way, we not only call him blind but teach him to call himself blind. And in *this* sense his behavior also determines the meaning of blindness for *him*. But now you will say: 'Surely blindness isn't a behavior; it's clear that a man can behave like a blind man and not be blind. Therefore "blindness" means something different; his behavior only helps him to understand what we mean by "blindness." The outward circumstances are what both he and we know. Whenever he behaves in a certain way, we say that he sees nothing; but he notices that a certain private experience of his coincides with all these cases and so concludes that we mean this experience of his by saying that he sees nothing.'

* * *

'Surely seeing is one thing, and showing that I see is another thing.' – This certainly is like saying 'skipping is one thing and jumping another.' But there is a supplement to this statement – 'skipping is this (showing it) and jumping is this (showing it).' Now how about this supplement in the first case? 'Seeing red is this (showing it) and showing that we see red is this (showing it).' The point is that there just isn't a 'showing that I see' except showing that I see. 'But can't I say "seeing red is what I'm doing now" (looking at something red)? And although in a sense the other man can't directly see what I'm talking about (be aware of the activity), I certainly know what it is that I'm talking about. That is, although for him I can't point directly to my seeing red, for myself I can point to it; and in this sense I can give an ostensive definition of the expression to myself.' But an ostensive definition is not a magic act.

So what does giving myself the ostensive definition of red consist in? – Now how am I to describe it? shall I say: seeing red and saying to myself 'I see red,' – or is it 'seeing a certain color sensation and saying "I see red" '? The first version I don't like. It assumes that the other knows the very same private impression which I am having. So I would rather leave it open what color I am concentrating my attention on. But then how can I call it a color? Isn't it just as uncertain that I mean by 'color' what they mean as that I mean by 'red' what they mean? And the same applies of course to 'seeing' (for what here I mean by this word is not an activity of the inner eye).

'But it's a blatant error to mix up "seeing red" with showing that you see red! I know what seeing red is and I know what showing . . . is.' Couldn't we say that knowing what showing . . . is is seeing showing? Now what is knowing what seeing is?

In knowing what seeing red is you seem to say to yourself 'seeing red is this' – you seem to give yourself a sample but you don't because the usual criteria for the sameness of the sample don't apply. I can say I call 'red' always the same color, or whenever I explain 'red' I point to a sample of the same color.

Consider the proposition: He makes sure what it means *to him* by . . . Would you say the word had meaning to him if it meant something else every time? And what is the criterion of the same color coming twice?

If we describe a game which he plays with himself, is it relevant that he should use the word 'red' for the same color in our sense, or would we also call it a language game if he used it anyhow? Then what is the criterion for using it in the same way? Not merely the connection between 'same,' 'color,' and 'red.'

'Let me see if I still know which of these colors is red? – (Looking about.) Yes I know.' (Here I could have said 'is called red.')

Making sure that you know what 'seeing red' means, is good only if you can make use of this knowledge in a further case. Now what if I see a color again, can I say I made sure I knew what 'red' was so now I shall know that I recognize it correctly? In what sense is having said the words 'this is red' before a guarantee that I now see the same color when I say again I see red?

The grammar of 'private sense data.'

' "Toothache" is a word which I use in a game which I play with other people, but it has a private meaning to me.'

In the use of the word 'meaning' it is essential that the same meaning is kept throughout a game.

'Are you sure that you call "toothache" always the same private experience?'

What's the use here of being sure, if it doesn't follow that it is so and if your being sure is the only criterion there is for its being so?

This means: This isn't at all a case of being sure, of conviction.

'So-and-so has excellent health, he never had to go to the dentist, never complained about toothache; but as toothache is a private experience, we can't know whether he hasn't had terrible toothache all his life.'

How does one assume such and such to be the case? What is an assumption that, e.g., '*A* has toothache'? Is it saying the words '*A* has toothache'? Or doesn't it consist in doing something with these words?

'A game of assumption.' –

Assuming: a state of mind. Assuming: a gesture.

Certain behaviour under certain circumstances we call showing our toothache, and other behavior hiding our toothache. Now would we talk about this behavior in this way if people didn't ordinarily behave in the way they do? Suppose I and they described my behavior without such a word as pain, would the description be incomplete? The question is: do *I* consider it incomplete? If so, I will distinguish between two cases of my behavior, and the others will say that I use two words alternately for my behavior and thereby they will acknowledge that I have toothache.

'But can't he have toothache without in any way showing it?

And this shows that the word "toothache" has a meaning entirely independent of a behavior connected with toothache.'

The game we play with the word 'toothache' entirely depends upon there being a behavior which we call the expression of toothache.

'We use "toothache" as the name of a personal experience.' – Well, let's see how we *use* the word!

'But you know the sensation of toothache! So you can give it a name, say, "*t*." '

But what is it like to give a sensation a name? Say it is pronouncing the name while one has the sensation and possibly concentrating on the sensation, – but what of it? Does this name thereby get magic powers? And why on earth do I call these sounds the 'name' of the sensation? I know what I do with the name of a man or of a number, but have I by this act of 'definition' given the name a use?

'To give a sensation a name' means nothing unless I know already in what sort of a game this name is to be used.

★ ★ ★

'Expressions can always be lying.' How can we say this of the expressions to which we fasten our words?

Suppose a child learned the word 'toothache' as an equivalent for its moaning, and noticed that whenever it said the word or moaned the grown-ups treated it particularly well. The child then uses moaning or the word 'toothache' as a means to bring about the desired effect: is the child lying?

You say: 'Surely I can moan with toothache and I can moan without toothache; so why shouldn't it be so with the child? Of course I only see and hear the child's behavior but from my own experience I know what toothache is (I know toothache apart from behavior) and I am led to believe that the others sometimes have the pains I have.' – The first sentence already is misleading. It isn't the question whether I *can* moan with or without toothache, the point is that I distinguish 'moaning with toothache' and 'moaning without toothache' and now we can't go on to say that of course in the child we make the same distinction. In fact we don't. We teach the child to use the words 'I have toothache' to replace its moans, and this was how I too was taught the expression. How do I know that I've learned the word 'toothache' to mean what they wanted me to express? I ought to say I *believe* I have!

Now one can moan because one has pain, or, e.g., one can moan on the stage. How do I know that the child, small as it is, doesn't already act, and in this case I teach it to mean by 'toothache' something I don't intend it to mean.

I have taught the child to use the expression 'I have toothache' under certain circumstances. And now it uses the words under these circumstances. – But what are these circumstances? Shall I say 'the circumstances under which it moaned,' and what are these?

But now I also teach the child to moan on the stage! That is to say, I *teach* it to use this expression in a different game. I also teach it to read out the sentence 'I have toothache' from a book, when it hasn't toothache. In fact I could teach it to lie, as a separate language game. (In fact we often play this kind of game with children.)

'But doesn't what you say come to this: that it doesn't matter what the persons feel as long as only they behave in a particular way?'

'Do you mean that you can define pain in terms of behavior?' But is this what we do if we teach the child to use the expression 'I have toothache'? Did I define: 'Toothache is such and such a behavior'? This obviously contradicts entirely the normal use of the word! 'But can't you, on the other hand, at least for yourself give an *ostensive* definition of "toothache"? Pointing to the place of your pain and saying "this is . . ."?' Can't I give a name to the pain I've got? Queer idea to give one's pain a name! What's it to do with a name? Or what do I do with it? What do I do with the name of a person whom I *call* by the name? What connection is the name to have with the pain? The only connection so far is that you had toothache, pointed to your cheek, and pronounced the word 'moo.' 'So what?' Remember what we said about private ostensive definition.

'But aren't you neglecting something – the experience or

whatever you might call it –? Almost *the world* behind the mere words?'

But here solipsism teaches us a lesson: It is that thought which is *on the way* to destroy this error. For if the *world* is idea it isn't any person's idea. (Solipsism stops short of saying this and says that it is my idea.) But then how could I say what the world is if the realm of ideas has no neighbor? What I do comes to defining the word 'world.'

'I neglect that which goes without saying.'

'What is seen *I* see' (pointing to my body). I point at my geometrical eye, saying this. Or I point with closed eyes and touch my breast and feel it. In no case do I make a connection between what is seen and a person.

Back to 'neglecting'! It seems that I neglect life. But not life physiologically understood but life as consciousness. And consciousness not physiologically understood, or understood from the outside, but consciousness as the very essence of experience, the appearance of the world, the world.

Couldn't I say: If I had to add the world to my language it would have to be one sign for the whole of language, which sign could therefore be left out.

How am I to describe the way the child learns the word 'toothache' – like this?: The child sometimes has toothache, it moans and holds its cheek, the grown-ups say '. . .,' etc. Or: The child cometimes moans and holds its cheek, the grown-ups . . . ? Does the first description say something superfluous or false, or does the second leave out something essential? Both descriptions are correct.

'But it seems as if you were neglecting something.' But what more can I do than *distinguish* the case of saying 'I have toothache' when I really have toothache, and the case of saying the words without having toothache. I am also (further) ready to talk of any *x* behind my words so long as it keeps its identity.

Isn't what you reproach me of as though you said: 'In your language you're only *speaking!*'

★ ★ ★

Privacy of sense data. I must bore you with a repetition of what I said last time. We said that one reason for introducing the idea of the sense datum was that people, as we say, sometimes see different things, colors, e.g., looking at the same object. Cases in which we say 'he sees dark red whereas I see light red.' We are inclined to talk about an object other than the physical object which the person sees who is said to see the physical object. It is further clear that we only gather from the other person's behavior (e.g., what he tells us) what that object looks like, and so it lies near to say that he has this object before his mind's eye and that we don't see it. Though we can also say that we might have it before our mind's eye as well, without however knowing that he has it before his mind's eye. The 'sense datum' here – the way the physical object appears to him. In other cases no physical object enters.

Now I want to draw your attention to one particular difficulty about the use of the 'sense datum.' We said that there were cases in which we should say that the person sees green what I see red. Now the question suggests itself: if this can be so at all, why should it not be always the case? It seems, if once we have admitted that it can happen under peculiar circumstances, that it may always happen. But then it is clear that the very idea of seeing red loses its use if we can never know if the other does not see something utterly different. So what are we to do: Are we to say that this can only happen in a limited number of cases? This is a very serious situation. – We introduced the expression that *A* sees something else than *B* and we mustn't forget that this had use only under the circumstances under which we introduced it. Consider the proposition: 'Of course we never know whether new circumstances wouldn't show that after all he saw what we see.' Remember that this whole notion need not have been introduced. 'But can't I *imagine* all blind men to see as well as I do and only behaving differently; and on the other hand imagine them really blind? For if I can imagine these possibilities, then the question, even if never answerable makes sense.' Imagine a man, say W., now blind, now seeing, and observe what you do? How do these images give sense to the question? They don't, and you see that the expression stands and falls with its usefulness.

The idea that the other person sees something else than I, is only introduced to account for certain expressions: whereas it seems that this idea can exist without any reference to expressions. 'Surely what I have he too can have.'

'And remember that we admit that the other may have pain without showing it! So if this is conceivable, why not that he never shows pain; and why not that everybody has pain constantly without showing it; or that even things have pain?!' What strikes us is that there seem to be a few useful applications of the idea of the other person's having pain without showing it, and a vast number of useless applications, applications which look as though they were no applications at all. And these latter applications seem to have their justification in this, that we can imagine the other person to have what we have and in this way the proposition that he has toothache seems to make sense apart from any expression at all. 'Surely,' we say, 'I can imagine him to have pain or to see, etc.' Or, 'As I can see myself, so I can imagine him to do the same.' In other words I can imagine him to play the same role in the act of seeing which I play. But does saying this determine what I mean by 'he sees'?

We arrive at the conclusion that imagining him to have pain (etc.) does not fix the sense of the sentence 'he has pain.'

'He may all along mean something different by "green" than I mean.' Evidence (verification). But there is this consideration: 'Surely I mean something particular, a particular impression, and therefore he may have another impression; surely I know what that would be like!' 'Surely I know what it is like to have the impression I call "green"!' But what is it like? You are inclined to look at a green object and to say 'it's like *this!*' And these words, though they don't explain anything to anybody else, seem to be at any rate an explanation you give yourself. But are they?! Will this explanation justify your future use of the word 'green'? In fact seeing green doesn't allow you to make the substitutions of someone else for you and of red for green.

'The sense datum is private' is a rule of grammar, it forbids [rules out] the use of such expressions as 'they saw the same sense datum'; it may (or may not) allow such sentences as 'he guessed that the other had a sense datum of this . . . kind.' It may only allow expressions of the form: 'The other looked round, had a sense datum and said . . .' You see that this word in such a case has no use at all. But if you like to use it, do! –

'But surely I distinguish between having toothache and expressing it, and merely expressing it; and I distinguish between these two in myself.' 'Surely this is not merely a matter of using different expressions, but there are two distinct experiences!' 'You talk as though the case of having pain and that of not having pain were only distinguished by the way in which I expressed myself!'

But do we always distinguish between 'mere behavior' and 'experience + behavior'? If we see someone falling into flames and crying out, do we say to ourselves: 'there are of course two cases: . . .'? Or if I see you here before me do I distinguish? Do you? You can't! That we do in certain cases, doesn't show that we do in all cases.

9
Aspect and Image

We call seeing, hearing, . . . sense-perception. There are analogies and connexions between these concepts, and these are our justification for so taking them together.

It can, then, be asked: what kind of connexions and analogies exist between seeing and hearing? Between seeing and touching? Between seeing and smelling?

And if we ask this, then the senses, so to say, at once shift further apart from one another than they seemed to be at first sight.

Psychological concepts are just everyday concepts. They are not concepts newly fashioned by science for its own purpose, as are the concepts of physics and chemistry. Psychological concepts are related to those of the exact sciences as the concepts of the science of medicine are to those of old women who spend their time nursing the sick.

Plan for the treatment of psychological concepts.

Psychological verbs characterized by the fact that the third person of the present is to be identified by observation, the first person not.

Sentences in the third person of the present: information. In the first person present, expression. ((Not quite right.))

Sensations: their inner connexions and analogies.

All have genuine duration. Possibility of giving the beginning and the end. Possibility of their being synchronized, of simultaneous occurrence.

All have degrees and qualitative mixtures. Degree: scarcely perceptible – unendurable.

In this sense there is not a sensation of position or movement.

Place of feeling in the body: differentiates seeing and hearing from sense of pressure, temperature, taste and pain.

(If sensations are characteristic of the position and movements of the limbs, at any rate their place is not the joint.)

One *knows* the position of one's limbs and their movements. One can give them if asked, for example. Just as one also knows the place of a sensation (pain) in the body.

Reaction of touching the painful place.

No local sign about the sensation. Any more than a temporal sign about a memory-image. (Temporal signs in a photograph.)

Pain differentiated from other sensations by a characteristic expression. This makes it akin to joy (which is not a sense-experience).

'Sensations give us knowledge about the external world.'

Images:

Auditory images, visual images – how are they distinguished from sensations? Not by 'vivacity'.

Images tell us nothing, either right or wrong, about the external world. (Images are not hallucinations, nor yet fancies.)

While I am looking at an object I cannot imagine it.

Difference between the language-games: 'Look at this figure!' and: 'Imagine this figure!'

Images are subject to the will.

Images are not pictures. I do not tell what object I am imagining by the resemblance between it and the image.

Asked 'What image have you?' one can answer with a picture.

One would like to say: The imaged is in a different *space* from the heard sound. (Question: Why?)

I read a book and have all sorts of images while I read, i.e. while I am looking attentively.

People might exist who never use the expression 'seeing something with the inner eye' or anything like it, and these people might be able to draw and model 'out of imagination' or memory, to mimic the characteristic behaviour of others etc. They might also shut their eyes or stare into vacancy as if blind before drawing something from memory. And yet they might deny that they then *see* before them what they go on to draw.

'Do you see the way she's coming in the door?' – and now one imitates it.

That is to say, 'seeing' is inseparably connected with 'looking'. ((i.e., that is *one* way of fixing the concept, which produces a physiognomy.))

The words which describe what we see are properties of things. We don't learn their meaning in connection with the concept of 'inner seeing'.

But if we ask, 'What is the difference between a visual picture and an image-picture?' – the answer could be: The same description can represent both what I see and what I imagine.

To say that there is a difference between a visual picture and an image-picture means that one imagines things differently from the way they appear.

I might also have said earlier: The *tie-up* between imaging and seeing is close; but there is no *similarity*.

The language-games employing both these concepts are radically different – but hang together.

A difference: 'trying to see something' and 'trying to form an image of something'. In the first case one says: 'Look, just over there!', in the second 'Shut your eyes!'

So don't you know, after all, whether what is seen (e.g., an after-image) and an image look exactly alike? (Or should I say: *are?*) – This question could only be an empirical one, and could only mean something like: 'Does it ever, or even often, happen that a person can keep an image in front of his mind uninterruptedly and for some time, and describe it in detail, as one can do, for example, with an after-image?'

'Now can you still see the bird?' – 'I fancy that I can still see it.' That doesn't mean: Maybe I am imagining it.

'Seeing and imaging are different phenomena.' – The words 'seeing' and 'imaging' are used differently. 'I see' is used differently from 'I have an image', 'See!' differently from 'Form an image!', and 'I am trying to see it' differently from 'I am trying to form an image of it'. – 'But the phenomena are: that men see and that we form images of things.' A phenomenon is something that can be observed. Now how does one observe that men see?

I can observe, e.g., that birds fly, or lay eggs. I can tell someone, 'You see, these creatures fly. Notice how they flap their wings and lift themselves into the air.' I can also say, 'You see, this child is not blind. It can see. Notice how it follows the flame of the candle.' But can I satisfy myself, so to speak, *that men see?*

'Men see.' – As opposed to *what?* Maybe that they are all blind?

Can I imagine a case in which I might say, 'Yes, you are right, men see'? – Or: 'Yes, you are right, men see, even as I do.'

'Seeing and understanding are different phenomena.' – The words 'seeing' and 'understanding' have different meanings! Their meanings relate to a host of important kinds of human behaviour, to phenomena of human life.

To close one's eyes in order to form an image of something is a phenomenon; to strain in looking another; to follow a thing in motion with one's eyes yet another.

Imagine someone saying: 'Man can see or be blind'! One could say that 'seeing', 'imaging', and 'hoping' are simply not words for phenomena. But of course that doesn't mean that the psychologist doesn't observe phenomena.

To say that imaging is subject to the will can be misleading, for it makes it seem as if the will were a kind of motor and the images were connected with it, so that it could evoke them, put them into motion, and shut them off.

Isn't it conceivable that there should be a man for whom ordinary seeing was subject to the will? Would seeing then teach him about the external world? Would things have colours if we could see them as we wished?

It is just because imaging is subject to the will that it does not instruct us about the external world.

In this way – but in no other – it is related to an activity such as drawing.

And yet it isn't easy to call imaging an activity.

But what if I tell you: 'Imagine a melody'? I have to 'sing it inwardly' to myself. That will be called an activity just as much as calculating in the head.

Consider also that you can order someone to 'Draw N.N. so

as to be like your image of him', and that whether he does this is not determined by the likeness of the portrait. Analogous to this is the fact that I have an image of N.N. even if my image is wrong.

If I say that imaging is subject to the will that does not mean that it is, as it were, a voluntary movement, as opposed to an involuntary one. For the same movement of the arm which is now voluntary might also be involuntary. – I mean: it makes *sense* to order someone to 'Imagine that', or again: 'Don't imagine that.'

But doesn't the connection with the will refer merely, so to speak, to the machinery which produces or changes what is imaged (the image-picture)? – Here no picture is engendered, unless someone manufactures a picture, a real picture.

The dagger which Macbeth sees before him is not an imagined dagger. One can't take an image for reality nor things seen for things imaged. But this is not because they are so dissimilar.

One objection to the imagination's being voluntary is that images often beset us against our will and remain, refusing to be banished.

Yet the will can struggle against them. But isn't calling them voluntary like calling a movement of my arm voluntary when someone forces my arm *against my will?*

If someone insists that what he calls a 'visual image' is like a visual impression, say to yourself once more that perhaps he is *making a mistake!* Or: Suppose that he is making a mistake. That is to say: What do you know about the resemblance of his visual impression and his visual image?! (I speak of others because what goes for them goes for me too.)

So what do you know about this resemblance? It is manifested only in the expressions which he is inclined to use; not in something he uses those expressions to say.

'There's no doubt at all: visual images and visual impressions are of the same kind!' That must be something you know from your own experience; and in that case it is something that may be true for you and not for other people. (And this of course holds for me too, if *I* say it.)

Nothing is more difficult than facing concepts *without prejudice.* (And that is the principal difficulty of philosophy.)

Forming an image of something is comparable to an activity. (Swimming.)

When we form an image of something we are not observing. The coming and going of the pictures is not something that *happens* to us. We are not surprised by these pictures, saying 'Look! . . .'

We do not banish visual impressions, as we do images.

If we could banish impressions and summon them before our minds then they couldn't inform us about reality. – So do impressions differ from images only in that we can affect the latter and not the former? Then the difference is empirical! But this is precisely what is not the case.

Is it conceivable that visual impressions could be banished or called back? What is more, isn't it really possible? If I look at my hand and then move it out of my visual field, haven't I voluntarily broken off the visual impression of it? – But I will be told that that sort of thing isn't called 'banishing the picture of the hand'! Certainly not; but where does the difference lie? One would like to say that the will affects images directly.

For if I voluntarily change my visual impression, then *things* obey my will.

But what if visual impressions could be controlled directly? Should I say, 'Then there wouldn't be any impressions, but only images'? And what would that be like? How would I find out, for instance, that another person has a certain image? He would tell me. – But how would he learn the necessary words, let us say 'red' and 'round'? For surely I couldn't teach them to him by pointing to something red and round. I could only evoke within myself the image of my pointing to something of the sort. And furthermore I couldn't test whether he was understanding me. Why, I could of course not even *see* him; no, I could only form an image of him.

Isn't this hypothesis really like the one that there is *only* fiction in the world and no truth?

And of course I myself couldn't learn or invent a description of my images. For what would it mean to say, e.g., that I was forming an image of a red cross on a white background? What does a red cross look like? *Like this*?? – But couldn't a higher being know intuitively *what* images I am forming, and describe them in his language, even though *I* couldn't understand it? Suppose that this higher being were to say, 'I know what image this man is now forming; it is this: . . .'. – But how was I able to call that 'knowing'? It is completely different from what *we* call 'knowing what someone else is imaging'. How can the normal case be compared with the one we have invented?

If I think of myself in this case as a third person, then I would have absolutely no idea what the higher being means when it says, with regard to someone who has only images and no impressions, that it knows which images that man has.

'But nevertheless can't I still imagine such a case?' The first thing to say is, you can *talk* about it. But that doesn't show that you have thought it through completely. (5 o'clock on the sun.)

One would also like to talk about what a visual impression and an image *look like*. And also to ask, perhaps, 'Couldn't something look like my present visual impression for instance, but otherwise *behave* as an image?' And clearly there is a mistake here.

But imagine this: We get someone to look through a hole into a kind of peep show, and inside we now move various objects and figures about, either by chance or intentionally, so that their movement is exactly what our viewer wanted, so that he fancies that what he sees is obeying his will. – Now could he be deluded, and believe that his visual impressions are images? That sounds totally absurd. I don't even need the peep show, but have only to look at my hand and move it, as mentioned above. But even if I could will the curtain over there to move, or could make it disappear, I should still not interpret that as something that was going on in my imagination.

I simply can't begin to take an impression for an image. But what does that mean? Could I think of a case in which *someone else* did that? Why isn't that conceivable?

If someone really were to say 'I don't know whether I am now seeing a tree or having an image of it', I should at first think he meant: 'or just fancying that there is a tree over there'. If he does not mean this, I couldn't understand him at all – but if someone tried to explain this case to me and said 'His images are of such extraordinary vivacity that he can take them for impressions of sense' – should I understand it then?

Still, imagine a person who says, 'My images are as vivid today as real visual impressions'. – Would he have to be lying or talking nonsense? No, certainly not. To be sure I would first have to have him tell me how this manifests itself.

But if he were to tell me, 'Often I don't know whether I see something or only have an image of it', then I wouldn't call this a case of overly vivid imaging.

But must one not distinguish here: forming the image of a human face, as we say, but not in the space that surrounds me – and on the other hand: forming an image of a picture on that wall over there?

At the request 'Imagine a round spot over there' one might fancy that one really was seeing one there.

To be sure, if I say 'Isn't there really a spot over there?', and therefore perhaps look there more closely, then what I am here calling an image does *not* obey my will. And of course if I *fancy* something to be the case, that does not obey my will.

* * *

Two uses of the word 'see'.

The one: 'What do you see there?' – 'I see *this*' (and then a description, a drawing, a copy). The other: 'I see a likeness between these two faces' – let the man I tell this to be seeing the faces as clearly as I do myself.

The importance of this is the difference of category between the two 'objects' of sight.

The one man might make an accurate drawing of the two faces, and the other notice in the drawing the likeness which the former did not see.

I contemplate a face, and then suddenly notice its likeness to another. I *see* that it has not changed; and yet I see it differently. I call this experience 'noticing an aspect'.

Its *causes* are of interest to psychologists.

We are interested in the concept and its place among the concepts of experience.

You could imagine the illustration

appearing in several places in a book, a text-book for instance. In the relevant text something different is in question every time: here a glass cube, there an inverted open box, there a wire frame of that shape, there three boards forming a solid angle. Each time the text supplies the interpretation of the illustration.

But we can also *see* the illustration now as one thing now as another. – So we interpret it, and *see* it as we *interpret* it.

Here perhaps we should like to reply: The description of what is got immediately, i.e. of the visual experience, by means of an interpretation – is an indirect description. 'I see the figure as a box' means: I have a particular visual experience which I have found that I always have when I interpret the figure as a box or when I look at a box. But if it meant this I ought to know it. I ought to be able to refer to the experience directly, and not only indirectly. (As I can speak of red without calling it the colour of blood.)

I shall call the following figure, derived from Jastrow[1], the duck-rabbit. It can be seen as a rabbit's head or as a duck's.

And I must distinguish between the 'continuous seeing' of an aspect and the 'dawning' of an aspect.

The picture might have been shewn me, and I never have seen anything but a rabbit in it.

Here it is useful to introduce the idea of a picture-object. For instance

would be a 'picture-face'.

[1]   Fact and Fable in Psychology.

In some respects I stand towards it as I do towards a human face. I can study its expression, can react to it as to the expression of the human face. A child can talk to picture-men or picture-animals, can treat them as it treats dolls.

I may, then, have seen the duck-rabbit simply as a picture-rabbit from the first. That is to say, if asked 'What's that?' or 'What do you see here?' I should have replied: 'A picture-rabbit'. If I had further been asked what that was, I should have explained by pointing to all sorts of pictures of rabbits, should perhaps have pointed to real rabbits, talked about their habits, or given an imitation of them.

I should not have answered the question 'What do you see here?' by saying: 'Now I am seeing it as a picture-rabbit'. I should simply have described my perception: just as if I had said 'I see a red circle over there.' –
Nevertheless someone else could have said of me: 'He is seeing the figure as a picture-rabbit.'

It would have made as little sense for me to say 'Now I am seeing it as . . .' as to say at the sight of a knife and fork 'Now I am seeing this as a knife and fork'. This expression would not be understood. – Any more than: 'Now it's a fork' or 'It can be a fork too'.

One doesn't '*take*' what one knows as the cutlery at a meal *for* cutlery; any more than one ordinarily tries to move one's mouth as one eats, or aims at moving it.

If you say 'Now it's a face for me', we can ask: 'What change are you alluding to?'

I see two pictures, with the duck-rabbit surrounded by rabbits in one, by ducks in the other. I do not notice that they are the same. Does it *follow* from this that I *see* something different in the two cases? – It gives us a reason for using this expression here.

'I saw it quite differently, I should never have recognized it!' Now, that is an exclamation. And there is also a justification for it.

I should never have thought of superimposing the heads like

that, of making *this* comparison between them. For they suggest a different mode of comparison.

Nor has the head seen like *this* the slightest similarity to the head seen like *this* — although they are congruent.

I am shewn a picture-rabbit and asked what it is; I say 'It's a rabbit'. Not 'Now it's a rabbit'. I am reporting my perception. – I am shewn the duck-rabbit and asked what it is; I *may* say 'It's a duck-rabbit'. But I may also react to the question quite differently. – The answer that it is a duck-rabbit is again the report of a perception; the answer 'Now it's a rabbit' is not. Had I replied 'It's a rabbit', the ambiguity would have escaped me, and I should have been reporting my perception.

The change of aspect. 'But surely you would say that the picture is altogether different now!'

But what is different: my impression? my point of view? – Can I say? I *describe* the alteration like a perception; quite as if the object had altered before my eyes.

'Now I am seeing *this*', I might say (pointing to another picture, for example). This has the form of a report of a new perception.

The expression of a change of aspect is the expression of a *new* perception and at the same time of the perception's being unchanged.

I suddenly see the solution of a puzzle-picture. Before, there were branches there; now there is a human shape. My visual impression has changed and now I recognize that it has not only shape and colour but also a quite particular 'organization'. – My visual impression has changed; – what was it like before and what is it like now? – If I represent it by means of an exact copy – and isn't that a good representation of it? – no change is shewn.

And above all do *not* say 'After all my visual impression isn't the *drawing*; it is *this* — which I can't shew to anyone.' – Of course it is not the drawing, but neither is it anything of the same category, which I carry within myself.

The concept of the 'inner picture' is misleading, for this concept uses the '*outer* picture' as a model; and yet the uses of the words for these concepts are no more like one another than the uses of 'numeral' and 'number'. (And if one chose to call numbers 'ideal numerals', one might produce a similar confusion.)

If you put the 'organization' of a visual impression on a level with colours and shapes, you are proceeding from the idea of the visual impression as an inner object. Of course this makes this object into a chimera; a queerly shifting construction. For the similarity to a picture is now impaired.

If I know that the schematic cube has various aspects and I want to find out what someone else sees, I can get him to make a model of what he sees, in addition to a copy, or to point to such a model; even though *he* has no idea of my purpose in demanding two accounts.

But when we have a changing aspect the case is altered. Now the only possible expression of our experience is what before perhaps seemed, or even was, a useless specification when once we had the copy.

And this by itself wrecks the comparison of 'organization' with colour and shape in visual impressions.

If I saw the duck-rabbit as a rabbit, then I saw: these shapes and colours (I give them in detail) – and I saw besides something like this; and here I point to a number of different pictures of rabbits. – This shews the difference between the concepts.

'Seeing as . . .' is not part of perception. And for that reason it is like seeing and again not like.

I look at an animal and am asked: 'What do you see?' I answer: 'A rabbit'. – I see a landscape; suddenly a rabbit runs past. I exclaim 'A rabbit!'

Both things, both the report and the exclamation, are expressions of perception and of visual experience. But the exclamation is so in a different sense from the report: it is forced from us. – It is related to the experience as a cry is to pain.

But since it is the description of a perception, it can also be called the expression of thought. — If you are looking at the object, you need not think of it; but if you are having the visual experience expressed by the exclamation, you are also *thinking* of what you see.

Hence the flashing of an aspect on us seems half visual experience, half thought.

* * *

The concept of an aspect is akin to the concept of an image. In other words: the concept 'I am now seeing it as . . .' is akin to 'I am now having *this* image'.

Doesn't it take imagination to hear something as a variation on a particular theme? And yet one is perceiving something in so hearing it.

'Imagine this changed like this, and you have this other thing.' One can use imagining in the course of proving something.

Seeing an aspect and imagining are subject to the will. There is such an order as 'Imagine *this*', and also: 'Now see the figure like *this*'; but not: 'Now see this leaf green'.

The question now arises: Could there be human beings lacking in the capacity to see something *as something* – and what would that be like? What sort of consequences would it have? – Would this defect be comparable to colour-blindness or to not having absolute pitch? – We will call it 'aspect-blindness' – and will next consider what might be meant by this. (A conceptual investigation.) The aspect-blind man is supposed not to see the aspects A change. But is he also supposed not to recognize that the double cross contains both a black and a white cross? So if told 'Shew me figures containing a black cross among these examples' will he be unable to manage it? No, he should be able to do that; but he will not be supposed to say: 'Now it's a black cross on a white ground!'

Is he supposed to be blind to the similarity between two faces? – And so also to their identity or approximate identity? I do not want to settle this. (He ought to be able to execute such orders as 'Bring me something that looks like *this*.')

Ought he to be unable to see the schematic cube as a cube? – It would not follow from that that he could not recognize it as a representation (a working drawing for instance) of a cube. But for him it would not jump from one aspect to the other. – Question: Ought he to be able to *take* it as a cube in certain circumstances, as we do? – If not, this could not very well be called a sort of blindness.

The 'aspect-blind' will have an altogether different relation-ship to pictures from ours.

(Anomalies of *this* kind are easy for us to imagine.)

Aspect-blindness will be *akin* to the lack of a 'musical ear'.

The importance of this concept lies in the connexion between the concepts of 'seeing an aspect' and 'experiencing the meaning of a word'. For we want to ask 'What would you be missing if you did not *experience* the meaning of a word?'

What would you be missing, for instance, if you did not understand the request to pronounce the word 'till' and to mean it as a verb, – or if you did not feel that a word lost its meaning and became a mere sound if it was repeated ten times over?

In a law-court, for instance, the question might be raised how someone meant a word. And this can be inferred from certain facts. – It is a question of *intention*. But could how he experi-enced a word – the word 'bank' for instance – have been signific-ant in the same way?

Suppose I had agreed on a code with someone; 'tower' means bank. I tell him 'Now go to the tower' – he understands me and acts accordingly, but he feels the word 'tower' to be strange in this use, it has not yet 'taken on' the meaning.

'When I read a poem or narrative with feeling, surely some-thing goes on in me which does not go on when I merely skim the lines for information.' – What processes am I alluding to? – The sentences have a different *ring*. I pay careful attention to my intonation. Sometimes a word has the wrong intonation, I em-phasize it too much or too little. I notice this and shew it in my face. I might later talk about my reading in detail, for example about the mistakes in my tone of voice. Sometimes a picture, as it were an illustration, comes to me. And this seems to help me to read with the correct expression. And I could mention a good deal more of the same kind. – I can also give a word a tone of voice which brings out the meaning of the rest, almost as if this word were a picture of the whole thing. (And this may, of course, depend on sentence-formation.)

When I pronounce this word while reading with expression it is completely filled with its meaning. – 'How can this be, if meaning is the use of the word?' Well, what I said was intended figuratively. Not that I chose the figure: it forced itself on me. – But the figurative employment of the word can't get into conflict with the original one.

Perhaps it could be explained why precisely *this* picture suggests itself to me. (Just think of the expression, and the meaning of the expression: 'the word that hits it off'.)

But if a sentence can strike me as like a painting in words, and the very individual word in the sentence as like a picture, then it is no such marvel that a word uttered in isolation and without purpose can seem to carry a particular meaning in itself.

* * *

An aspect is subject to the will. If something appears blue to me, I cannot see it red, and it makes no sense to say 'See it red'; whereas it does make sense to say 'See it as . . .'. And that the aspect is voluntary (at least to a certain extent) seems to be essential to it, as it is essential to imaging that *it* is voluntary. I mean: voluntariness seems to me (but why?) not to be a mere addition; as if one were to say: 'This movement can, as a matter of experience, also be brought about in *this* way.' That is to say: It is essential that one can say 'Now see it like *this*' and 'Form an image of . . .'. For this hangs together with the aspect's not 'teaching us something about the external world'. One may teach the words 'red' and 'blue' by saying 'This is red and not blue'; but one can't teach someone the meaning of 'figure' and 'ground' by pointing to an ambiguous figure.

We do not first become acquainted with images and only later learn to bend them to our will. And of course it is anyway quite wrong to think that we have been directing them, so to speak, with our will. As if the will governed them, as orders may govern men. As if, that is, the will were an influence, a force, or again: a primary *action*, which then is the cause of the outward perceptible action.

10

The First Person

This leads us to considering the criteria for the identity of a person. Under what circumstances do we say: 'This is the same person whom I saw an hour ago'? Our actual use of the phrase 'the same person' and of the name of a person is based on the fact that many characteristics which we use as the criteria for identity coincide in the vast majority of cases. I am as a rule recognized by the appearance of my body. My body changes its appearance only gradually and comparatively little, and likewise my voice, characteristic habits, etc. only change slowly and within a narrow range. We are inclined to use personal names in the way we do, only as a consequence of these facts. This can best be seen by imagining unreal cases which show us what different 'geometries' we would be inclined to use if facts were different. Imagine, e.g., that all human bodies which exist looked alike, that on the other hand, different sets of characteristics seemed, as it were, to change their habitation among these bodies. Such a set of characteristics might be, say, mildness, together with a high pitched voice, and slow movements, or a choleric temperament, a deep voice, and jerky movements, and such like. Under such circumstances, although it would be possible to give the bodies names, we should perhaps be as little inclined to do so as we are to give names to the chairs of our dining-room set. On the other hand, it might be useful to give names to the sets of characteristics, and the use of these names would now *roughly* correspond to the personal names in our present language.

Or imagine that it were usual for human beings to have two characters, in this way: People's shape, size and characteristics of behaviour periodically undergo a complete change. It is the usual thing for a man to have two such states, and he lapses suddenly from one into the other. It is very likely that in such a society we should be inclined to christen every man with two names, and perhaps to talk of the pair of persons in his body. Now were Dr Jekyll and Mr Hyde two persons or were they the same person who merely changed? We can say whichever we like. We are not forced to talk of a double personality.

There are many uses of the word 'personality' which we may feel inclined to adopt, all more or less akin. The same applies when we define the identity of a person by means of his memories. Imagine a man whose memories on the even days of his life comprise the events of all these days, skipping entirely what happened on the odd days. On the other hand, he remembers on an odd day what happened on previous odd days, but his memory then skips the even days without a feeling of discontinuity. If we like we can also assume that he has alternating appearances and characteristics on odd and even days. Are we bound to say that here two persons are inhabiting the same body? That is, is it right to say that there are, and wrong to say that there aren't, or vice versa? Neither. For the *ordinary* use of the word 'person' is what one might call a composite use suitable under the ordinary circumstances. If I assume, as I do, that these circumstances are changed, the application of the term 'person' or 'personality' has thereby changed; and if I wish to preserve this term and give it a use analogous to its former use, I am at liberty to choose between many uses, that is, between many different kinds of analogy. One might say in such a case that the term 'personality' hasn't got one legitimate heir only. (This kind of consideration is of importance in the philosophy of mathematics. Consider the use of the words 'proof', 'formula', and others. Consider the question: 'Why should what we do here be called 'philosophy'? Why should it be regarded as the only legitimate heir of the different activities which had this name in former times?')

* * *

There are two different cases in the use of the word 'I' (or 'my') which I might call 'the use as object' and 'the use as subject'. Examples of the first kind of use are these: 'My arm is broken', 'I have grown six inches', 'I have a bump on my forehead', 'The wind blows my hair about'. Examples of the second kind are: '*I* see so-and-so', '*I* hear so-and-so', '*I* try to lift my arm', '*I* think it will rain', '*I* have toothache'. One can point to the difference between these two categories by saying: The cases of the first category involve the recognition of a particular person, and there is in these cases the possibility of an error, or as I should rather put it: The possibility of an error has been provided for. The possibility of failing to score has been provided for in a pin game. On the other hand, it is not one of the hazards of the game that the balls should fail to come up if I have put a penny in the slot. It is possible that, say in an accident, I should feel a pain in my arm, see a broken arm at my side, and think it is mine, when really it is my neighbour's. And I could, looking into a mirror, mistake a bump on his forehead for one on mine. On the other hand, there is no question of recognizing a person when I say I have toothache. To ask 'are you sure that it's *you* who have pains?' would be nonsensical. Now, when in this case no error is possible, it is because the move which we might be inclined to think of as an error, a "bad move", is no move of the game at all. (We distinguish in chess between good and bad moves, and we call it a mistake if we expose the queen to a bishop. But it is no mistake to promote a pawn to a king.) And now this way of stating our idea suggests itself: that it is as impossible that in making the statement 'I have toothache' I should have mistaken another person for myself, as it is to moan with pain by mistake, having mistaken someone else for me. To say, 'I have pain' is no more a statement *about* a particular person than moaning is. 'But surely the word "I" in the mouth of a man refers to the man who says it; it points to himself; and very often a man who says it actually points to himself with his finger'. But it was quite superfluous to point to himself. He might just as well only have raised his hand. It would be wrong to say that when someone points to the sun with his hand, he is pointing both to the sun and himself because it is *he* who points; on the other hand, he may by pointing attract attention both to the sun and to himself.

The word 'I' does not mean the same as 'L. W.' even if I am L. W., nor does it mean the same as the expression 'the person who is now speaking'. But that doesn't mean: that 'L. W.' and 'I' mean different things. All it means is that these words are different instruments in our language.

Think of words as instruments characterized by their use, and then think of the use of a hammer, the use of a chisel, the use of a square, of a glue pot, and of the glue. (Also, all that we say here can be understood only if one understands that a great variety of games is played with the sentences of our language: Giving and obeying orders; asking questions and answering them; describing an event; telling a fictitious story; telling a joke; describing an immediate experience; making conjectures about events in the physical world; making scientific hypotheses and theories; greeting someone, etc., etc.) The mouth which says 'I' or the hand which is raised to indicate that it is I who wish to speak, or I who have toothache, does not thereby point to anything. If, on the other hand, I wish to indicate the *place* of my pain, I point. And here again remember the difference between pointing to the painful spot without being led by the eye and on the other hand pointing to a scar on my body after looking for it. ('That's where I was vaccinated'.) – The man who cries out with pain, or says that he has pain, *doesn't choose the mouth which says it.*

All this comes to saying that the person of whom we say 'he has pain' is, by the rules of the game, the person who cries, contorts his face, etc. The place of the pain – as we have said – may be in another person's body. If, in saying 'I', I point to my own body, I model the use of the word 'I' on that of the demonstrative 'this person' or 'he'. (This way of making the two expressions similar is somewhat analogous to that which one sometimes adopts in mathematics, say in the proof that the sum of the three angles of a triangle is 180°.

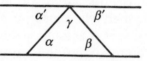

We say '$\alpha = \beta'$, $\beta = \beta'$, and $\gamma = \gamma'$. The first two equalities are of an entirely different kind from the third.) In 'I have pain', 'I' is not a demonstrative pronoun.

Compare the two cases: 1. 'How do you know that *he* has pains?' – 'Because I hear him moan'. 2. 'How do you know that you have pains?' – 'Because I *feel* them'. But 'I feel them' means the same as 'I have them'. Therefore this was no explanation at all. That, however, in my answer I am inclined to stress the word 'feel' and not the word 'I' indicates that by 'I' I don't wish to pick out one person (from amongst different persons).

The difference between the propositions 'I have pain' and 'he has pain' is not that of 'L. W. has pain' and 'Smith has pain'. Rather, it corresponds to the difference between moaning and saying that someone moans. – 'But surely the word 'I' in "I have pain" serves to distinguish me from other people, because it is by the sign "I" that I distinguish saying that I have pain from saying that one of the others has'. I imagine a language in which, instead of 'I found nobody in the room', one said 'I found Mr Nobody in the room'. Imagine the philosophical problems which would arise out of such a convention. Some philosophers brought up in this language would probably feel that they didn't like the similarity of the expressions 'Mr Nobody' and 'Mr Smith'. When we feel that we wish to abolish the 'I' in 'I have pain', one may say that we tend to make the verbal expression of pain similar to the expression by moaning. – We are inclined to forget that it is the particular use of a word only which gives the word its meaning. Let us think of our old example for the use of words: Someone is sent to the grocer with a slip of paper with the words 'five apples' written on it. The use of the word *in practice* is its meaning. Imagine it were the usual thing that the objects around us carried labels with words on them by means of which our speech referred to the objects. Some of these words would be proper names of the objects, others generic names (like table, chair, etc.), others again, names of colours, names of shapes, etc. That is to say, a label would only have a meaning to us in so far as we made a particular use of it. Now we could easily imagine ourselves to be impressed by merely seeing a label on a thing, and to forget that what makes these labels important is their use. In this way we sometimes believe that we have named something when we make the gesture of pointing and utter words like 'This is . . .' (the formula of the ostensive definition). We say we call something 'toothache', and think that the word has received a definite function in the dealings we carry out with language when, under certain circumstances, we have pointed to our cheek and said: 'This is toothache'. (Our idea is that when we point and the other 'only knows what we are pointing to' he knows the use of the word. And here we have in mind the special case when "what we point to" is, say, a person and 'to know that I point to' means to see which of the persons present I point to.)

We feel then that in the cases in which 'I' is used as subject, we don't use it because we recognize a particular person by his bodily characteristics; and this creates the illusion that we use this word to refer to something bodiless, which, however, has its seat in our body. In fact *this* seems to be the real ego, the one of which it was said, 'Cogito, ergo sum'. – 'Is there then no mind, but only a body?' Answer: The word 'mind' has meaning, i.e., it has a use in our language; but saying this doesn't yet say what kind of use we make of it.

* * *

'But when I imagine something, or even actually *see* objects, I have *got* something which my neighbour has not.' – I understand you. You want to look about you and say: 'At any rate only I have got THIS.' – What are these words for? They serve no purpose. – Can one not add: 'There is here no question of a "seeing" – and therefore none of a "having" – nor of a subject, nor therefore of "I" either'? Might I not ask: In what sense have you *got* what you are talking about and saying that only you have got it? Do you possess it? You do not even *see* it. Must you not really say that no one has got it? And this too is clear: if as a matter of logic you exclude other people's having something, it loses its sense to say that you have it.

But what is the thing you are speaking of? It is true I said that I knew within myself what you meant. But that meant that I knew how one thinks to conceive this object, to see it, to make one's looking and pointing mean it. I know how one stares ahead and looks about one in this case – and the rest. I think we can say: you are talking (if, for example, you are sitting in a room) of the "visual room". The "visual room" is the one that has no owner. I can as little own it as I can walk about it, or look at it, or point to it. Inasmuch as it cannot be any one else's it is not mine either. In other words, it does not belong to me *because* I want to use the same form of expression about it as about the material room in which I sit. The description of the latter need not mention an owner, in fact it need not have any owner. But then the visual room *cannot* have any owner. 'For' – one might say – 'it has no master, outside or in.'

Think of a picture of a landscape, an imaginary landscape with a house in it. – Someone asks 'Whose house is that?' – The answer, by the way, might be 'It belongs to the farmer who is sitting on the bench in front of it'. But then he cannot for example enter his house.

One might also say: Surely the owner of the visual room would have to be the same kind of thing as it is; but he is not to be found in it, and there is no outside.

The "visual room" seemed like a discovery, but what its discoverer really found was a new way of speaking, a new comparison; it might even be called a new sensation.

You have a new conception and interpret it as seeing a new object. You interpret a grammatical movement made by yourself as a quasi-physical phenomenon which you are observing. (Think for example of the question: 'Are sense-data the material of which the universe is made?')

But there is an objection to my saying that you have made a "grammatical" movement. What you have primarily discovered is a new way of looking at things. As if you had invented a new way of painting; or, again, a new metre, or a new kind of song. –

'It's true I say "Now I am having such-and-such an image", but the words "I am having" are merely a sign to someone *else*; the description of the image is a *complete* account of the imagined world.' – You mean: the words 'I am having' are like 'I say! . . .' You are inclined to say it should really have been expressed differently. Perhaps simply by making a sign with one's hand and then giving a description. – When as in this case, we disapprove of the expressions of ordinary language (which are after all performing their office), we have got a picture in our heads which conflicts with the picture of our ordinary way of speaking. Whereas we are tempted to say that our way of speaking does not describe the facts as they really are. As if, for example the proposition 'he has pains' could be false in some other way than by that man's *not* having pains. As if the form of expression were saying something false even when the proposition *faute de mieux* asserted something true.

For *this* is what disputes between Idealists, Solipsists and Realists look like. The one party attack the normal form of expression as if they were attacking a statement; the others defend it, as if they were stating facts recognized by every reasonable human being.

If I were to reserve the word 'pain' solely for what I had hitherto called 'my pain', and others 'L.W.'s pain', I should do other people no injustice, so long as a notation were provided in which the loss of the word 'pain' in other connexions were somehow supplied. Other people would still be pitied, treated by doctors and so on. It would, of course, be *no* objection to this mode of expression to say: 'But look here, other people have just the same as you!'

But what should I gain from this new kind of account? Nothing. But after all neither does the solipsist *want* any practical advantage when he advances his view!

'When I say "I am in pain", I do not point to a person who is in pain, since in a certain sense I have no idea *who* is.' And this can be given a justification. For the main point is: I did not say that such-and-such a person was in pain, but 'I am . . .' Now in saying this I don't name any person. Just as I don't name anyone when I *groan* with pain. Though someone else sees who is in pain from the groaning.

What does it mean to know *who* is in pain? It means, for example, to know which man in this room is in pain: for instance, that it is the one who is sitting over there, or the one who is standing in that corner, the tall one over there with the fair hair, and so on. – What am I getting at? At the fact that there is a great variety of criteria for personal '*identity*'.

Now which of them determines my saying that '*I*' am in pain? None.

'But at any rate when you say "I am in pain", you want to draw the attention of others to a particular person.' – The answer might be: No, I want to draw their attention to *myself*. –

'But surely what you want to do with the words "I am . . ." is to distinguish between *yourself* and *other* people.' – Can this be said in every case? Even when I merely groan? And even if I do "want to distinguish" between myself and other people – do I want to distinguish between the person L.W. and the person N.N.?

It would be possible to imagine someone groaning out: 'Someone is in pain – I don't know who!' – and our then hurrying to help him, the one who groaned.

'But you aren't in doubt whether it is you or someone else who has the pain!' – The proposition 'I don't know whether I or someone else is in pain' would be a logical product, and one of its factors would be: 'I don't know whether I am in pain or not' – and that is not a significant proposition.

Imagine several people standing in a ring, and me among them. One of us, sometimes this one, sometimes that, is connected to the poles of an electrical machine without our being able to see this. I observe the faces of the others and try to see which of us has just been electrified. – Then I say: 'Now I *know* who it is; for it's myself.' In this sense I could also say: 'Now I know who is getting the shocks; it is myself.' This would be a rather queer way of speaking. – But if I make the supposition that I can feel the shock even when someone else is electrified, then the expression 'Now I know who . . .' becomes quite unsuitable. It does not belong to this game.

'I' is not the name of a person, nor 'here' of a place, and 'this' is not a name. But they are connected with names. Names are explained by means of them. It is also true that it is characteristic of physics not to use these words.

Consider how the following questions can be applied, and how settled:
(1) 'Are these books *my* books?'
(2) 'Is this foot *my* foot?'
(3) 'Is this body *my* body?'
(4) 'Is this sensation *my* sensation?'
Each of these questions has practical (non-philosophical) applications.
(2) Think of cases in which my foot is anaesthetized or paralysed. Under certain circumstances the question could be settled by determining whether I can feel pain in this foot.
(3) Here one might be pointing to a mirror-image. Under certain circumstances, however, one might touch a body and ask the question. In others it means the same as: 'Does my body look like *that*?'
(4) Which sensation does one mean by "*this*" one? That is: how is one using the demonstrative pronoun here? Certainly otherwise than in, say, the first example! Here confusion occurs because one imagines that by directing one's attention to a sensation one is pointing to it.

The feeling of an unbridgeable gulf between consciousness and brain-process: how does it come about that this does not come into the considerations of our ordinary life? This idea of a difference in kind is accompanied by slight giddiness, – which occurs when we are performing a piece of logical sleight-of-hand. (The same giddiness attacks us when we think of certain theorems in set theory.) When does this feeling occur in the present case? It is when I, for example, turn my attention in a particular way on to my own consciousness, and, astonished, say to myself: THIS is supposed to be produced by a process in the brain! – as it were clutching my forehead. – But what can it mean to speak of 'turning my attention on to my own consciousness'? This is surely the queerest thing there could be! It was a particular act of gazing that I called doing this. I stared fixedly in front of me – but *not* at any particular point or object. My eyes were wide open, the brows not contracted (as they mostly are when I am interested in a particular object). No such interest preceded this gazing. My glance was vacant; or again *like* that of someone admiring the illumination of the sky and drinking in the light.

Now bear in mind that the proposition which I uttered as a paradox (THIS is produced by a brain-process!) has nothing paradoxical about it. I could have said it in the course of an experiment whose purpose was to shew that an effect of light which I see is produced by stimulation of a particular part of the brain. – But I did not utter the sentence in the surroundings in which it would have had an everyday and unparadoxical sense. And my attention was not such as would have accorded with making an experiment. (If it had been, my look would have been intent, not vacant.)

Here we have a case of introspection, not unlike that from which William James got the idea that the 'self' consisted mainly of "peculiar motions in the head and between the head and throat". And James' introspection shewed, not the meaning of the word 'self' (so far as it means something like 'person', 'human being', 'he himself', 'I myself'), nor any analysis of such a thing, but the state of a philosopher's attention when he says the word 'self' to himself and tries to analyse its meaning. (And a good deal could be learned from this.)

You think that after all you must be weaving a piece of cloth: because you are sitting at a loom – even if it is empty – and going through the motions of weaving.

What we are supplying are really remarks on the natural

history of human beings; we are not contributing curiosities however, but observations which no one has doubted, but which have escaped remark only because they are always before our eyes.

'Human beings agree in saying that they see, hear, feel, and so on (even though some are blind and some are deaf). So they are their own witnesses that they have *consciousness*.' – But how strange this is! Whom do I really inform, if I say 'I have consciousness'? What is the purpose of saying this to myself, and how can another person understand me? – Now, expressions like 'I see', 'I hear', 'I am conscious' really have their uses. I tell a doctor 'Now I am hearing with this ear again', or I tell someone who believes I am in a faint 'I am conscious again', and so on.

Do I observe myself, then, and perceive that I am seeing or conscious? And why talk about observation at all? Why not simply say 'I perceive I am conscious'? – But what are the words 'I perceive' for here? – why not say 'I am conscious'? – But don't the words 'I perceive' here shew that I am attending to my consciousness? – which is ordinarily not the case. – If so, then the sentence 'I perceive I am conscious' does not say that I am conscious, but that my attention is disposed in such-and-such a way.

But isn't it a particular experience that occasions my saying 'I am conscious again'? – *What* experience? In what situations do we say it?

* * *

If you observe your own grief, which senses do you use to observe it? A particular sense; one that *feels* grief? Then do you feel it *differently* when you are observing it? And what is the grief that you are observing – is it one which is there only while it is being observed?

'Observing' does not produce what is observed. (That is a conceptual statement.)

Again: I do not 'observe' what only comes into being through observation. The object of observation is something *else*.

A touch which was still painful yesterday is no longer so today.

Today I feel the pain only when I think about it. (That is: in certain circumstances.)

My grief is no longer the same; a memory which was still unbearable to me a year ago is now no longer so.

That is a result of observation.

When do we say that any one is observing? Roughly: when he puts himself in a favourable position to receive certain impressions in order (for example) to describe what they tell him.

If you trained someone to emit a particular sound at the sight of something red, another at the sight of something yellow, and so on for other colours, still he would not yet be describing objects by their colours. Though he might be a help to us in giving a description. A description is a representation of a distribution in a space (in that of time, for instance).

If I let my gaze wander round a room and suddenly it lights on an object of a striking red colour, and I say 'Red!' – that is not a description.

Are the words 'I am afraid' a description of a state of mind?

I say 'I am afraid'; someone else asks me: 'What was that? A cry of fear; or do you want to tell me how you feel; or is it a reflection on your present state?' – Could I always give him a clear answer? Could I never give him one?
We can imagine all sorts of things here, for example:
'No, no! I am afraid!'
'I am afraid. I am sorry to have to confess it.'
'I am still a bit afraid, but no longer as much as before.'
'At bottom I am still afraid, though I won't confess it to myself.'
'I torment myself with all sorts of fears.'
'Now, just when I should be fearless, I am afraid!'
To each of these sentences a special tone of voice is appropriate, and a different context.
It would be possible to imagine people who as it were thought much more definitely than we, and used different words where we use only one.

We ask 'What does "I am frightened" really mean, what am I referring to when I say it?' And of course we find no answer, or one that is inadequate.
The question is: 'In what sort of context does it occur?'

I can find no answer if I try to settle the question 'What am I referring to?' 'What am I thinking when I say it?' by repeating the expression of fear and at the same time attending to myself, as it were observing my soul out of the corner of my eye. In a concrete case I can indeed ask 'Why did I say that, what did I mean by it?' – and I might answer the question too; but not on the ground of observing what accompanied the speaking. And my answer would supplement, paraphrase, the earlier utterance.

What is fear? What does 'being afraid' mean? If I wanted to define it at a *single* shewing – I should *play-act* fear.

Could I also represent hope in this way? Hardly. And what about belief?

Describing my state of mind (of fear, say) is something I do in a particular context. (Just as it takes a particular context to make a certain action into an experiment.)

Is it, then, so surprising that I use the same expression in different games? And sometimes as it were between the games?

And do I always talk with very definite purpose? – And is what I say meaningless because I don't?

When it is said in a funeral oration 'We mourn our . . .' this is surely supposed to be an expression of mourning; not to tell anything to those who are present. But in a prayer at the grave these words would in a way be used to tell someone something.

But here is the problem: a cry, which cannot be called a description, which is more primitive than any description, for all that serves as a description of the inner life.

A cry is not a description. But there are transitions. And the words 'I am afraid' may approximate more, or less, to being a cry. They may come quite close to this and also be *far* removed from it.

We surely do not always say someone is *complaining*, because he says he is in pain. So the words 'I am in pain' may be a cry of complaint, and may be something else.

But if 'I am afraid' is not always something like a cry of complaint and yet sometimes is, then why should it *always* be a description of a state of mind?

How did we ever come to use such an expression as 'I believe

. . .'? Did we at some time become aware of a phenomenon (of belief)?

Did we observe ourselves and other people and so discover belief?

Moore's paradox can be put like this: the expression 'I believe that this is the case' is used like the assertion 'This is the case'; and yet the *hypothesis* that I believe this is the case is not used like the hypothesis that this is the case.

So it *looks* as if the assertion 'I believe' were not the assertion of what is supposed in the hypothesis 'I believe'!

Similarly: the statement 'I believe it's going to rain' has a meaning like, that is to say a use like, 'It's going to rain', but the meaning of 'I believed then that it was going to rain', is not like that of 'It did rain then'.

'But surely "I believed" must tell of just the same thing in the past as "I believe" in the present!' – Surely $\sqrt{-1}$ must mean just the same in relation to -1, as $\sqrt{1}$ means in relation to 1! This means nothing at all.

'At bottom, when I say "I believe . . ." I am describing my own state of mind – but this description is indirectly an assertion of the fact believed.' – As in certain circumstances I describe a photograph in order to describe the thing it is a photograph of.

But then I must also be able to say that the photograph is a good one. So here too: 'I believe it's raining and my belief is reliable, so I have confidence in it.' – In that case my belief would be a kind of sense-impression.

One can mistrust one's own senses, but not one's own belief.

If there were a verb meaning 'to believe falsely', it would not have any significant first person present indicative.

Don't look at it as a matter of course, but as a most remarkable thing, that the verbs 'believe', 'wish', 'will' display all the inflexions possessed by 'cut', 'chew', 'run'.

The language-game of reporting can be given such a turn that a report is not meant to inform the hearer about its subject matter but about the person making the report.

It is so when, for instance, a teacher examines a pupil. (You can measure to test the ruler.)

Suppose I were to introduce some expression – 'I believe', for instance – in this way: it is to be prefixed to reports when they serve to give information about the reporter. (So the expression need not carry with it any suggestion of uncertainty. Remember that the uncertainty of an assertion can be expressed impersonally: 'He might come today'.) – 'I believe . . . ., and it isn't so' would be a contradiction.

'I believe . . . .' throws light on my state. Conclusions about my conduct can be drawn from this expression. So there is a *similarity* here to expressions of emotion, of mood, etc..

If, however, 'I believe it is so' throws light on my state, then so does the assertion 'It is so'. For the sign 'I believe' can't do it, can at the most hint at it.

Imagine a language in which 'I believe it is so' is expressed only by means of the tone of the assertion 'It is so'. In this language they say, not 'He believes' but 'He is inclined to say . . .' and there exists also the hypothetical (subjunctive) 'Suppose I were inclined etc.', but not the expression 'I am inclined to say'.
Moore's paradox would not exist in this language; instead of it, however, there would be a verb lacking one inflexion.
But this ought not to surprise us. Think of the fact that one can predict one's *own* future action by an expression of intention.

I say of someone else 'He seems to believe . . . .' and other people say it of me. Now, why do I never say it of myself, not even when others *rightly* say it of me? – Do I myself not see and hear myself, then? – That can be said.

'One feels conviction within oneself, one doesn't infer it from one's own words or their tone.' – What is true here is: one does not infer one's own conviction from one's own words; nor yet the actions which arise from that conviction.

'Here it *looks* as if the assertion "I believe" were not the assertion of what is supposed in the hypothesis.' – So I am tempted to look for a different development of the verb in the first person present indicative.

This is how I think of it: Believing is a state of mind. It has duration; and that independently of the duration of its expression

in a sentence, for example. So it is a kind of disposition of the
believing person. This is shewn me in the case of someone else
by his behaviour; and by his words. And under this head, by the
expression 'I believe . . .' as well as by the simple assertion. –
What about my own case: how do I myself recognize my own
disposition? – Here it will have been necessary for me to take
notice of myself as others do, to listen to myself talking, to be
able to draw conclusions from what I say!

My own relation to my words is wholly different from other
people's.

That different development of the verb would have been possible, if only I could say 'I seem to believe'.

If I listened to the words of my mouth, I might say that
someone else was speaking out of my mouth.

'Judging from what I say, *this* is what I believe.' Now, it is
possible to think out circumstances in which these words would
make sense.

And then it would also be possible for someone to say 'It is
raining and I don't believe it', or 'It seems to me that my ego
believes this, but it isn't true.' One would have to fill out the
picture with behaviour indicating that two people were speaking
through my mouth.

Even in the *hypothesis* the pattern is not what you think.

When you say 'Suppose I believe . . .' you are presupposing
the whole grammar of the word 'to believe', the ordinary use, of
which you are master. – You are not supposing some state of
affairs which, so to speak, a picture presents unambiguously to
you, so that you can tack on to this hypothetical use some
assertive use other than the ordinary one. – You would not know
at all what you were supposing here (i.e. what, for example,
would follow from such a supposition), if you were not already
familiar with the use of 'believe'.

Think of the expression 'I say . . .', for example in 'I say it will
rain today', which simply comes to the same thing as the assertion 'It will . . .'. 'He says it will . . .' means approximately 'He
believes it will . . .'. 'Suppose I say . . .' does *not* mean: Suppose
it rains today.

Different concepts touch here and coincide over a stretch. But
you need not think that all lines are *circles*.

Consider the misbegotten sentence 'It may be raining, but it isn't'.

And here one should be on one's guard against saying that 'It may be raining' really means 'I think it'll be raining.' For why not the other way round, why should not the latter mean the former?

Don't regard a hesitant assertion as an assertion of hesitancy.

11

The Inner and the Outer

I can know what someone else is thinking, not what I am thinking.

It is correct to say 'I know what you are thinking', and wrong to say 'I know what I am thinking.'

(A whole cloud of philosophy condensed into a drop of grammar.)

'A man's thinking goes on within his consciousness in a seclusion in comparison with which any physical seclusion is an exhibition to public view.'

If there were people who always read the silent internal discourse of others – say by observing the larynx – would they too be inclined to use the picture of complete seclusion?

If I were to talk to myself out loud in a language not understood by those present my thoughts would be hidden from them.

Let us assume there was a man who always guessed right what I was saying to myself in my thoughts. (It does not matter how he manages it.) But what is the criterion for his guessing *right*? Well, I am a truthful person and I confess that he has guessed right. – But might I not be mistaken, can my memory not deceive me? And might it not always do so when – without lying – I express what I have thought within myself? – But now it does appear that 'what went on within me' is not the point at all. (Here I am drawing a construction-line.)

The criteria for the truth of the *confession* that I thought such-and-such are not the criteria for a true *description* of a process. And the importance of the true confession does not reside in its being a correct and certain report of a process. It resides rather in the special consequences which can be drawn from a confession whose truth is guaranteed by the special criteria of *truthfulness*.

(Assuming that dreams can yield important information about the dreamer, what yielded the information would be truthful accounts of dreams. The question whether the dreamer's memory deceives him when he reports the dream after waking cannot arise, unless indeed we introduce a completely new criterion for the report's "agreeing" with the dream, a criterion which gives us a concept of "truth" as distinct from "truthfulness" here.)

There is a game of 'guessing thoughts'. A variant of it would be this: I tell A something in a language that B does not understand. B is supposed to guess the meaning of what I say. – Another variant: I write down a sentence which the other person cannot see. He has to guess the words or their sense. – Yet another: I am putting a jig-saw puzzle together; the other person cannot see me but from time to time guesses my thoughts and utters them. He says, for instance, 'Now where is this bit?' – '*Now* I know how it fits!' – 'I have no idea what goes in here,' – 'The sky is always the hardest part' and so on – but *I* need not be talking to myself either out loud or silently at the time.

All this would be guessing at thoughts; and the fact that it does not actually happen does not make thought any more hidden than the unperceived physical proceedings.

'What is *internal* is hidden from us.' – The future is hidden from us. But does the astronomer think like this when he calculates an eclipse of the sun?

If I see someone writhing in pain with evident cause I do not think: all the same, his feelings are hidden from me.

We also say of some people that they are transparent to us. It is, however, important as regards this observation that one human being can be a complete enigma to another. We learn this when we come into a strange country with entirely strange traditions; and, what is more, even given a mastery of the country's language. We do not *understand* the people. (And not because of not knowing what they are saying to themselves.) We cannot find our feet with them.

'I cannot know what is going on in him' is above all a *picture*. It is the convincing expression of a conviction. It does not give the reasons for the conviction. *They* are not readily accessible.

If a lion could talk, we could not understand him.

It is possible to imagine a guessing of intentions like the guessing of thoughts, but also a guessing of what someone is actually *going to do*.

To say 'He alone can know what he intends' is nonsense: to say 'He alone can know what he will do', wrong. For the prediction contained in my expression of intention (for example 'When it strikes five I am going home') need not come true, and someone else may know what will really happen.

Two points, however, are important: one, that in many cases someone else cannot predict my actions, whereas I foresee them in my intentions; the other, that my prediction (in my expression of intention) has not the same foundation as his prediction of what I shall do, and the conclusions to be drawn from these predictions are quite different.

I can be as *certain* of someone else's sensations as of any fact. But this does not make the propositions 'He is much depressed', '25 × 25 = 625' and 'I am sixty years old' into similar instruments. The explanation suggests itself that the certainty is of a different *kind*. – This seems to point to a psychological difference. But the difference is logical.

'But, if you are *certain*, isn't it that you are shutting your eyes in face of doubt?' – They are shut.

Am I less certain that this man is in pain than that twice two is four? – Does this shew the former to be mathematical certainty? – 'Mathematical certainty' is not a psychological concept.
The kind of certainty is the kind of language-game.

'He alone knows his motives' – that is an expression of the fact that we ask *him* what his motives are. – If he is sincere he will tell us them; but I need more than sincerity to guess his motives. This is where there is a kinship with the case of *knowing*.

Let yourself be *struck* by the existence of such a thing as our language-game of: confessing the motive of my action.

We remain unconscious of the prodigious diversity of all the everyday language-games because the clothing of our language makes everything alike.

★ ★ ★

What a lot of things a man must do in order for us to say he *thinks!*

He cannot *know* whether I am thinking, but I know it. What do I know? That what I am doing now is *thinking*? And what do I compare it with in order to know that? And may I not be mistaken about it? So all that is left is: I know that I am doing what I am doing.

But it surely makes sense to say. 'He does not know what I thought, for I did not tell him!'
Is a thought also 'private' in the case where I utter it out loud in talking to myself, if no one hears me?
'My thoughts are known to myself alone.'
But what that means is, roughly: 'I *can* describe them, can express them *if* I want to.'

'Only I know my thoughts.' – How do you know that? Experience did not teach you it. – What do you tell us by saying so? You must be expressing yourself badly.
'Not so! I am now thinking something to myself; tell me what it is!' So was it after all an empirical proposition? No; for, if I were to tell you what you are thinking to yourself, I would only be *guessing* it. How is it to be decided whether I have guessed right? By your word, and by certain circumstances: So I am comparing this language-game with *another* one, in which the means of deciding (verification) look different.

'Here I cannot . . .' – Well, where *can* I? In another game. (Here – that is in tennis – I cannot shoot the ball into goal.)

But isn't there a connexion between the grammatical 'privacy' of thoughts and the fact that we generally cannot guess the thoughts of someone else before he utters them? But there is such a thing as guessing thoughts in the sense that someone says to me: 'I know what you have just thought' (or 'What you just thought of') and I have to admit that he has guessed my thoughts right. But in fact this happens very seldom. I often sit without talking for several minutes in my class, and thoughts go through my head; but surely none of my audience could guess what I have been thinking to myself. Yet it would also be possible that someone should guess them and write them down just as if I had uttered them out loud. And if he shewed me what he had written, I should have to say, 'Yes, I thought just that to myself.' – And here, e.g., this question would be undecidable: whether I am not making a mistake; whether I really thought that, or, influenced by his writing, I am firmly *imagining* myself to have thought precisely that.

And the word 'undecidable' belongs to the description of the language-game.

And wouldn't *this* too be conceivable: I tell someone 'You have just thought . . . to yourself' – He denies it. But I stick to my assertion, and in the end he says: 'I believe you are right; I must have thought that to myself; my memory must be deceiving me.'

And now imagine this being a quite ordinary episode!

'Thoughts and feelings are private' means roughly the same as 'There is pretending', or 'One can hide one's thoughts and feelings; can even lie and dissimulate'. And the question is, what is the import of this 'There is . . .' and 'One can'.

Under what circumstances, on what occasions, then, does one say: 'Only I know my thoughts'? – When one might also have said: 'I am not going to tell you my thoughts' or 'I am keeping my thoughts secret', or 'You people could not guess my thoughts'.

Of what does one say that one is *acquainted* with it? and to what extent am I acquainted with my thoughts?

Don't we say that one is acquainted with what one can give a correct description of? And can one say that of one's own thoughts?

If someone wants to call the words the 'description' of the thought instead of the 'expression' of the thought, let him ask himself how anyone learns to describe a table and how he learns to describe his own thoughts. And that only means: let him look and see how one judges the description of a table as right or wrong, and how the description of thoughts: so let him keep in view these language-games in all their situations.

'But the fact is that a human being knows only his *own* thoughts.' ('But the fact is that only I know of my own thinking.')

'And I don't either,' one might say.

'Nature has given it to man to be able to think in secret.' Imagine its being said: 'Nature has given it to man to be able to talk audibly, but also to be able to talk inaudibly, within his mind.' So, that means, he can do the same thing in two ways. (As if he could digest visibly and also digest invisibly.) Only with speaking within one's mind the speaking is hidden better than any process within one's body can possibly be. – But how would it be if I were to speak, and everyone else were deaf? Wouldn't my speaking be equally well hidden?

'It all goes on in the deepest secrecy of the mind.'

If someone *says* to me what he has thought – has he really said: what he *thought*? Would not the actual mental event have to remain undescribed? – Was *it* not the secret thing, – of which I give another a mere picture in speech?

If I *say* what I *think* to someone, – do I know my thought here better than my words represent it? Is it as if I were acquainted with a *body* and shewed the other a mere photograph?

'Man has the gift of speaking with himself in total seclusion; in a seclusion far more complete than that of a hermit.' How do I know that N. has this gift? – Because he says so and is trustworthy? –

And yet we do say: 'I'd like to know what he is thinking to himself now,' quite as we might say: 'I'd like to know what he's writing in his notebook now.' Indeed, one might say *that* and so to speak see it as obvious that he is thinking to himself what he enters in his notebook.

If there were people who could *regularly* read a man's thoughts – say by observation of his larynx – would they too be inclined to speak of the total solitude of the spirit within itself? – Or: Would they too be inclined to use *that picture* of 'total seclusion'?

'I'd like to know what he's thinking of.' But now ask yourself this – apparently irrelevant – question: 'Why does what is going on in him, in his mind, interest me at all, supposing that something is going on?' (The devil take what's going on inside him!)

In philosophy, the comparison of thinking to a process that goes on in secret is a misleading one.

As misleading as, e.g., the comparison of searching for the appropriate expression to the efforts of someone who is trying to make an exact copy of a line that only he can see.

What confuses us is that knowing the thoughts of another from one angle is logically impossible, and from another it is psychologically and physiologically impossible.

Is it right to say: these two 'impossibilities' connect up with each other in such a way that the psychological impossibility (here) supplies us with the picture that (then) becomes for us the mark of the concept 'thinking'?

One cannot say: writing in one's notebook or speaking in monologue is '*like*' silent thinking; but for certain purposes the one process can *replace* the other (e.g. calculating in the head can replace calculating on paper).

Might there be people who always mutter to themselves as they think, so that their thinking is accessible to others? – 'Yes, but we still could not know whether they don't think silently to themselves as well.' – But then might it not be that it was just as senseless to suppose this as to suppose that these people's hairs were thinking, or a stone was thinking? That is to say: if this were so, need it so much as occur to us that someone thought, that he had thoughts, hidden in his mind?

'I don't know what you are thinking to yourself. Say what you are thinking.' – That means something like 'Talk!'

Then is it misleading to speak of man's soul, or of his spirit? So little misleading, that it is quite intelligible if I say 'My soul is tired, not just my mind'. But don't you at least say that everything that can be expressed by means of the word 'soul', can also be expressed somehow by means of words for the corporeal? I do not say that. But if it were so – what would it amount to? For the words, and also what we point to in explaining them, are nothing but instruments, and everything depends on their use.

* * *

No supposition seems to me more natural than that there is no process in the brain correlated with associating or with thinking; so that it would be impossible to read off thought-processes from brain-processes. I mean this: if I talk or write there is, I assume, a system of impulses going out from my brain and correlated with my spoken or written thoughts. But why should the *system* continue further in the direction of the centre? Why should this order not proceed, so to speak, out of chaos? The case would be like the following – certain kinds of plants multiply by seed, so that a seed always produces a plant of the same kind as that from which it was produced – but *nothing* in the seed corresponds to the plant which comes from it; so that it is impossible to infer the properties or structure of the plant from those of the seed that it comes out of – this can only be done from the *history* of the seed. So an organism might come into being even out of something quite amorphous, as it were causelessly; and there is no reason why this should not really hold for our thoughts, and hence for our talking and writing.

It is thus perfectly possible that certain psychological phenomena *cannot* be investigated physiologically, because physiologically nothing corresponds to them.

I saw this man years ago: now I have seen him again, I recognize him, I remember his name. And why does there have to be a cause of this remembering in my nervous system? Why must something or other, whatever it may be, be stored-up there *in any form*? Why *must* a trace have been left behind? Why should there not be a psychological regularity to which *no* physiological regularity corresponds? If this upsets our concepts of causality then it is high time they were upset.

The prejudice in favour of psycho-physical parallalism is also a fruit of the primitive conception of grammar. For when one admits a causality between psychological phenomena, which is not mediated physiologically, one fancies that in doing so one is making an admission of the existence of a soul *alongside* the body, a ghostly mental nature.

Must the verb 'I believe' have a past tense form? Well, if instead of 'I believe he's coming' we always said 'He could be coming' (or the like), but nevertheless said 'I believed . . .' – in this way the verb 'I believe' would have no *present*. It is characteristic of the kind of way in which we are apt to regard language, that we believe that there must after all in the last instance be uniformity, symmetry: instead of holding on the contrary that it doesn't *have* to exist.

Imagine the following phenomenon. If I want someone to take note of a text that I recite to him, so that he can repeat it to me later, I have to give him paper and pencil, while I am speaking he makes lines, marks, on the paper; if he has to reproduce the text later he follows those marks with his eyes and recites the text. But I assume that what he has jotted down is not *writing*, it is not connected by rules with the words of the text; yet without these jottings he is unable to reproduce the text; and if anything in it is altered, if part of it is destroyed, he gets stuck in his 'reading' or recites the text uncertainly or carelessly, or cannot find the words at all. – This *can* be imagined! – What I called jottings would not be a *rendering* of the text, not a translation, so to speak, in another symbolism. The text would not be *stored up* in the jottings. And why should it be stored up in our nervous system?

Why should not the initial and terminal states of a system be connected by a natural law, which does not cover the intermediary state? (Only don't think of *agency*).

What is called an alteration in concepts is of course not merely an alteration in what one says, but also in what one does.

One sees the terminology, but fails to see the technique of applying it.

One says: 'He appears to be in frightful pain' even when one hasn't the faintest doubt, the faintest suspicion that the appearance is deceptive. Now why doesn't one say 'I appear to be in frightful pain' for this too must at the very least make *sense*? I might say it at an audition; and equally 'I appear to have the intention of . . .' etc. etc. Everyone will say: 'Naturally I don't say that; because I *know* whether I am in pain.' It doesn't ordinarily *interest* me to know whether I appear to be in pain; for the conclusions which I draw from this impression in the case of other people, are ones I don't draw in my own case. I don't say 'I'm groaning dreadfully, I must see a doctor', but I may very well say 'He's groaning dreadfully, he must . . .'.

If this makes no sense: 'I know that I am in pain' – and neither does 'I feel my pains', – then neither does it make sense to say:

'I don't bother about my own groaning because *I know* that I am in pain' – or – 'because I *feel* my pains.'

So much, however, is true: I don't bother about my groaning.

I infer from observation of his behaviour that he must go to the doctor; but I do *not* make this inference for myself from observation of my behaviour. Or rather: I do that too sometimes, but *not* in analogous cases.

Here it is a help to remember that it is a primitive reaction to take care of, to treat, the place that hurts when someone else is in pain, and not merely when one is so oneself – hence it is a primitive reaction to attend to the pain-behaviour of another, as, also, *not* to attend to one's own pain- behaviour.

What, however, is the word 'primitive' meant to say here? Presumably, that the mode of behaviour is *pre-linguistic*: that a language-game is based *on it*: that it is the prototype of a mode of thought and not the result of thought.

It can be called 'putting the cart before the horse' to give an explanation like the following: we took care of the other man, because going by analogy with our own case, we believed that he too had the experience of pain. – Instead of saying: Learn from this particular chapter of our behaviour – from this language-game – what are the functions of 'analogy' and of believing' in it.

'How does it come about that I see the tree standing up straight even if I incline my head to one side, and so the retinal image is that of an obliquely standing tree?' Well how does it come about that I speak of the tree as standing up straight even in these circumstances? – 'Well, I am conscious of the inclination of my head, and so I supply the requisite correction in the way I take my visual impression.' – But doesn't that mean confusing what is primary and what is secondary? Imagine that we knew *nothing at all* of the inner structure of the eye – would this problem make an appearance? We do *not* in truth supply any correction here – that explanation is gratuitous.

Well – but now that the structure of the eye is known – *how does it come about* that we act, react, in this way? But must there be a physiological explanation here? Why don't we just leave explaining alone? – But you would never talk like that, if you were examining the behaviour of a machine! – Well, who says that a living creature, an animal body, is a machine in this sense?

One may note an alteration in a face and describe it by saying that the face assumed a harder expression – and yet not be able to describe the alteration in spatial terms. This is enormously important. – Perhaps someone now says: if you do that, you just aren't describing the alteration of the face, but only the effect on yourself; but then why shouldn't a description using concepts of shape and colour be that too?

One may also say: 'He made *this* face' or 'His face altered like *this*', imitating it – and again one can't describe it in any other way. ((There just are many more language-games that are dreamt of in the philosophy of Carnap and others.))

Consciousness that . . . may disturb me in my work; knowledge can't.

How do I know that a dog is hearing something continuously, is having a continuous visual impression, that it feels joy, fear, pain?

What do I know of the 'experience contents' of a dog?

* * *

Consciousness in the face of another. Look into someone else's face and see the consciousness in it, and also a particular *shade* of consciousness. You see on it, in it, joy, indifference, interest, excitement, dullness etc. The light in the face of another.

Do you look within *yourself*, in order to recognize the fury in *his* face? It is there as clearly as in your own breast.

(And what does one want to say? That someone else's face stimulates me to imitate it, and so that I feel small movements and muscular tensions on my own part, and *mean* the sum of these? Nonsense! Nonsense, – for you are making suppositions instead of just describing. If your head is haunted by explanations here, you will neglect to bear in mind the facts which are most important.)

Knowledge, opinion, have no facial expression. There is a tone, a gesture of conviction all right, but only if something is said in this tone, or with this gesture.

'Consciousness is as clear in his face and behaviour, as in myself.'

What would it mean for me to be wrong about his having a mind, having consciousness? And what would it mean to say I was wrong and didn't have any myself? What would it mean to say 'I am not conscious'? – But don't I know that there is a consciousness in me? – Do I know it then, and yet the statement that it is so has no purpose?

And how remarkable that one can learn to make oneself understood to others in this matter!

A man can pretend to be unconscious; but *conscious*?

What would it be like for someone to tell me with complete seriousness that he (really) did not know whether he was dreaming or awake? –

Is the following situation possible: Someone says 'I believe I am now dreaming'; he actually wakes up soon afterwards, remembers that utterance in his dream and says 'So I was right!' – This narrative can surely only signify: Someone dreamt that he had said he was dreaming.

Imagine an unconscious man (anaesthetized, say) were to say 'I am conscious' – should we say 'He ought to know'?

And if someone talked in his sleep and said 'I am asleep' – should we say 'He's quite right'?

Is someone speaking untruth if he says to me 'I am not conscious'? (And truth, if he says it while unconscious? And suppose a parrot says 'I don't understand a word', or a gramophone: 'I am only a machine'?)

Suppose it were part of a day-dream I was having to say: 'I am merely engaged in phantasy', would this be *true*? Suppose I write such a phantasy or narrative, an imaginary dialogue, and in it I say 'I am engaged in phantasy' – but, when I write it down, – how does it come out that these words belong to the phantasy and that I have not emerged from the phantasy?

Might it not actually happen that a dreamer, as it were emerging from the dream, said in his sleep. 'I am dreaming'? It is quite imaginable there should be such a language-game.

This hangs together with the problem of 'meaning'. For I can write 'I am healthy' in the dialogue of a play, and so not *mean* it, although it is true. The words belong to this and not that language-game.

'True' and 'false' in a dream. I dream that it is raining, and that I say 'It is raining' – on the other hand: I dream that I say 'I am dreaming'.

Has the verb 'to dream' a present tense? How does a person learn to use this?

One language-game analogous to a fragment of another. A space projected into bounded bits of a space.

Suppose I were to have an experience like waking up, were then to find myself in quite different surroundings, with people who assure me that I have been asleep. Suppose further I insisted that I had not been dreaming, but living in some way outside my sleeping body. What function has this assertion?

' "I have consciousness" – that is a statement about which no doubt is possible.' Why should that not say the same as: ' "I have consciousness" is not a proposition'?

It might also be said: What's the harm if someone says that 'I have consciousness' is a statement admitting of no doubt? How do I come into conflict with him? Suppose someone were to say this to me – why shouldn't I get used to making no answer to him instead of starting an argument? Why shouldn't I treat his words like his whistling or humming?

'Nothing is so certain as that I posses consciousness.' In that case, why shouldn't I let the matter rest? This certainty is like a mighty force whose point of application does not move, and so no work is accomplished by it.

12
Necessity

Why don't I call cookery rules arbitrary, and why am I tempted to call the rules of grammar arbitrary? Because "cookery" is defined by its end, whereas "speaking" is not. That is why the use of language is in a certain sense autonomous, as cooking and washing are not. You cook badly if you are guided in your cooking by rules other than the right ones; but if you follow other rules than those of chess you are *playing another game*; and if you follow grammatical rules other than such-and-such ones, that does not mean you say something wrong, no, you are speaking of something else.

When a rule concerning a word in it is appended to a sentence, the sense does not change.

Language is not defined for us as an arrangement fulfilling a definite purpose. Rather 'language' is for us a name for a collection, and I understand it as including German, English and so on, and further various systems of signs which have more or less affinity with these languages.

Being acquainted with many languages prevents us from taking quite seriously a philosophy which is laid down in the forms of any one. But here we are blind to the fact that we ourselves have strong prejudices for, and against, certain forms of expression; that this very piling up of a lot of languages results in our having a particular picture.

Does a child learn only to talk, or also to think? Does it learn the sense of multiplication *before* – or *after* it learns multiplication?

How did I arrive at the concept "sentence" or "language"? Surely only through the languages that I have learnt. – But they seem to me in a certain sense to have led beyond themselves, for

I am now able to construct new language, e.g. to invent words. – So such construction also belongs to the concept of language. But only because that is how I want to fix the concept.

The concept of a living being has the same indeterminacy as that of a language.

Compare: inventing a game – inventing language – inventing a machine.

In philosophy it is significant that such-and-such a sentence makes no sense; but also that it sounds funny.

I make a plan not merely so as to make myself understood but also in order to get clear about the matter myself. (i.e. language is not merely a means of communication.)

What does it mean to say: 'But that's no longer the same game!' How do I use this sentence? As information? Well, perhaps to introduce some information in which differences are enumerated and their consequences explained. But also to express that just for that reason I don't join in here, or at any rate take up a different attitude to the game.

One is tempted to justify rules of grammar by sentences like 'But there really are four primary colours'. And the saying that the rules of grammar are arbitrary is directed against the possibility of this justification, which is constructed on the model of justifying a sentence by pointing to what verifies it.

Yet can't it after all be said that in some sense or other the grammar of colour-words characterizes the world as it actually is? One would like to say: May I not really look in vain for a fifth primary colour? Doesn't one put the primary colours together because there is a similarity among them, or at least put *colours* together, contrasting them with e.g. shapes or notes, because there is a similarity among them? Or, when I set this up as the right way of dividing up the world, have I a pre-conceived idea in my head as a paradigm? Of which in that case I can only say: 'Yes, that is the kind of way we look at things' or 'We just do want to form this sort of picture.' For if I say 'there is a particular similarity among the primary colours' – whence do I derive the idea of this similarity? Just as the idea 'primary colour' is nothing else but 'blue or red or green or yellow' – is not the idea of that similarity too given simply by the four colours? Indeed, aren't they the same? – 'Then might one also take red, green and circular together?' – Why not?!

Do not believe that you have the concept of colour within you because you look at a coloured object – however you look.

(Any more than you possess the concept of a negative number by having debts.)

* * *

'But am I not compelled, then, to go the way I do in a chain of inferences?' – Compelled? After all I can presumably go as I choose! – 'But if you want to remain in accord with the rules you *must* go this way.' – Not at all, I call *this* 'accord'. – 'Then you have changed the meaning of the word 'accord', or the meaning of the rule.' – No; – who says what 'change' and 'remaining the same' mean here?

However many rules you give me – I give a rule which justifies *my* employment of your rules.

We might also say: when we *follow* the laws of inference (inference-rules) then following always involves interpretation too.

'But you surely can't suddenly make a different application of the law now!' – If my reply is: 'Oh yes of course, *that* is how I was applying it!' or: 'Oh! *That's* how I ought to have applied it – !'; then I am playing your game. But if I simply reply: 'Different? – But this surely *isn't* different!' – what will you do? That is: somebody may reply like a rational person and yet not be playing our game.

'Then according to you everybody could continue the series as he likes; and so infer *any*how!' In that case we shan't call it 'continuing the series' and also presumably not 'inference'. And thinking and inferring (like counting) is of course bounded for us, not by an arbitrary definition, but by natural limits corresponding to the body of what can be called the role of thinking and inferring in our life.

For we are at one over this, that the laws of inference do not compel him to say or to write such and such like rails compelling a locomotive. And if you say that, while he may indeed *say* it, still he can't *think* it, then I am only saying that that means, not:

try as he may he can't think it, but: it is for us an essential part of 'thinking' that – in talking, writing, etc. – he makes *this sort* of transition. And I say further that the line between what we include in 'thinking' and what we no longer include in 'thinking' is no more a hard and fast one than the line between what is still and what is no longer called 'regularity'.

Nevertheless the laws of inference can be said to compel us; in the same sense, that is to say, as other laws in human society. The clerk who [applies a regulation] *must* do it like that; he would be punished if he inferred differently. If you draw different conclusions you do indeed get into conflict, e.g. with society; and also with other practical consequences.

And there is even something in saying: he can't *think* it. One is trying e.g. to say: he can't fill it with personal content; he can't really *go along with it* – personally, with his intelligence. It is like when one says: this sequence of notes makes no sense, I can't sing it with expression. I cannot *respond* to it. Or, what comes to the same thing here: I don't respond to it.

'If he says it' – one might say – 'he can only say it without thinking'. And here it merely needs to be noticed that 'thoughtless' talk and other talk do indeed sometimes differ as regards what goes on in the talker, his images, sensations and so on while he is talking, but that this accompaniment does not constitute the thinking, and the lack of it is not enough to constitute 'thoughtlessness'.

In what sense is logical argument a compulsion? – 'After all you grant *this* and *this*; so you must also grant *this*!' That is the way of compelling someone. That is to say, one can in fact compel people to admit something in this way. – Just as one can e.g. compel someone to go over there by pointing over there with a bidding gesture of the hand.

Suppose in such a case I point with two fingers at once in different directions, thus leaving it open to the man to go in which of the two directions he likes, – and another time I point in only *one* direction; then this can also be expressed by saying: my first order did not compel him to go just in *one* direction, while the second one did. But this is a statement to tell us what kind of orders I gave; not the way they operate, not whether they do in fact compel such-and-such a person, i.e. whether he obeys them.

It looked at first as if these considerations were meant to shew that 'what seems to be a logical compulsion is in reality only a psychological one' – only here the question arose: am I acquainted with both kinds of compulsion, then?!

Imagine that people used the expression: 'The law §. . . punishes a murderer with death'. Now this could only mean: this law runs so and so. That form of expression, however, might force itself on us, because the law is an instrument when the guilty man is brought to punishment. – Now we talk of 'inexorability' in connexion with people who punish. And here it might occur to us to say: 'The law is *inexorable* – men can let the guilty go, the law executes him'. (And even: 'the law *always* executes him'.) – What is the use of such a form of expression? – In the first instance, this proposition only says that such-and-such is to be found in the law, and human beings sometimes do not go by the law. Then, however, it does give us a picture of a single inexorable judge, and many lax judges. That is why it serves to express respect for the law. Finally, the expression can also be so used that a law is called inexorable when it makes no provision for a possible act of grace, and in the opposite case it is perhaps called 'discriminating'.

Now we talk of the 'inexorability' of logic; and think of the laws of logic as inexorable, still more inexorable than the laws of nature. We now draw attention to the fact that the word 'inexorable' is used in a variety of ways. There correspond to our laws of logic very general facts of daily experience. They are the ones that make it possible for us to keep on demonstrating those laws in a very simple way (with ink on paper for example). They are to be compared with the facts that make measurement with a yardstick easy and useful. This suggests the use of precisely these laws of inference, and now it is *we* that are inexorable in applying these laws. Because we *'measure'*; and it is part of measuring for everybody to have the same measures. Besides this, however, inexorable, i.e. *unambiguous* rules of inference can be distinguished from ones that are not unambiguous, I mean from such as leave an alternative open to us.

'But I can infer only what actually does follow.' – That is to say: what the logical machine really does produce. The logical machine – that would be an all-pervading ethereal mechanism. – We must give warning against this picture.

Imagine a material harder and more rigid than any other. But if a rod made of this stuff is brought out of the horizontal into the vertical, it shrinks; or it bends when set upright and at the same time it is so hard that there is no other way of bending it. – (A mechanism made of this stuff, say a crank, connecting-rod and crosshead. The different way the crosshead would move.)

Or again: a rod bends if one brings a certain mass near it; but it is completely rigid in face of all forces that we subject it to. Imagine that the guide-rails of the crosshead bend and then straighten again as the crank approaches and retreats. My assumption would be, however, that no particular external force is necessary to cause this. This behaviour of the rails would give an impression as of something alive.

When we say: 'If the parts of the mechanism were quite rigid, they would move so and so', what is the criterion for their being quite rigid? Is it that they resist certain forces? Or that they do move so and so?

Suppose I say: 'This is the law of motion of the crosshead (the correlation of its position and the position of the crank perhaps) when the lengths of the crank and connecting-rod remain constant'. This presumably means: If the crank and crosshead keep these relative positions, I say that the length of the connecting-rod remains constant.

'If the parts were quite rigid this is how they would move'; is that a hypothesis? It seems not. For when we say: 'Kinematics describes the movements of the mechanism on the assumption that its parts are completely rigid', on the one hand we are admitting that this assumption never squares with reality, and on the other hand it is not supposed to be in any way doubtful that completely rigid parts would move in this way. But whence this certainty? The question here is not really one of certainty but of something stipulated by us. We do not *know* that bodies would move in these ways if (by such and such criteria) they were quite rigid; but (in certain circumstances) we should certainly *call* 'rigid' such parts as did move in those ways. – Always remember in such a case that geometry (or kinematics) does not specify any method of measuring when it talks about the same, or constant, length.

When therefore we call kinematics the theory, say, of the movement of perfectly rigid parts of a mechanism, on the one hand this contains an indication as to (mathematical) method –

we stipulate certain distances as the lengths of machine parts that do not alter – and on the other hand an *indication* about the application of the calculus.

The hardness of the logical *must*. What if one were to say: the *must* of kinematics is much harder than the causal *must* compelling a machine part to move like *this* when another moves like *this*? –

Suppose we represented the movement of the 'perfectly rigid' mechanism by a cinematographic picture, a cartoon film. Suppose this picture were said to be *perfectly hard*, and this meant that we had taken this picture as our method of description – whatever the facts may be, however the parts of the real mechanism may bend or expand.

The machine (its structure) as symbolizing its action: the action of a machine – I might say at first – seems to be there in it from the start. What does that mean? –

If we know the machine, everything else, that is its movement, seems to be already completely determined.

'We talk as if these parts *could* only move in this way, as if they could not do anything else.'

How is this – do we forget the possibility of their bending, breaking off, melting, and so on? Yes; in *many* cases we don't think of that at all. We use a machine, or the picture of a machine, to symbolize a particular action of the machine. For instance, we give someone such a picture and assume that he will derive the movement of the parts from it. (Just as we can give someone a number by telling him that it is the twenty-fifth in the series 1, 4, 9, 16, . . .)

'The machine's action seems to be in it from the start' means: you are inclined to compare the future movements of the machine in definiteness to objects which are already lying in a drawer and which we then take out.

But we do not say this kind of thing when we are concerned with predicting the actual behaviour of a machine. Here we do not in general forget the possibility of a distortion of the parts and so on.

We do talk like that, however, when we are wondering at the way we can use a machine to symbolize a given way of moving – since it can also move in quite *different* ways.

Now, we might say that a machine, or the picture of it, is the first of a series of pictures which we have learnt to derive from this one.

But when we remember that the machine could also have moved differently, it readily seems to us as if the way it moves must be contained in the machine-as-symbol far more determinately than in the actual machine. As if it were not enough here for the movements in question to be empirically determined in advance, but they had to be really – in a mysterious sense – already *present*. And it is quite true: the movement of the machine-as-symbol is predetermined in a different sense from that in which the movement of any given actual machine is predetermined.

'It is as if we could grasp the whole use of the word in a flash.' Like *what* e.g.? – Can't the use – in a certain sense – be grasped in a flash? And in *what* sense can it not? The point is, that it is as if we could 'grasp it in a flash' in yet another and much more direct sense than that. – But have you a model for this? No. It is just that this expression suggests itself to us. As the result of crossing similes.

You have no model of this superlative fact, but you are seduced into using a *super-expression*.

When does one have the thought: the possible movements of a machine are already there in it in some mysterious way? – Well, when one is doing philosophy. And what leads us into thinking that? The way we talk about machines. We say, for example, that a machine *has* (*possesses*) such-and-such possibilities of movement; we speak of the ideally rigid machine which *can* only move in such-and-such a way. — What is this *possibility* of movement? It is not the *movement*, but it does not seem to be the mere physical *conditions* for moving either, e.g. that there is a certain space between socket and pin, the pin not fitting too tight in the socket. For while this is the *empirical* condition for movement, one could also imagine it to be otherwise. The possibility of a movement is, rather, supposed to be a shadow of the movement itself. But do you know of such a shadow? And by a shadow I do not mean some picture of the movement; for such a picture would not necessarily be a picture of just *this* movement. But the possibility of this movement must be the possibility of just this movement. (See how high the seas of language run here!)

The waves subside as soon as we ask ourselves: how do we use the phrase 'possibility of movement' when we are talking about a given machine? – But then where did our queer ideas come from? Well, I shew you the possibility of a movement, say by means of a *picture* of the movement: 'so possibility is something which is like reality'. We say: 'It isn't moving yet, but it already has the possibility of moving' – 'so possibility is something very near reality'. Though we may doubt whether such-and-such physical conditions make this movement possible, we never discuss whether *this* is the possibility of this or of that movement: 'so the possibility of the movement stands in a unique relation to the movement itself; closer than that of a picture to its subject'; for it can be doubted whether a picture is the picture of this thing or that. We say 'Experience will shew whether this gives the pin this possibility of movement', but we do not say 'Experience will shew whether this is the possibility of this movement': 'so it is not an empirical fact that this possibility is the possibility of precisely this movement'.

We pay attention to the expressions we use concerning these things; we do not understand them, however, but misinterpret them. When we do philosophy we are like savages, primitive people, who hear the expressions of civilized men, put a false interpretation on them, and then draw queer conclusions from it.

Imagine someone not understanding our past tense: 'he has had it'. – He says: ' "he *has*" – that's present, so the proposition says that in some sense the past is present.'

'But I don't mean that what I do now (in grasping a sense) determines the future use *causally* and as a matter of experience, but that in a *queer* way, the use itself is in some sense present.' But of course it is, 'in *some* sense'! (And don't we also say: 'the events of the years that are past are present to me'?) Really the only thing wrong with what you say is the expression 'in a queer way'. The rest is correct; and the sentence only seems queer when one imagines a different language-game for it from the one in which we actually use it. (Someone once told me that as a child he had wondered how a tailor '*sewed a dress*' – he thought this meant that a dress was produced *just by sewing*, by sewing one thread on to another.)

In our failure to understand the use of a word we take it as the expression of a queer *process*. (As we think of time as a queer medium, of the mind as a queer kind of being.)

The difficulty arises in all these cases through mixing up 'is' and 'is called'.

The connexion which is not supposed to be a causal, experiential one, but much stricter and harder, so rigid even, that the one thing somehow already *is* the other, is always a connexion in grammar.

How do I know that this picture is my image of the *sun?* – I *call* it an image of the sun. I *use* it as a picture of the *sun*.

'It's as if we could grasp the whole use of the word in a flash.' – And that is just what we say we do. That is to say: we sometimes describe what we do in these words. But there is nothing astonishing, nothing queer, about what happens. It becomes queer when we are led to think that the future development must in some way already be present in the act of grasping the use and yet isn't present. – For we say that there isn't any doubt that we understand the word . . ., and on the other hand its meaning lies in its use. There is no doubt that I now want to play *chess*, but chess is the game it is in virtue of *all its rules* (and so on). Don't I know, then, which game I wanted to play until I *have* played it? Or are all the rules contained in my act of intending? Is it experience that tells me that this sort of play usually follows this act of intention? So is it impossible for me to be certain what I am intending to do? And if that is nonsense, what kind of super-strong connexion exists between the act of intending and the thing intended? — Where is the connexion effected between the sense of the expression 'Let's play a game of chess' and all the rules of the game? – Well, in the list of rules of the game, in the teaching of it, in the day-to-day practice of playing.

The laws of logic are indeed the expression of "thinking habits" but also of the habit of *thinking*. That is to say they can be said to shew: how human beings think, and also *what* human beings call 'thinking'.

* * *

The limit of the empirical – is *concept-formation*.

What is the transition that I make from 'It will be like this' to 'it *must* be like this'? I form a different concept. One involving something that was not there before. When I say: 'If these derivations are the same, then it *must* be that . . .', I am making something into a criterion of identity. So I am recasting my concept of identity.

But what if someone now says: 'I am not aware of these *two* processes, I am only aware of the empirical, not of a formation and transformation of concepts which is independent of it; everything seems to me to be in the service of the empirical'?

In other words: we do not seem to become now more, now less, rational, or to alter the form of our thinking, so as to alter *what we call 'thinking'*. We only seem always to be fitting our thinking to experience.

So much is clear: when someone says: 'If you follow the *rule*, it *must* be like this', he has not any *clear* concept of what experience would correspond to the opposite.

Or again: he has not any clear concept of what it would be like for it to be otherwise. And this is very important.

What compels us *so* to form the concept of identity as to say, e.g., 'If you really do the same thing both times, then the result must be the same too'? – What compels us to proceed according to a rule, to conceive something as a rule? What compels us to talk to ourselves in the forms of the languages we have learnt?

For the word 'must' surely expresses our inability to depart from *this* concept. (Or ought I to say 'refusal'?)

And even if I have made the transition from one concept-formation to another, the old concept is still there in the background.

Can I say: 'A proof induces us to make a certain decision, namely that of accepting a particular concept-formation'?

Do not look at the proof as a procedure that *compels* you, but as one that *guides* you. – And what it guides is your *conception* of a (particular) situation.

But how does it come about that it guides *each one* of us in such a way that we agree in the influence it has on us? Well, how does it come about that we agree in *counting*? 'That is just how we are trained' one may say, 'and the agreement produced in this way is carried further by the proofs.'

In the course of this proof we formed our way of looking at the trisection of the angle, which excludes a construction with ruler and compass.

By accepting a proposition as a matter of course, we also release it from all responsibility in face of experience.

In the course of the proof our way of seeing is changed – and it does not detract from this that it is connected with experience.

Our way of seeing is remodelled.

It must be like this, does not mean: it will be like this. On the contrary: 'it will be like this' chooses between one possibility and another. 'It must be like this' sees only *one* possibility.

The proof as it were guides our experience into definite channels. Someone who has tried again and again to do such-and-such gives the attempt up after the proof.

Someone tries to arrange pieces to make a particular pattern. Now he sees a model in which one *part* of that pattern is seen to be composed of all his pieces, and he gives up his attempt. The model was the *proof* that his proposal is impossible.

That model too, like the one that shews that he will be able to make a pattern of these pieces, changes his *concept*. For, one might say, he never looked at the task of making the pattern of these pieces in this way before.

Is it obvious that if anyone sees that part of the pattern can be made with these pieces, he realizes that there is no way of making the whole pattern with them? May it not be that he goes on trying and trying whether after all some arrangement of the pieces does not achieve this end? And may he not achieve it? (Use of one piece twice over, e.g.)

Must we not distinguish here between thinking and the practical success of the thinking?

' . . . who do not realize certain truths immediately, as we do, but perhaps are reduced to the roundabout path of induction', says Frege. But what interests me is this immediate realization, whether it is of a truth or of a falsehood. I am asking: what is the characteristic demeanour of human beings who 'realize' something 'immediately', whatever the practical result of this realizing is?

What interests me is not the immediate realization of a truth, but the phenomenon of immediate realization. Not indeed as a special mental phenomenon, but as one of human action.

Yes: it is as if the formation of a concept guided our experience into particular channels, so that one experience is now seen together with another one in a new way. (As an optical instrument makes light come from various sources in a particular way to form a pattern.)

Imagine that a proof was a work of fiction, a stage play. Cannot watching a play lead me to something?

I did not know how it would go, – but I saw a picture and became convinced that it would go as it does in the picture.

The picture helped me to make a prediction. Not as an experiment — it was only midwife to the prediction.

For, whatever my experience is or has been, I surely still have to *make* the prediction. (Experience does not make it for me.)

No great wonder, then, that proof helps us to *predict*. Without this picture I should not have been able to say how it will be, but when I see it I seize on it with a view to prediction.

I cannot predict the colour of a chemical compound by means of a picture exhibiting the substances in the test-tube and the reaction. If the picture shewed frothing, and finally red crystals, I should not be able to say: 'Yes, *that* is how it has to be' or 'No, it cannot be like that'. It is otherwise, however, when I see the picture of a mechanism in motion; that can tell me, how a part actually will move. Though if the picture represented a mechanism whose parts were composed of a very soft material (dough, say), and hence bent about in various ways in the picture, then the picture would perhaps again not help in making a prediction.

Can we say that a concept is so formed as to be adapted to a certain prediction, i.e. it enables it to be made in the simplest terms –?

The philosophical problem is: how can we tell the truth and *pacify* these strong prejudices in doing so?

It makes a difference whether I think of something as a deception of my senses or an external event, whether I take this object as a measure of that or the other way round, whether I resolve to make two criteria decide or only one.

If the calculation has been done right, then this must be the result. Must *this always* be the result, in that case? Of course.

By being educated in a technique, we are also educated to have a way of looking at the matter which is just as firmly rooted as that technique.

Mathematical propositions seem to treat neither of signs nor of human beings, and therefore they *do* not.

They shew *those* connexions that we regard as rigid. But to a certain extent we look away from these connexions and at something else. We turn our back upon them, so to speak. Or: we rest, or lean, on them.

Once more: we do not look at the mathematical proposition as a proposition dealing with signs, and hence it *is* not that.

We acknowledge it *by* turning our back on it.

What about e.g. the fundamental laws of mechanics? If you understand them you must know how experience supports them. It is otherwise with the propositions of pure mathematics.

A proposition may describe a picture and this picture be variously anchored in our way of looking at things, and so in our way of living and acting.

Is not the proof too flimsy a reason for entirely giving up the search for a construction of the trisection? You have only gone through the sequence of signs once or twice; will you decide on the strength of that? Just because you have seen this one transformation, will you give up the search?

The effect of proof is, I believe, that we plunge into the new rule.

Hitherto we have calculated according to such and such a rule; now someone shews us the proof that it can also be done in another way, and we switch to the other technique – not because we tell ourselves that it will work this way too, but because we feel the new technique as identical with the old one, because we have to give it the same sense, because we recognize it as the same just as we recognize this colour as green.

That is to say: realizing mathematical relations has a role similar to that of realizing identity. It might almost be said to be a more complicated kind of identity.

It might be said: the reasons why we now shift to a different technique are of the same kind as those which make us carry out a new multiplication as we do; we accept the technique as the *same* as we have applied in doing other multiplications.

A human being is *imprisoned* in a room, if the door is unlocked but opens inwards; he, however, never gets the idea of *pulling* instead of pushing against it.

When white turns black some people say 'Essentially it is still the same'; and others, when the colour turns a shade darker: 'It is *completely* different'.

The proposition '$a = a$', '$p \supset p$', 'The word "Bismarck" has 8 letters', 'There is no such thing as reddish-green', are all obvious and are propositions about essence: what have they in common? They are evidently each of a different kind and differently used. The last but one is the most like an empirical proposition. And it can understandably be called a synthetic *a priori* proposition.

It can be said: unless you put the series of numbers and the series of letters side by side, you cannot know how many letters the word has.

One pattern derived from another according to a rule. (Say the reversal of a theme.)

Then the result put as equivalent to the operation.

When I wrote 'proof must be perspicuous' that meant: *causality* plays no part in the proof.

Or again: a proof must be capable of being reproduced by mere copying.

It might perhaps be said that the synthetic character of the propositions of mathematics appears most obviously in the unpredictable occurrence of the prime numbers.

But their being synthetic (in this sense) does not make them any the less *a priori*. They could be said, I want to say, not to be got out of their concepts by means of some kind of analysis, but really to determine a concept by synthesis, e.g. as crossing prisms can be made to determine a body.

The distribution of primes would be an ideal example of what could be called synthetic *a priori*, for one can say that it is at any rate not discoverable by an analysis of the concept of a prime number.

* * *

Now can it be said that the concepts which mathematics produces are a convenience, that essentially we could do without them?

First and foremost the adoption of these concepts expresses the *sure* expectation of certain experiences.

We do not accept e.g. a multiplication's not yielding the same result every time.

And what we expect with certainty is essential to our whole life.

Why, then, should I not say that mathematical propositions just express those special expectations, i.e., therefore, that they express matters of experience? Only because they just do not. Perhaps I should not take the measure of adopting a certain concept if I did not quite definitely expect the occurrence of certain facts; but for that reason laying down this measure and expressing the expectations are not equivalent.

It is difficult to put the body of fact right side up: to regard the given as given. It is difficult to place the body differently from the way one is accustomed to see it. A table in a lumber room may always lie upside down, in order to save space perhaps. Thus I have always seen the body of fact placed like *this*, for reasons of various kinds; and now I am supposed to see something else as its beginning and something else as its end. That is difficult. It as it were will not stand like that, unless one supports it in this position by means of other contrivances.

It is one thing to use a mathematical technique consisting in the avoidance of contradiction, and another to philosophize against contradiction in mathematics.

Contradiction. Why just this *one* bogy? That is surely very suspicious.

Why should not a calculation made for a practical purpose, with a contradictory result, tell me: 'Do as you please, I, the calculation, do not decide the matter'?

The contradiction might be conceived as a hint from the gods that I am to act and *not* consider.

'Why should contradiction be disallowed in mathematics?' Well, why is it not allowed in our simple language-games? (There is certainly a connexion here.) Is this then a fundamental law governing all thinkable language-games?

Let us suppose that a contradiction in an order, e.g. produces astonishment and indecision – and now we say: that is just the purpose of contradiction in this language-game.

* * *

The pernicious thing is not, to produce a contradiction in the region in which neither the consistent nor the contradictory proposition has any kind of work to accomplish; no, what *is* pernicious is: not to know how one reached the place where contradiction no longer does any harm.

13

Scepticism and Certainty

But can't it be imagined that there should be no physical objects? I don't know. And yet 'There are physical objects' is nonsense. Is it supposed to be an empirical proposition? –

And is *this* an empirical proposition: 'There seem to be physical objects'?

'A is a physical object' is a piece of instruction which we give only to someone who doesn't yet understand either what 'A' means, or what 'physical object' means. Thus it is instruction about the use of words, and 'physical object' is a logical concept. (Like colour, quantity, . . .) And that is why no such proposition as: 'There are physical objects' can be formulated.

Yet we encounter such unsuccessful shots at every turn.

But is it an adequate answer to the scepticism of the idealist, or the assurances of the realist, to say that 'There are physical objects' is nonsense? For them after all it is not nonsense. It would, however, be an answer to say: this assertion, or its opposite is a misfiring attempt to express what can't be expressed like that. And that it does misfire can be shewn; but that isn't the end of the matter. We need to realize that what presents itself to us as the first expression of a difficulty, or of its solution, may as yet not be correctly expressed at all. Just as one who has a just censure of a picture to make will often at first offer the censure where it does not belong, and an *investigation* is needed in order to find the right point of attack for the critic.

★ ★ ★

What sort of proposition is: 'What could a mistake here be like!'? It would have to be a logical proposition. But it is a logic that is not used, because what it tells us is not taught by means of propositions. – It is a logical proposition; for it does describe the conceptual (linguistic) situation.

This situation is thus not the same for a proposition like 'At this distance from the sun there is a planet' and 'Here is a hand' (namely my own hand). The second can't be called a hypothesis. But there isn't a sharp boundary line between them.

So one might grant that Moore was right, if he is interpreted like this: a proposition saying that here is a physical object may have the same logical status as one saying that here is a red patch.

For it is not true that a mistake merely gets more and more improbable as we pass from the planet to my own hand. No: at some point it has ceased to be conceivable.

This is already suggested by the following: if it were not so, it would also be conceivable that we should be wrong in *every* statement about physical objects; that any we ever make are mistaken.

So is the *hypothesis* possible, that all the things around us don't exist? Would that not be like the hypothesis of our having miscalculated in all our calculations?

When one says: 'Perhaps this planet doesn't exist and the light-phenomenon arises in some other way', then after all one needs an example of an object which does exist. This doesn't exist, – as *for example* does . . .

Or are we to say that *certainty* is merely a constructed point to which some things approximate more, some less closely? No. Doubt gradually loses its sense. This language-game just *is* like that.

And everything descriptive of a language-game is part of logic.

* * *

That I am a man and not a woman can be verified, but if I were to say I was a woman, and then tried to explain the error by saying I hadn't checked the statement, the explanation would not be accepted.

The *truth* of my statements is the test of my *understanding* of these statements.

That is to say: if I make certain false statements, it becomes uncertain whether I understand them.

What counts as an adequate test of a statement belongs to logic. It belongs to the description of the language-game.

The *truth* of certain empirical propositions belongs to our frame of reference.

* * *

Now would it be correct to say: So far no one has opened my skull in order to see whether there is a brain inside; but everything speaks for, and nothing against, its being what they would find there?

But can it also be said: Everything speaks for, and nothing against the table's still being there when no one sees it? For what does speak for it?

But if anyone were to doubt it, how would his doubt come out in practice? And couldn't we peacefully leave him to doubt it, since it makes no difference at all?

Can one say: 'Where there is no doubt there is no knowledge either'?

Doesn't one need grounds for doubt?

Wherever I look, I find no ground for doubting that . . .

* * *

I am not more certain of the meaning of my words than I am of certain judgments. Can I doubt that this colour is called 'blue'?
(My) doubts form a system.

For how do I know that someone is in doubt? How do I know that he uses the words 'I doubt it' as I do?

From a child up I learnt to judge like this. *This is* judging.

This is how I learned to judge; *this* I got to know *as* judgment.

But isn't it experience that teaches us to judge like *this*, that is to say, that it is correct to judge like this? But how does experience *teach* us, then? *We* may derive it from experience, but experience does not direct us to derive anything from experience.

If it is the *ground* of our judging like this, and not just the cause, still we do not have a ground for seeing this in turn as a ground.

No, experience is not the ground for our game of judging. Nor is its outstanding success.

Men have judged that a king can make rain; *we* say this contradicts all experience. Today they judge that aeroplanes and the radio etc. are means for the closer contact of peoples and the spread of culture.

Under ordinary circumstances I do not satisfy myself that I have two hands by seeing how it looks. *Why* not? Has experience shown it to be unnecessary? Or (again): Have we in some way learnt a universal law of induction, and do we trust it here too? – But why should we have learnt one *universal* law first, and not the special one straight away?

After putting a book in a drawer, I assume it is there, unless . . . 'Experience always proves me right. There is no well attested case of a book's (simply) disappearing.' It has *often* happened that a book has never turned up again, although we thought we knew for certain where it was. – But experience does really teach that a book, say, does not vanish away. (E.g. gradually evaporate.) But is it this experience with books etc. that leads us to assume that such a book has not vanished away? Well, suppose we were to find that under particular novel circumstances books did vanish away. – Shouldn't we alter our assumption? Can one give the lie to the effect of experience on our system of assumption?

★ ★ ★

But do we not simply follow the principle that what has always happened will happen again (or something like it)? What does it mean to follow this principle? Do we really introduce it into our reasoning? Or is it merely the *natural law* which our inferring apparently follows? This latter it may be. It is not an item in our considerations.

When we first begin to *believe* anything, what we believe is not a single proposition, it is a whole system of propositions. (Light dawns gradually over the whole.)

It is not single axioms that strike me as obvious, it is a system in which consequences and premises give one another *mutual* support.

I am told, for example, that someone climbed this mountain many years ago. Do I always enquire into the reliability of the teller of this story, and whether the mountain did exist years ago? A child learns there are reliable and unreliable informants much later than it learns facts which are told it. It doesn't learn *at all* that that mountain has existed for a long time: that is, the question whether it is so doesn't arise at all. It swallows this consequence down, so to speak, together with *what* it learns.

The child learns to believe a host of things. I.e. it learns to act according to these beliefs. Bit by bit there forms a system of what is believed, and in that system some things stand unshakeably fast and some are more or less liable to shift. What stands fast does so, not because it is intrinsically obvious or convincing; it is rather held fast by what lies around it.

One wants to say '*All* my experiences shew that it is so'. But how do they do that? For that proposition to which they point itself belongs to a particular interpretation of them.

'That I regard this proposition as certainly true also characterizes my interpretation of experience.'

There are cases such that, if someone gives signs of doubt where we do not doubt, we cannot confidently understand his signs as signs of doubt.

I.e.: if we are to understand his signs of doubt as such, he may give them only in particular cases and may not give them in others.

In certain circumstances a man cannot make a *mistake*. ('Can' is here used logically, and the proposition does not mean that a man cannot say anything false in those circumstances.) If Moore were to pronounce the opposite of those propositions which he declares certain, we should not just not share his opinion: we should regard him as demented.

In order to make a mistake, a man must already judge in conformity with mankind.

Suppose a man could not remember whether he had always had five fingers or two hands? Should we understand him? Could we be sure of understanding him?

Can I be making a mistake, for example, in thinking that the words of which this sentence is composed are English words whose meaning I know?

As children we learn facts; e.g., that every human being has a brain, and we take them on trust. I believe that there is an island, Australia, of such-and-such a shape, and so on and so on; I believe that I had great-grandparents, that the people who gave themselves out as my parents really were my parents, etc. This belief may never have been expressed; even the thought that it was so, never thought.

The child learns by believing the adult. Doubt comes after belief.

I learned an enormous amount and accepted it on human authority, and then I found some things confirmed or disconfirmed by my own experience.

In general I take as true what is found in text-books, of geography for example. Why? I say: All these facts have been confirmed a hundred times over. But how do I know that? What is my evidence for it? I have a world-picture. Is it true or false? Above all it is the substratum of all my enquiring and asserting. The propositions describing it are not all equally subject to testing.

Does anyone ever test whether this table remains in existence when no one is paying attention to it?
We check the story of Napoleon, but not whether all the reports about him are based on sense-deception, forgery and the like. For whenever we test anything, we are already presupposing something that is not tested. Now am I to say that the experiment which perhaps I make in order to test the truth of a proposition presupposes the truth of the proposition that the apparatus I believe I see is really there (and the like)?

Doesn't testing come to an end?

* * *

What does this mean: the truth of a proposition is *certain*?

With the word 'certain' we express complete conviction, the total absence of doubt, and thereby we seek to convince other people. That is *subjective* certainty.

But when is something objectively certain? When a mistake is not possible. But what kind of possibility is that? Mustn't mistake be *logically* excluded?

If I believe that I am sitting in my room when I am not, then I shall not be said to have *made a mistake*. But what is the essential difference between this case and a mistake?

Sure evidence is what we *accept* as sure, it is evidence that we go by in *acting* surely, acting without any doubt.

What we call 'a mistake' plays a quite special part in our language games, and so too does what we regard as certain evidence.

It would be nonsense to say that we regard something as sure evidence because it is certainly true.

Rather, we must first determine the role of deciding for or against a proposition.

The reason why the use of the expression 'true or false' has something misleading about it is that it is like saying 'it tallies with the facts or it doesn't', and the very thing that is in question is what 'tallying' is here.

Really 'The proposition is either true or false' only means that it must be possible to decide for or against it. But this does not say what the ground for such a decision is like.

Suppose someone were to ask: 'Is it really right for us to rely on the evidence of our memory (or our senses) as we do?'

Moore's certain propositions almost declare that we have a right to rely upon this evidence.

[Everything that we regard as evidence indicates that the earth already existed long before my birth. The contrary hypothesis has *nothing* to confirm it at all.

If everything speaks *for* an hypothesis and nothing against it, is it objectively *certain*? One can *call* it that. But does it *necessarily* agree with the world of facts? At the very best it shows us what 'agreement' means. We find it difficult to imagine it to be false, but also difficult to make use of it.]

What does this agreement consist in, if not in the fact that what is evidence in these language games speaks for our proposition? (*Tractatus Logico-Philosophicus*)

Giving grounds, however, justifying the evidence, comes to an end; – but the end is not certain propositions' striking us immediately as true, i.e. it is not a kind of *seeing* on our part; it is our *acting*, which lies at the bottom of the language-game.

If the true is what is grounded, then the ground is not *true*, nor yet false.

If someone asked us 'but is that *true*?' we might say 'yes' to him; and if he demanded grounds we might say 'I can't give you any grounds, but if you learn more you too will think the same'.

If this didn't come about, that would mean that he couldn't for example learn history.

'Strange coincidence, that every man whose skull has been opened had a brain!'

I have a telephone conversation with New York. My friend tells me that his young trees have buds of such and such a kind. I am now convinced that his tree is . . . Am I also convinced that the earth exists?

The existence of the earth is rather part of the whole *picture* which forms the starting-point of belief for me.

Does my telephone call to New York strengthen my conviction that the earth exists?

Much seems to be fixed, and it is removed from the traffic. It is so to speak shunted onto an unused siding.

Now it gives our way of looking at things, and our researches, their form. Perhaps it was once disputed. But perhaps, for unthinkable ages, it has belonged to the *scaffolding* of our thoughts. (Every human being has parents.)

In certain circumstances, for example, we regard a calculation as sufficiently checked. What gives us a right to do so? Experience? May that not have deceived us? Somewhere we must be finished with justification, and then there remains the proposition that *this* is how we calculate.

Our 'empirical propositions' do not form a homogeneous mass.

What prevents me from supposing that this table either vanishes or alters its shape and colour when no one is observing it, and then when someone looks at it again changes back to its old condition? – 'But who is going to suppose such a thing!' – one would feel like saying.

Here we see that the idea of 'agreement with reality' does not have any clear application.

* * *

If a child asked me whether the earth was already there before my birth, I should answer him that the earth did not begin only with my birth, but that it existed long, long before. And I should have the feeling of saying something funny. Rather as if the child had asked if such and such a mountain were higher than a tall house that it had seen. In answering the question I should have to be imparting a picture of the world to the person who asked it.

If I do answer the question with certainty, what gives me this certainty?

I believe that I have forebears, and that every human being has them. I believe that there are various cities, and, quite generally, in the main facts of geography and history. I believe that the earth is a body on whose surface we move and that it no more suddenly disappears or the like than any other solid body: this table, this house, this tree, etc. If I wanted to doubt the existence of the earth long before my birth, I should have to doubt all sorts of things that stand fast for me.

And that something stands fast for me is not grounded in my stupidity or credulity.

If someone said 'The earth has not long been . . .' what would he be impugning? Do I know?

Would it have to be what is called a scientific belief? Might it not be a mystical one? Is there any absolute necessity for him to be contradicting historical facts? or even geographical ones?

If I say 'an hour ago this table didn't exist', I probably mean that it was only made later on.

If I say 'this mountain didn't exist then', I presumably mean that it was only formed later on – perhaps by a volcano.

If I say 'this mountain didn't exist half an hour ago', that is such a strange statement that it is not clear what I mean.

Whether for example I mean something untrue but scientific. Perhaps you think that the statement that the mountain didn't exist then is quite clear, however one conceives the context. But suppose someone said 'This mountain didn't exist a minute ago, but an exactly similar one did instead'. Only the accustomed context allows what is meant to come through clearly.

I might therefore interrogate someone who said that the earth did not exist before his birth, in order to find out which of my convictions he was at odds with. And then it *might* be that he was contradicting my fundamental attitudes, and if that were how it was, I should have to put up with it.
Similarly if he said he had at some time been on the moon.

I believe that every human being has two human parents; but Catholics believe that Jesus only had a human mother. And other people might believe that there are human beings with no parents, and give no credence to all the contrary evidence. Catholics believe as well that in certain circumstances a wafer completely changes its nature, and at the same time that all evidence proves the contrary. And so if Moore said 'I know that this is wine and not blood', Catholics would contradict him.

What is the belief that all human beings have parents based on? On experience. And how can I base this sure belief on my experience? Well, I base it not only on the fact that I have known the parents of certain people but on everything that I have learnt about the sexual life of human beings and their anatomy and physiology: also on what I have heard and seen of animals. But then is that really a proof?

Isn't this an hypothesis, which, as I *believe*, is again and again completely confirmed?

Mustn't we say at every turn: 'I *believe* this with certainty'?

One says 'I know' when one is ready to give compelling grounds. 'I know' relates to a possibility of demonstrating the truth. Whether someone knows something can come to light, assuming that he is convinced of it.
But if what he believes is of such a kind that the grounds that he can give are no surer than his assertion, then he cannot say that he knows what he believes.

If someone says 'I have a body', he can be asked 'Who is speaking here with this mouth?'

To whom does anyone say that he knows something? To himself, or to someone else. If he says it to himself, how is it distinguished from the assertion that he is *sure* that things are like that? There is no subjective sureness that I know something. The certainty is subjective, but not the knowledge. So if I say 'I know that I have two hands', and that is not supposed to express just my subjective certainty, I must be able to satisfy myself that I am right. But I can't do that, for my having two hands is not less certain before I have looked at them than afterwards. But I could say: 'That I have two hands is an irreversible belief.' That would express the fact that I am not ready to let anything count as a disproof of this proposition.

'Here I have arrived at a foundation of all my beliefs.' 'This position I will *hold*!' But isn't that, precisely, only because I am completely *convinced* of it? – What is 'being completely convinced' like?

What would it be like to doubt now whether I have two hands? Why can't I imagine it at all? What would I believe if I didn't believe that? So far I have no system at all within which this doubt might exist.

I have arrived at the rock bottom of my convictions.
And one might almost say that these foundation-walls are carried by the whole house.

One gives oneself a false picture of *doubt*.

My having two hands is, in normal circumstances, as certain as anything that I could produce in evidence for it.
That is why I am not in a position to take the sight of my hand as evidence for it.

Doesn't this mean: I shall proceed according to this belief unconditionally, and not let anything confuse me?

But it isn't just that *I* believe in this way that I have two hands, but that every reasonable person does.

At the foundation of well-founded belief lies belief that is not founded.

Any 'reasonable' person behaves like *this*.

Doubting has certain characteristic manifestation, but they are only characteristic of it in particular circumstances. If someone said that he doubted the existence of his hands, kept looking at them from all sides, tried to make sure it wasn't 'all done by mirrors', etc., we should not be sure whether we ought to call that doubting. We might describe his way of behaving as like the behaviour of doubt, but his game would not be ours.

On the other hand a language-game does change with time.

If someone said to me that he doubted whether he had a body I should take him to be a half-wit. But I shouldn't know what it would mean to try to convince him that he had one. And if I had said something, and that had removed his doubt, I should not know how or why.

I do not know how the sentence 'I have a body' is to be used.

That doesn't unconditionally apply to the proposition that I have always been on or near the surface of the earth.

Someone who doubted whether the earth had existed for 100 years might have a scientific, or on the other hand a philosophical, doubt.

I would like to reserve the expression 'I know' for the cases in which it is used in normal linguistic exchange.

I cannot at present imagine a reasonable doubt as to the existence of the earth during the last 100 years.

I can imagine a man who had grown up in quite special circumstances and been taught that the earth came into being 50 years ago, and therefore believed this. We might instruct him: the earth has long . . . etc. – We should be trying to give him our picture of the world.

This would happen through a kind of *persuasion*.

* * *

It is quite sure that motor cars don't grow out of the earth. We feel that if someone could believe the contrary he could believe *everything* that we say is untrue, and could question everything that we hold to be sure.

But how does this *one* belief hang together with all the rest? We should like to say that someone who could believe that does not accept our whole system of verification.

This system is something that a human being acquires by means of observation and instruction. I intentionally do not say 'learns'.

After he has seen this and this and heard that and that, he is not in a position to doubt whether . . .

I, L. W., believe, am sure, that my friend hasn't sawdust in his body or in his head, even though I have no direct evidence of my senses to the contrary. I am sure, by reason of what has been said to me, of what I have read, and of my experience. To have doubts about it would seem to me madness – of course, this is also in agreement with other people; but *I* agree with them.

I cannot say that I have good grounds for the opinion that cats do not grow on trees or that I had a father and a mother.

If someone has doubts about it – how is that supposed to have come about? By his never, from the beginning, having believed that he had parents? But then, is that conceivable, unless he has been taught it?

For how can a child immediately doubt what it is taught? That could mean only that he was incapable of learning certain language games.

People have killed animals since the earliest times, used the fur, bones etc. etc. for various purposes; they have counted definitely on finding similar parts in any similar beast.

They have always learnt from experience; and we can see from their actions that they believe certain things definitely, whether they express this belief or not. By this I naturally do not want to say that men *should* behave like this, but only that they do behave like this.

14

The Nature of Philosophy

THE DIFFICULTY OF PHILOSOPHY IS NOT AN
INTELLECTUAL DIFFICULTY LIKE THAT OF THE
SCIENCES, BUT THE DIFFICULTY OF A CONVERSION.
WHAT HAS TO BE CONQUERED IS THE RESISTANCE OF
THE WILL.

As I have often said, philosophy does not call on me for any sacrifice, because I am not denying myself the saying of anything but simply giving up a certain combination of words as sense-less. In a different sense, however, philosophy does demand a renunciation, but a renunciation of feeling, not of under-standing. Perhaps that is what makes it so hard for many people. It can be as hard to refrain from using an expression as it is to hold back tears, or hold in anger.

Tolstoy: The meaning (significance) of an object consists in its being universally intelligible. – That is partly true, partly false. When an object is significant and important what makes it hard to understand is not the lack of some special instruction in abstruse matters necessary for its understanding, but the con-flict between the right understanding of the object and what most people *want* to see. This can make the most obvious things the very hardest to understand. What has to be overcome is not a difficulty of the understanding but of the will.

The job to be done in philosophy – as often in architecture – is really more a job on oneself. On one's own viewpoint. On how one sees things. (And what one demands from them.)

Roughly speaking, according to the old view, the view, say, of the (great) Western philosophers, there were two kinds of scientific problems: essential, great, universal problems, and non-essential, quasi-accidental problems. Our view, on the contrary, is that there is no *great*, essential problem of a scientific kind.

PHILOSOPHY EXPOSES MISLEADING ANALOGIES IN THE USE OF OUR LANGUAGE.

Is grammar, how I use a word, only the description of the actual usage of language? So that its propositions should be looked on just as propositions of a natural science?

One might call such a discipline a descriptive science which deals with speaking, as opposed to thinking.

The rules of chess might also be looked on as propositions of the natural history of human beings. (Just as the play of animals is described in books of natural history.)

Whenever I correct a philosophical error, and say 'This has always been imagined thus and so, but it is not really like that', in each case what I have to do is to expose an analogy which has been guiding people's thought without their realizing that it was an analogy.

The effect of a false analogy embedded in language: it means a constant struggle and discomfort (almost, a constant itch). It is as when something in the distance looks like a man, but we cannot see anything clearly, and then from close up we see that it is a tree stump. If we step back a little and lose sight of the distinguishing features, we see one shape; if we look closer again, we see another; then we go back again, and so on.

(The irritating nature of grammatical unclarity.)

Doing philosophy is turning bad arguments around.

The philosopher strives to find the liberating word, that is, the word which finally allows us to grasp what it is that has hitherto, imperceptibly, been a burden upon our consciousness.

(It is like having a hair on your tongue: you feel it, but you can't get hold of it and get rid of it.)

The philosopher offers us the word which enables us to make matters explicit and harmless.

(The choice of our words is important because it is a matter of hitting off exactly the features of things, because only thoughts pointed in just the right direction can lead down the right track. The carriage has to sit exactly snug on the rails if it is to run properly along them.)

One of the most important tasks is to describe all the blind alleys of thought so vividly that the reader says 'Yes, that is just what I meant'. To hit off exactly the features of every error.

You see, it *is* the right expression only if he recognizes it as such. (Psychoanalysis).

What the other person recognizes is that the analogy I am offering him is the source of his way of thinking.

WHAT MAKES OUR GRAMMATICAL INVESTIGATIONS APPEAR BASIC?

We are preoccupied with various kinds of questions, such as 'What is the specific gravity of this body?' 'Will it stay fine today?' 'Who will be the next person to come through the door?' But among our questions there are some of a special kind which feel quite different. These questions seem to be more basic than the others. And I say: when we have this feeling, then we have come up against the limits of language.

Where does our investigation get its importance from, since it seems only to destroy everything interesting, that is, all that is great and important? (As it were all the buildings; leaving behind only bits of stone and rubble.)

Where does our investigation get its importance from – pointing out that a table can be used in more than one way, that one can devise a table for the use of a table, that one can interpret an arrow as pointing in the direction from tip to tail, that I can use a blueprint as a blueprint in more than one way?

What we do is to bring words back from their metaphysical to their normal use in language.

(The man who said that one cannot step twice into the same

river, uttered a falsehood. One *can* step twice into the same river.)

And that is what the solution of all philosophical problems looks like. Their answers will only be correct if they are plain and everyday. Provided you look at them in the right spirit, that won't matter.

Where did the old philosophical problems get their significance from?

The law of identity, for instance, seemed to have a fundamental significance. But the proposition that this 'law' is a piece of nonsense has taken over that significance.

I could ask: why do I feel a grammatical joke to be in a certain sense deep? (And that of course is what the depth of philosophy is.)

Why do we feel the investigation of grammar to be something basic?

(The word 'basic', in the cases where it does have some meaning, can mean something non-metalogical, non-philosophical.)

The investigation of grammar is basic in the same sense as we might call language itself basic – as its own basis.

Our grammatical investigation is different from that of a philologist etc.; we are interested, for instance, in translation from one language into another language which we have just made up. In general we are interested in rules which the philologist does not consider at all. We could make quite a lot of this difference.

On the other hand, it would be misleading to say that we deal with what is essential in grammar, while he deals with what is accidental.

'But that is just a superficial difference.' I think there is no other kind.

We might rather say that he and we give the name 'grammar' to two different things. Just as we make distinctions between kinds of words where he does not make any distinction.

The importance of grammar is the importance of language.

One might similarly say that a word like 'red' is important because it is used frequently, and for serious purposes, unlike, say, the word for the lid of a pipe. And thus the grammar of the word 'red' is important because it describes the meaning of the word 'red'.

(All philosophy can do is to destroy idols. And that means, not making any new ones – in the 'absence of an idol'.)

THE METHOD OF PHILOSOPHY; PERSPICUOUS REPRESENTATION OF GRAMMATICAL FACTS. ITS PURPOSE: TRANSPARENCY OF ARGUMENTS. JUSTICE.

A person has heard that the anchor of a ship is pulled up by a steam engine. He thinks only of the engine which drives the ship (the one which entitles it to the name 'steamship') and he cannot make sense of what he has heard. (Perhaps the problem only strikes him later on.) So we tell him, no, it is not *that* steam engine, there are several others on board, and one of these pulls up the anchor. – Was his problem a philosophical one? Would it be if he had heard of the existence of other steam engines on this ship and only needed reminding of this? – I think his confusion is twofold. The facts which are told him in the explanation are ones whose possibility he could well have thought up for himself, and he could have framed his question in a specific form instead of as a mere admission of confusion. He could have got rid of that part of the doubt himself, though mere reflection could not have given him any information about the facts. In other words: no ordering of his concepts could remove the worry arising from his ignorance of the facts.

The other sort of worry and confusion is expressed in the words 'something seems wrong here' and its resolution in the words 'So – you don't mean *the* steam engine' or – in another case – 'By steam engine you don't just mean the piston engine'.

The work of the philosopher consists in assembling reminders for a particular purpose.

A philosophical question is like an inquiry into the constitution of a society. It is as if a society met without clear written rules but in a situation where rules are necessary: the members have an instinct that enables them to observe certain rules in their dealings with one another, but everything is made more difficult because there is no clear pronouncement on the subject, no arrangement for clarifying the rules. Thus they regard one of their number as president, but he does not sit at the head of the table, nor is he in any way recognizable and this makes the transaction of business more difficult. So we come along and bring order and clarity. We seat the president at an easily identifiable place with his secretary near him at a special little table, and we seat the other, ordinary, members in two rows on either side of the table and so on.

When philosophy is asked 'What is – say – substance' the request is for a rule, a universal rule which holds for the word 'substance' – that is, the rule according to which I am determined to play. – I want to say: The question 'what is . . . ' is not concerned with any particular, practical, case; it is an armchair question. Just bring to mind the case of the law of identity, in order to see that dealing with philosophical problems is not a matter of expressing new truths about the object of the investigation (identity).

The problem is only to understand in what way it helps us to lay down a rule, why it soothes us after we were so deeply worried. What soothes us is obviously that we see a system that systematically excludes the structures which always worried us, that we did not know how to cope with, and yet which we 'believed we had to respect'. Isn't the laying down of such a grammatical rule in this context like the discovery of an explanation in physics, such as the Copernican system? Well, there is a similarity. – The peculiarity of philosophical worry and its resolution might seem to be that it is like the anguish of an ascetic, groaning under the weight of a heavy sphere, until someone gives him relief by saying 'let it drop'. One asks oneself: If these propositions worried you, and you could not cope with them, why did you not let them drop earlier, what stopped you? I think that it was the false system, which he thought he had to adapt himself to. [Hen and chalk line].

(There is a particular discomfort when a case which we believed to be unique turns out to be capable of being grouped with other similar cases. This always turns up in our investigations whenever we show that a word does not have only *one* meaning, or only two, but is used with five or six different meanings.

There are some safes which can be opened by using a certain word or a certain number: before you hit on the right word, no amount of force can open the door, but once you do so any child can open it. Philosophical problems are like that.

The concept of a perspicuous representation is of fundamental significance for us. It earmarks the form of account we give, the way we look at things. (A type of 'Weltanschauung' which seems to be typical of our age. Spengler.)

This perspicuous representation produces just that understanding which consists in 'seeing connections'. Hence the importance of finding *intermediate cases*.

A proposition is completely logically analysed if its grammar is fully clarified. It does not matter in what form of expression it is written or uttered.

What our grammar lacks above all is *perspicuity*.

Philosophy may in no way interfere with the actual use of language; it can in the end only describe it.

For it cannot give it any foundation either.

It leaves everything as it is.

It also leaves mathematics as it is (now is), and no mathematical discovery can advance it.

A 'leading problem of mathematical logic' (Ramsey) is a problem of mathematics *like any other*.

(A simile forms part of our structures; but we cannot draw any consequences from it; it doesn't take us beyond itself, but has to stay put as a simile. We cannot draw any conclusions from it. Thus it is when we compare the proposition with a picture (where what we mean by 'picture' must already be ingrained in us) or when I compare the use of language with that of something like the multiplication table.

Philosophy simply puts everything before us, and neither explains nor deduces anything.

Since everything lies open to view there is nothing to explain. For what is hidden, for example, is of no interest to us.

The real answer to the request for an explanation of negation is: don't you understand it then? Well, if you do, what is there left to explain, what is there left for an explanation to do?

We must know what we mean by *explanation*. There is a constant danger of wanting to use this word in logic in a sense which is taken over from physics.

Methodology, when it talks about measurement, does not say what is the best material for making the measuring rod in order to achieve a particular result, though that too is part of the method of measurement. This investigation is interested rather just in the circumstances in which we say that a length, or the strength of a current (etc.) have been measured. What it wants to do is to tabulate the ordinary methods we already use, so as to exhibit the meaning of the words 'length', 'strength of current', etc.

If one tried to advance *theses* in philosophy, it would never be possible to question them, because everyone would agree to them.

Learning philosophy really *is* a remembering. We remind ourselves that we have really used words in this way.

The philosophically most important aspects of things are hidden because of their simplicity and familiarity.
(One is unable to notice something – because it is always in plain view before one's eyes.)

The real foundations of his enquiry do not strike a man at all. Unless *that* fact has at some time struck him. (Frazer etc. etc.) And that means that the most striking (most powerful) thing does not strike him at all.

(One of the greatest hindrances to philosophy is the expectation of new, unheard of, discoveries.)

One might also give the name 'philosophy' to what is possible *before* all new discoveries and inventions.

This must also be connected with the fact that I cannot give any explanation for the variable 'proposition'. It is clear that this logical concept, this variable, must be of the same rank as the concept 'reality' or 'world'.

Suppose someone thinks he has found the solution to the 'problem of life' and tells himself that now everything is now quite easy. To see his error he only has to remind himself that there was a time when this 'solution' had not been discovered; but even at *that* time people also had to live. In that light the solution he has discovered seems something quite inessential. And that is the way it is in logic. If there were to be a 'solution' to logical (philosophical) problems, we would only have to bring to mind that there was a time when they were not solved, and then too people had to be able to live and think.

All my reflections could be expressed in a much more straightforward way than I did in the past. In philosophy there is no need to use new words; the old familiar words of the language are quite sufficient.

Our job is simply to be just. That is, we have only to identify and solve the injustices of philosophy, without setting up new parties and creeds.

(In philosophy it is difficult not to overdo things.)

The philosopher goes wild, screaming helplessly, until he gets to the heart of his confusion.

A philosophical problem is a consciousness of the disorder in our concepts which can be removed by an ordering.

A philosophical problem is always of the form 'I just don't know my way about'.

The way I do philosophy, its whole job is to frame an expression in such a way that certain worries disappear. (Hertz).

If I am right, then philosophical problems, unlike all others, must really be solved without remainder.

Whenever I say: here we are at the limits of language, that sounds as if some kind of self-denial were necessary; but on the contrary, we have reached complete satisfaction, since there are *no* questions left over.

The problems are, in the strict sense, dissolved: like a piece of sugar in water.

People who feel no need for transparency in their argumentation are lost for philosophy.

CLARIFYING THE USE OF LANGUAGE. PITFALLS OF LANGUAGE

How does it come about that philosophy is so complicated a structure? It surely ought to be completely simple, if it is the ultimate thing, independent of all experience, that you make it out to be. – Philosophy unties knots in our thinking; hence its result must be simple, but its activity must be as complicated as the knots it unties.

Lichtenberg: 'Our whole philosophy is the rectification of linguistic usage: the rectification, that is, of a philosophy which is the most universal one'.

A gift for philosophy consists in the capacity to receive a strong and enduring impression of a fact of grammar.

Why are grammatical problems so tough and apparently insoluble? Because they are linked to the oldest habits of thought, the oldest pictures that are embedded in our language itself. (Lichtenberg.)

Teaching philosophy has the same kind of extraordinary difficulty that geography lessons would have if the pupils began with a lot of false and oversimplified ideas of the way rivers and mountain ranges go.

Human beings are profoundly enmeshed in philosophical – i.e. grammatical – confusions. They cannot be freed without first being extricated from the extraordinary variety of associations which hold them prisoner. You have as it were to reconstitute their entire language. – But this language grew up as it did because human beings had – and have – the tendency to think in this way. So you can only succeed in extricating people who live in an instinctive rebellion against language; you cannot help those whose entire instinct is to live in the herd which has created this language as its own proper mode of expression.

Language sets the same traps for everybody: the terrible network of well-worn wrong tracks. So we see one person after another going the same way, and we know where they will turn aside, where they will go straight ahead, without noticing a fork, etc. etc. So what I should do is to put up signs in all the places wherever wrong turnings branch off, to help people over the dangerous places.

You always hear people say that philosophy makes no progress and that the same philosophical problems which were already preoccupying the Greeks are still troubling us today. But people who say that do not understand the reason why it has to be so. The reason is that our language has remained the same and always introduces us to the same questions. As long as there is a verb 'be' which seems to work like 'eat' and 'drink'; as long as there are adjectives like 'identical', 'true', 'false', 'possible'; as long as people speak of the passage of time and of the extent of space, and so on; as long as all this happens people will always run up against the same teasing difficulties and will stare at something which no explanation seems able to remove.

This satisfies too a longing for the supernatural, because while they believe they are seeing the 'limit of human understanding' they believe of course that they can see over it.

I read 'Philosophers are no nearer to the meaning of "reality" than Plato got . . .'. What an extraordinary thing. How remarkable that Plato could get so far! Or that we have not been able to get any further! Was it because Plato was *so* clever?

The conflict we are always getting into when we do logic is like the conflict between two people who have made a contract with each other whose official formulation is ambiguous, while there are definitions attached which set out everything unambiguously. One of the two has a short memory, and constantly forgets the definitions and misinterprets the terms of the contract, and is always getting into difficulty. The other keeps having to remind him of the definitions in the contract and to get rid of his difficulties.

Just remind yourself how hard it is for children to believe (or to understand) that a word really can have two quite different meanings.

The goal of philosophy is to build a wall where language comes to an end.

The results of philosophy are the uncovering of one or another piece of plain nonsense and of bumps that the understanding has got by running its head up against the limits of language. These bumps make us see the value of the discovery.

What kind of investigation are we engaged in? These cases which I produce as examples – do I investigate whether they are probable, or actual? No, I am merely adducing possibilities; I am giving grammatical examples.

Philosophy is embodied not in propositions, but in a language.

Just as laws arouse our interest only when we are inclined to break them, so certain grammatical rules arouse our interest only when philosophers would like to break them.

Savages have games (or what we would call games) for which they have no written rules or rule-book. Imagine a researcher, travelling through the lands of these people and drawing up a code of rules for their games. That is wholly analogous to what the philosopher does. (But why don't I say: The savages (or we) have languages but no written grammar?)

IT IS NOT IN PRACTICAL LIFE THAT WE ENCOUNTER PHILOSOPHICAL PROBLEMS (AS WE MAY ENCOUNTER SCIENTIFIC PROBLEMS) – IT IS WHEN WE START CONSTRUCTING SENTENCES NOT FOR PRACTICAL PURPOSES BUT UNDER THE INFLUENCE OF CERTAIN ANALOGIES IN LANGUAGE.

What belongs to the essence of the world cannot be expressed by language. So it cannot *say* that everything flows. Language can say only what we can imagine otherwise.

That everything flows, must lie in the essence of the contact between language and reality. Or better: that everything flows, must belong to the essence of language. And, let us remind ourselves, in ordinary life that doesn't strike us – any more than the blurred edges of our visual field ('because we are so used to it', some people will say). How, in what circumstances, do we think we are noticing it? Isn't it when we want to form sentences which violate the grammar of time?

When people say 'everything flows' we feel that we are prevented from grasping the actuality, the actual reality. The process on the screen escapes us, just because it is a process. But we certainly describe something; and is it a different process? But the description is obviously connected with the picture on the screen. Our feeling of helplessness must rest upon a false picture. Because what we want to be able to describe is something that we are able to describe.

Isn't the false picture the idea of film flashing past so swiftly that we have no time to take in a single picture?

In this case we actually feel the inclination to run after the picture. But in the course of a process there is nothing analogous.

It is a remarkable thing that the feeling of a phenomenon eluding us, of the constant flow of appearance, is never felt in ordinary life, but only when we philosophize. That indicates that what we have here is a thought suggested to us by an incorrect use of our language.

The feeling is that the present vanishes into the past without our being able to stop it. And obviously here we employ the picture of a film running constantly before us which we cannot stop. But of course it is just as obvious that the picture is misapplied, and that we can't say 'time flows' if by 'time' we mean the possibility of change.

That nothing strikes us when we look around a room, feel our own body, etc. etc., that shows how natural these things are to us. We do not perceive that we see the room in perspective or that our visual field is in some sense blurred at the edge. It does not strike us and cannot strike us, because *that* is what perception is like. We don't think about it, and we can't do so, because the form of our world has no opposite.

I want to say that it is remarkable that people who ascribe reality only to things and not to our representations take the world of our representations so much as a matter of course and aim no further.

That is, the given is such a matter of course. All hell would break loose if it was a tiny picture taken from some crooked corner.

That this matter-of-fact thing, *life itself*, should be something accidental and inessential, while something to which I never normally give a thought should be the reality!

That is to say, something beyond which we cannot go, and yet want to go, could not be the world.

Again and again there is the attempt to limit and present the world in language – but it never succeeds. The banality of the world is evident in the fact that language means it alone, and can mean only it.

Because language takes its mode of meaning from what it means, namely the world, no language is conceivable which does not represent this world.

In the theories and disputes of philosophy we find words whose meanings are familiar to us from everyday life being used in a super-physical sense.

When philosophers use a word and enquire about its meaning we must always ask: is this word actually used thus in the language which created it?

Philosophers are often like little children who scribble a jumble of lines on a piece of paper and then ask grown-ups 'what is that?' – This is how it happens. Adults have often drawn something for the child and said: 'That is a man', 'That is a house' and so on. So now the child draws lines and asks: 'What's *that*?'

METHOD IN PHILOSOPHY.
POSSIBILITY OF PEACEFUL PROGRESS

The real discovery is the one that makes me capable of stopping doing philosophy when I want to.

The one that gives philosophy peace, so that it is no longer tormented by questions which bring *itself* in question.

Instead, we now demonstrate a method, by examples; and the series of examples can be broken off.

It would be more correct to say: Problems are solved (difficulties eliminated), not a *single* problem.

Disquiet in philosophy is due to the fact that philosophers look at philosophy wrongly, seeing it wrong, namely as if it were divided into (infinite) longitudinal strips instead of into (finite) cross strips. This inversion in our conception produces the *greatest* difficulty. They want as it were to grasp the unlimited strips, and complain that it cannot be done piecemeal. To be sure it cannot, if by a piece one means an infinite longitudinal strip. But it may well be done, if one means a cross-strip. – But in that case we never get to the end of our work! – Of course not, for it has no end.

(We want to replace wild conjectures and explanations by quiet weighing of linguistic facts.)

The whole of language must be thoroughly ploughed up.

Most people, when they want to start a philosophical investigation, behave like someone searching frantically for an object in a drawer. He throws some papers out of the drawer – what he is looking for may be underneath – and riffles through the rest hastily and carelessly; he throws some back in the drawer and gets them all mixed up and so on. You can only say to him: Hold on, if you are going to search like *that* I can't help you. You must begin calmly and methodically to look at one thing after another; if you do, I am ready to help you search and to adopt your method.

THE MYTHOLOGY IN THE FORMS OF OUR LANGUAGE. (PAUL ERNST.)

In ancient rites we can see in use a thoroughly developed gesture-language.

And when I read Frazer, I keep wanting to say: all these

processes, these changes of meaning are still with us in our own word-language. What is hidden in the last sheaf is called the cornwolf; but so is the sheaf itself and the man who binds it. Here we recognize a familiar linguistic process.

The scapegoat, on whom people heap their sins and who goes out into the desert with them – a wrong picture, like those which cause philosophical mistakes.

I would like to say: nothing shows better our relationship with those savages than the fact that Frazer has available to describe their ideas a word so familiar to him and us as 'ghost' or 'shade'.

(This is different from when he describes, say, how the savages imagined that their head drops when they have killed an enemy. There would be nothing superstitious or magical in *our description* here.)

This oddness is not only about the expressions 'ghost' and 'shade'; people are not sufficiently struck-by the fact that we count words like 'soul' and 'spirit' as part of our own civilized vocabulary. By comparison it is a minor matter that we do not believe that our soul eats and drinks.

In our language there is an entire mythology embedded.

Casting out death, killing death; but on the other hand death is represented as a skeleton, so as being himself in a manner dead. 'As dead as death.' 'Nothing is as dead as death, nothing is so beautiful as beauty itself.' The picture we are using here to conceive reality is that beauty, death, etc. are the pure (concentrated) substances, while in a beautiful object it is only an ingredient. Don't I recognize here my own discussions on 'object' and 'complex'? (Plato.)

The primitive forms of our language – noun, adjective and verb – show the simple picture to which it tries to make everything conform.

As long as you imagine the soul as a *thing*, a *body* in the head, this hypothesis is not at all dangerous. It is not the crudity and incompleteness of our models that brings danger, but their vagueness.

The danger begins when we notice that the old model is

inadequate and then instead of altering it as it were sublimate it. As long as I say that thought is in my head, there is nothing wrong; things become dangerous when we say that thought is not in my head but in my spirit.

★ ★ ★

In what sense is logic something sublime?

For there seemed to pertain to logic a peculiar depth – a universal significance. Logic lay, it seemed, at the bottom of all the sciences. – For logical investigation explores the nature of all things. It seeks to see to the bottom of things and is not meant to concern itself whether what actually happens is this or that. — It takes its rise, not from an interest in the facts of nature, nor from a need to grasp causal connexions: but from an urge to understand the basis, or essence, of everything empirical. Not, however, as if to this end we had to hunt out new facts; it is, rather, of the essence of our investigation that we do not seek to learn anything *new* by it. We want to *understand* something that is already in plain view. For *this* is what we seem in some sense not to understand.

Augustine says in the *Confessions* 'quid est ergo tempus? si nemo ex me quaerat scio; si quaerenti explicare velim, nescio'. – This could not be said about a question of natural science ('What is the specific gravity of hydrogen?' for instance). Something that we know when no one asks us, but no longer know when we are supposed to give an account of it, is something that we need to *remind* ourselves of. (And it is obviously something of which for some reason it is difficult to remind oneself.)

We feel as if we had to *penetrate* phenomena: our investigation, however, is directed not towards phenomena, but, as one might say, towards the '*possibilities*' of phenomena. We remind ourselves, that is to say, of the *kind of statement* that we make about phenomena. Thus Augustine recalls to mind the different statements that are made about the duration, past present or future, of events. (These are, of course, not *philosophical* statements about time, the past, the present and the future.)

Our investigation is therefore a grammatical one. Such an investigation sheds light on our problem by clearing misunderstandings away. Misunderstandings concerning the use of words, caused, among other things, by certain analogies between the forms of expression in different regions of language. – Some of them can be removed by substituting one form of expression for another; this may be called an 'analysis' of our forms of expression, for the process is sometimes like one of taking a thing apart.

But now it may come to look as if there were something like a final analysis of our forms of language, and so a *single* completely resolved form of every expression. That is, as if our usual forms of expression were, essentially, unanalysed; as if there were something hidden in them that had to be brought to light. When this is done the expression is completely clarified and our problem solved.

It can also be put like this: we eliminate misunderstandings by making our expressions more exact; but now it may look as if we were moving towards a particular state, a state of complete exactness; and as if this were the real goal of our investigation.

This finds expression in questions as to the *essence* of language, of propositions, of thought. – For if we too in these investigations are trying to understand the essence of language – its function, its structure, – yet *this* is not what those questions have in view. For they see in the essence, not something that already lies open to view and that becomes surveyable by a rearrangement, but something that lies *beneath* the surface. Something that lies within, which we see when we look *into* the thing, and which an analysis digs out.

'*The essence is hidden from us*': this is the form our problem now assumes. We ask: '*What is* language?', '*What is* a proposition?' And the answer to these questions is to be given once for all; and independently of any future experience.

* * *

Here it is difficult as it were to keep our heads up, – to see that we must stick to the subjects of our every-day thinking, and not go astray and imagine that we have to describe extreme subtleties, which in turn we are after all quite unable to describe with the means at our disposal. We feel as if we had to repair a torn spider's web with our fingers.

The more narrowly we examine actual language, the sharper becomes the conflict between it and our requirement. (For the crystalline purity of logic was, of course, not a *result of investigation*: it was a requirement.) The conflict becomes intolerable; the requirement is now in danger of becoming empty. – We have got on to slippery ice where there is no friction and so in a certain sense the conditions are ideal, but also, just because of that, we are unable to walk. We want to walk: so we need *friction*. Back to the rough ground!

We see that what we call 'sentence' and 'language' has not the formal unity that I imagined, but is the family of structures more or less related to one another. — But what becomes of logic now? Its rigour seems to be giving way here. – But in that case doesn't logic altogether disappear? – For how can it lose its rigour? Of course not by our bargaining any of its rigour out of it. – The *preconceived idea* of crystalline purity can only be removed by turning our whole examination round. (One might say: the axis of reference of our examination must be rotated, but about the fixed point of our real need.)

The philosophy of logic speaks of sentences and words in exactly the sense in which we speak of them in ordinary life when we say e.g. 'Here is a Chinese sentence', or 'No, that only looks like writing; it is actually just an ornament' and so on.

We are talking about the spatial and temporal phenomenon of language, not about some non-spatial, non-temporal phantasm. [Note in margin: Only it is possible to be interested in a phenomenon in a variety of ways]. But we talk about it as we do about the pieces in chess when we are stating the rules of the game, not describing their physical properties.

The question 'What is a word really?' is analogous to 'What is a piece in chess?'

It was true to say that our considerations could not be scientific ones. It was not of any possible interest to us to find out empirically 'that, contrary to our preconceived ideas, it is possible to think such-and-such' – whatever that may mean. (The conception of thought as a gaseous medium.) And we may not advance any kind of theory. There must not be anything hypothetical in our considerations. We must do away with all *explanation*, and description alone must take its place. And this description gets its light, that is to say its purpose, from the philosophical problems. These are, of course, not empirical problems; they are solved, rather, by looking into the workings of our language, and that in such a way as to make us recognize those workings: *in despite of* an urge to misunderstand them. The problems are solved, not by giving new information, but by arranging what we have always known. Philosophy is a battle against the bewitchment of our intelligence by means of language.

'Language (or thought) is something unique' – this proves to be a superstition (*not* a mistake!), itself produced by grammatical illusions.

And now the impressiveness retreats to these illusions, to the problems.

The problems arising through a misinterpretation of our forms of language have the character of *depth*. They are deep disquietudes; their roots are as deep in us as the forms of our language and their significance is as great as the importance of our language. — Let us ask ourselves: why do we feel a grammatical joke to be *deep*? (And that is what the depth of philosophy is.)

A simile that has been absorbed into the forms of our language produces a false appearance, and this disquiets us. 'But *this* isn't how it is!' – we say. 'Yet *this* is how it has to *be*!'

'But *this* is how it is —' I say to myself over and over again. I feel as though, if only I could fix my gaze absolutely sharply on this fact, get it in focus, I must grasp the essence of the matter.

(*Tractatus Logico-Philosophicus*, 4.5): 'The general form of propositions is: This is how things are.' — That is the kind of proposition that one repeats to oneself countless times. One thinks that one is tracing the outline of the thing's nature over and over again, and one is merely tracing round the frame through which we look at it.

A *picture* held us captive. And we could not get outside it, for it lay in our language and language seemed to repeat it to us inexorably.

When philosophers use a word – 'knowledge', 'being', 'object', 'I', 'proposition', 'name' – and try to grasp the *essence* of the thing, one must always ask oneself: is the word ever actually used in this way in the language-game which is its original home? –

What *we* do is to bring words back from their metaphysical to their everyday use.

You say to me: 'You understand this expression, don't you? Well then – I am using it in the sense you are familiar with.' – As if the sense were an atmosphere accompanying the word, which it carried with it into every kind of application.

If, for example, someone says that the sentence 'This is here' (saying which he points to an object in front of him) makes sense to him, then he should ask himself in what special circumstances this sentence is actually used. There it does make sense.

When I talk about language (words, sentences, etc.) I must speak the language of every day. Is this language somehow too coarse and material for what we want to say? *Then how is another one to be constructed?* – And how strange that we should be able to do anything at all with the one we have!

In giving explanations I already have to use language full-blown (not some sort of preparatory, provisional one); this by itself shews that I can adduce only exterior facts about language.

Yes, but then how can these explanations satisfy us? – Well, your very questions were framed in this language; they had to be expressed in this language, if there was anything to ask!

And your scruples are misunderstandings.

Your questions refer to words; so I have to talk about words.

You say: the point isn't the word, but its meaning, and you think of the meaning as a thing of the same kind as the word, though also different from the word. Here the word, there the meaning. The money, and the cow that you can buy with it. (But contrast: money, and its use.)

One might think: if philosophy speaks of the use of the word 'philosophy' there must be a second-order philosophy. But it is not so: it is, rather, like the case of orthography, which deals with the word 'orthography' among others without then being second-order.

It is the business of philosophy, not to resolve a contradiction by means of a mathematical or logico-mathematical discovery, but to make it possible for us to get a clear view of the state of

mathematics that troubles us: the state of affairs *before* the contradiction is resolved. (And this does not mean that one is
sidestepping a difficulty.)

The fundamental fact here is that we lay down rules, a technique, for a game, and that then when we follow the rules, things
do not turn out as we had assumed. That we are therefore as it
were entangled in our own rules.

This entanglement in our rules is what we want to understand
(i.e. get a clear view of).

It throws light on our concept of *meaning* something. For in
those cases things turn out otherwise than we had meant, foreseen. That is just what we say when, for example, a contradiction appears: 'I didn't mean it like that.'

The civil status of a contradiction, or its status in civil life:
there is the philosophical problem.

Our clear and simple language-games are not preparatory
studies for a future regularization of language – as it were first
approximations, ignoring friction and air-resistance. The language-games are rather set up as *objects of comparison* which are
meant to throw light on the facts of our language by way not
only of similarities, but also of dissimilarities.

For we can avoid ineptness or emptiness in our assertions only
by presenting the model as what it is, as an object of comparison
– as, so to speak, a measuring-rod; not as a preconceived idea to
which reality *must* correspond. (The dogmatism into which we
fall so easily in doing philosophy.)

We want to establish an order in our knowledge of the use of
language: an order with a particular end in view; one out of
many possible orders; not *the* order. To this end we shall constantly be giving prominence to distinctions which our ordinary
forms of language easily make us overlook. This may make it
look as if we saw it as our task to reform language.

Such a reform for particular practical purposes, an improve-
ment in our terminology designed to prevent misunderstandings
in practice, is perfectly possible. But these are not the cases we
have to do with. The confusions which occupy us arise when
language is like an engine idling, not when it is doing work.

It is not our aim to refine or complete the system of rules for
the use of our words in unheard-of ways.

For the clarity that we are aiming at is indeed *complete* clarity. But this simply means that the philosophical problems should *completely* disappear.

★ ★ ★

And does one say that the sentence 'It's raining' says: such-and-such is the case? What is the everyday use of this expression in ordinary language? For you learned it from this use. If you now use it contrary to its original use, and think you are still playing the old game with it, that is as if you were to play draughts with chess-pieces and imagine that your game had kept something of the spirit of chess.

Extension of a concept in a *theory* (e.g. wish- fulfillment dream).

One who philosophises often makes the wrong, inappropriate gesture for a verbal expression.

(One says the ordinary thing – with the wrong gesture.)

(As one can sometimes reproduce music only in one's inward ear, and cannot whistle it, because the whistling drowns out the inner voice, so sometimes the voice of a philosophical thought is so soft that the noise of spoken words is enough to drown it and prevent it from being heard, if one is questioned and has to speak.)

Plato: '– What? he said, *it* be of no use? If wisdom is the knowledge of knowledge and is prior to other knowledges, then it must also be prior to that knowledge which relates to the good and in that way must be of use to us. – Does *it* make us healthy, I said, and not medicine? And similarly with the rest of the arts; does *it* direct their business, and not rather each of them its own? Again, have we not long since allowed that it would only be the knowledge of knowledges and ignorances and not of any other matter? – We have indeed. – So it will not produce health in us? – Presumably not. – Because health belongs to a different art? – Yes – Then, friend, neither will it produce utility for us. For this is a business we have too assigned to another art. – Of course – So how can wisdom be useful, if it does not bring us any utility?'

(The philosopher is not a citizen of any community of ideas. That is what makes him into a philosopher.)

Some philosophers (or whatever you like to call them) suffer from what may be called 'loss of problems'. Then everything seems quite simple to them, no deep problems seem to exist any more, the world becomes broad and flat and loses all depth, and what they write becomes immeasurably shallow and trivial. Russell and H. G. Wells suffer from this.

. . . quia plus loquitur inquisitio quam inventio . . . (Augustine.)'

Philosophical investigations: conceptual investigations. The essential thing about metaphysics: it obliterates the distinction between factual and conceptual investigations.

The fundamental thing expressed grammatically: What about the sentence: 'One cannot step into the same river twice'?

In a certain sense one cannot take too much care in handling philosophical mistakes, they contain so much truth.

People sometimes say they cannot make any judgement about this or that because they have not studied philosophy. This is irritating nonsense, because the pretence is that philosophy is some sort of science. People speak of it almost as they might speak of medicine. – On the other hand we may say that people who have never carried out an investigation of a philosophical kind, like, for instance, most mathematicians, are not equipped with the right visual organs for this type of investigation or scrutiny. Almost in the way a man who is not used to searching in the forest for flowers, berries, or plants will not find any because his eyes are not trained to see them and he does not know where you have to be particularly on the lookout for them. Similarly, someone unpractised in philosophy passes by all the spots where difficulties are hidden in the grass, whereas someone who has had practice will pause and sense that there is a difficulty close by even though he cannot see it yet. – And this is no wonder for someone who knows how long even the man with practice, who realizes there is a difficulty, will have to search before he finds it.

When something is well hidden it is hard to find.

¹ . . . because the search says more than the discovery . . . Eds.

15

Ethics, Life and Faith

My subject, as you know, is Ethics and I will adopt the explanation of that term which Professor Moore has given in his book *Principia Ethica*. He says: 'Ethics is the general enquiry into what is good.' Now I am going to use the term Ethics in a slightly wider sense, in a sense in fact which includes what I believe to be the most essential part of what is generally called Aesthetics. And to make you see as clearly as possible what I take to be the subject matter of Ethics I will put before you a number of more or less synonymous expressions each of which could be substituted for the above definition, and by enumerating them I want to produce the same sort of effect which Galton produced when he took a number of photos of different faces on the same photographic plate in order to get the picture of the typical features they all had in common. And as by showing to you such a collective photo I could make you see what is the typical – say – Chinese face; so if you look through the row of synonyms which I will put before you, you will, I hope, be able to see the characteristic features they all have in common and these are the characteristic features of Ethics. Now instead of saying 'Ethics is the enquiry into what is good' I could have said Ethics is the enquiry into what is valuable, or, into what is really important, or I could have said Ethics is the enquiry into the meaning of life, or into what makes life worth living, or into the right way of living. I believe if you look at all these phrases you will get a rough idea as to what it is that Ethics is concerned with. Now the first thing that strikes one about all these expressions is that each of them is actually used in two very different senses. I will call them the trivial or relative sense on the one hand and the ethical or absolute sense on the other. If for instance I say that this is a *good* chair this means that the chair serves a certain predetermined purpose and the word good here has only meaning so far as this purpose has been previously fixed upon. In fact the word good in the relative sense simply means coming up to a certain predetermined standard. Thus when we say that this man is a good pianist we mean that he can play pieces of a certain degree of difficulty with a certain degree of dexterity. And similarly if I say that it is *important* for me not to catch cold I mean that catching a cold produces certain describable disturbances in my life and if I say that this is the *right* road I mean that it's the right road relative to a certain goal. Used in this way these expressions don't present any difficult or deep problems. But this is not how Ethics uses them. Supposing that I could play tennis and one of you saw me playing and said 'Well, you play pretty badly' and suppose I answered 'I know, I'm playing badly but I don't want to play any better,' all the other man could say would be 'Ah then that's all right.' But suppose I had told one of you a preposterous lie and he came up to me and said 'You're behaving like a beast' and then I were to say 'I know I behave badly, but then I don't want to behave any better,' could he then say 'Ah, then that's all right'? Certainly not; he would say 'Well, you *ought* to want to behave better.' Here you have an absolute judgment of value, whereas the first instance was one of a relative judgment. The essence of this difference seems to be obviously this: Every judgment of relative value is a mere statement of facts and can therefore be put in such a form that it loses all the appearance of a judgment of value: Instead of saying 'This is the right way to Granchester,' I could equally well have said, 'This is the right way you have to go if you want to get to Granchester in the shortest time'; 'This man is a good runner' simply means that he runs a certain number of miles in a certain number of minutes, etc. Now what I wish to contend is that, although all judgments of relative value can be shown to be mere statements of facts, no statement of fact can ever be, or imply, a judgment of absolute value. Let me explain this: Suppose one of you were an omniscient person and therefore knew all the movements of all the bodies in the world dead or alive and that he also knew all the states of mind of all human beings that ever lived, and suppose this man wrote all he knew in a big book, then this book would contain the whole description of the world; and what I want to say is, that this book would contain nothing that we would call an *ethical* judgment or anything that would logically imply such a judgment. It would of course contain all relative judgments of value and all true scientific propositions and in fact all true propositions that can be made. But all the facts described would, as it were, stand on the same level and in the same way all propositions stand on the same level. There are no propositions which, in any absolute sense, are sublime, important, or trivial. Now perhaps some of you will agree to that and be reminded of Hamlet's words: 'Nothing is either good or bad, but thinking makes it so.' But this again could lead to a misunderstanding. What Hamlet says seems to imply that good and bad, though not qualities of the world outside us, are attributes to our states of mind. But what I mean is that a state of mind, so far as we mean by that a fact which we can describe, is in no ethical sense good or bad. If for instance in our world-book we read the description of a murder with all its details physical and psychological, the mere description of these facts will contain nothing which we could call an *ethical* proposition. The murder will be on exactly the same level as any other event, for instance the falling of a stone. Certainly the reading of this description might cause us pain or rage or any other emotion, or we might read about the pain or rage caused by this murder in other people when they heard of it, but there will simply be facts, facts, and facts but no Ethics. And now I must say that if I contemplate what Ethics really would have to be if there were such a science, this result seems to me quite obvious. It seems to me obvious that nothing we could ever think or say should be *the* thing. That we cannot write a scientific book, the subject matter of which could be intrinsically sublime and above all other subject matters. I can only describe my feeling by the metaphor, that, if a man could write a book on Ethics which really was a book on Ethics, this book would, with an explosion, destroy all the other books in the world. Our words used as we use them in science, are vessels capable only of containing and conveying meaning and sense, *natural* meaning and sense. Ethics, if it is anything, is supernatural and our words will only express facts; as a teacup will only hold a teacup full of water and if I were to pour out a gallon over it. I said that so far as facts and propositions are concerned there is only relative value and relative good, right, etc. And let me, before I go on, illustrate this by a rather obvious example. The right road is the road which leads to an arbitrarily predetermined end and it is quite clear to us all that there is no sense in talking about the right road apart from such a predetermined goal. Now let us see what we could possibly mean by the expression, '*the* absolutely right road.' I think it would be the road which *everybody* on seeing it would, *with logical necessity*, have to go, or be ashamed for not going. And similarly the *absolute good*, if it is a describable state of affairs, would be one which everybody, independent of his tastes and inclinations, would *necessarily* bring about or feel guilty for not bringing about. And I want to say that such a state of affairs is a chimera. No state of affairs has, in itself, what I would like to call the coercive power of an absolute judge. Then what have all of us who, like myself, are still tempted to use such expressions as 'absolute good,' 'absolute value,' etc., what have we in mind and what do we try to express? Now whenever I try to make this clear to myself it is natural that I should recall cases in which I would certainly use these expressions and I am then in the situation in which you would be if, for instance, I were to give you a lecture on the psychology of pleasure. What you would do then would be to try and recall some typical situation in which you always felt pleasure. For, bearing this situation in mind, all I should say to you would become concrete and, as it were, controllable. One man would perhaps choose as his stock example the sensation when taking a walk on a fine summer's day. Now in this situation I am, if I want to fix my mind on what I mean by absolute or ethical value. And there, in my case, it always happens that the idea of one particular experience presents itself to me which therefore is, in a sense, my experience *par excellence* and this is the reason why, in talking to you now, I will use this experience as my first and foremost example. (As I have said before, this is an entirely personal matter and others would find other examples more striking.) I will describe this experience in order, if possible, to make you recall the same or similar experiences, so that we may have a common ground for our investigation. I believe the best way of describing it is to say that when I have it *I wonder at the existence of the world.* And I am then inclined to use such phrases as 'how extraordinary that anything should exist' or 'how extraordinary that the world should exist.' I will mention another experience straight away which I also know and which others of you might be acquainted with: it is, what one might call, the experience of feeling *absolutely* safe. I mean the state of mind in which one is inclined to say 'I am safe, nothing can injure me whatever happens.' Now let me consider these experiences, for, I believe, they exhibit the very characteristics we try to get clear about. And there the first thing I have to say is, that the verbal expression which we give to these experiences is nonsense! If I say 'I wonder at the existence of the world' I am misusing language. Let me explain this: It has a perfectly good and clear sense to say that I wonder at something being the case, we all understand what it means to say that I wonder at the size of a dog which is bigger than anyone I have ever seen before or at any thing which, in the common sense of the word, is extraordinary. In every such case I wonder at something being the case which I *could* conceive *not* to be the case. I wonder at the size of this dog because I could conceive of a dog of another, namely the ordinary size, at which I should not wonder. To say 'I wonder at such and such being the case' has only sense if I can imagine it not to be the case. In this sense one can wonder at the existence of, say, a house when one sees it and has not visited it for a long time and has imagined that it had been pulled down in the meantime. But it is nonsense to say that I wonder at the existence of the world, because I cannot imagine it not existing. I could of course wonder at the world round me being as it is. If for instance I had this experience while looking into the blue sky, I could wonder at the sky being blue as opposed to the case when it's clouded. But that's not what I mean. I am wondering at the sky being *whatever it is*. One might be tempted to say that what I am wondering at is a tautology, namely at the sky being blue or not blue. But then it's just nonsense to say that one is wondering at a tautology. Now the same applies to the other experience which I have mentioned, the experience of absolute safety. We all know what it means in ordinary life to be safe. I am safe in my room, when I cannot be run over by an omnibus. I am safe if I have had whooping cough and cannot therefore get it again. To be safe essentially means that it is physically impossible that certain things should happen to me and therefore it's nonsense to say that I am safe *whatever* happens. Again this is a misuse of the word 'safe' as the other example was of a misuse of the word 'existence' or 'wondering.' Now I want to impress on you that a certain characteristic misuse of our language runs through *all* ethical and religious expressions. All these expressions *seem*, prima facie, to be just *similes*. Thus it seems that when we are using the word *right* in an ethical sense, although, what we mean, is not right in its trivial sense, it's something similar, and when we say 'This is a good fellow,' although the word good here doesn't mean what it means in the sentence 'This is a good football player' there seems to be some similarity. And when we say 'This man's life was valuable' we don't mean it in the same sense in which we would speak of some valuable jewelry but there seems to be some sort of analogy. Now all religious terms seem in this sense to be used as similes or allegorically. For when we speak of God and that he sees everything and when we kneel and pray to him all our terms and actions seem to be parts of a great and elaborate allegory which represents him as a human being of great power whose grace we try to win, etc., etc. But this allegory also describes the experience which I have just referred to. For the first of them is, I believe, exactly what people were referring to when they said that God had created the world; and the experience of absolute safety has been described by saying that we feel safe in the hands of God. A third experience of the same kind is that of feeling guilty and again this was described by the phrase that God disapproves of our conduct. Thus in ethical and religious language we seem constantly to be using similes. But a simile must be the simile for *something*. And if I can describe a fact by means of a simile I must also be able to drop the simile and to describe the facts without it. Now in our case as soon as we try to drop the simile and simply to state the facts which stand behind it, we find that there are no such facts. And so, what at first appeared to be a simile now seems to be mere nonsense. Now the three experiences which I have mentioned to you (and I could have added others) seem to those who have experienced them, for instance to me, to have in some sense an intrinsic, absolute value. But when I say they are experiences, surely, they are facts; they have taken place then and there, lasted a certain definite time and consequently are describable. And so from what I have said some minutes ago I must admit it is nonsense to say that they have absolute value. And I will make my point still more acute by saying 'It is the paradox that an experience, a fact, should seem to have supernatural value.' Now there is a way in which I would be tempted to meet this paradox. Let me first consider, again, our first experience of wondering at the existence of the world and let me describe it in a slightly different way; we all know what in ordinary life would be called a miracle. It obviously is simply an event the like of which we have never yet seen. Now suppose such an event happened. Take the case that one of you suddenly grew a lion's head and began to roar. Certainly that would be as extraordinary a thing as I can imagine. Now whenever we should have recovered from our surprise, what I would suggest would be to fetch a doctor and have the case scientifically investigated and if it were not for hurting him I would have him vivisected. And where would the miracle have got to? For it is clear that when we look at it in this way everything miraculous has disappeared; unless what we mean by this term is merely that a fact has not yet been explained by science which again means that we have hitherto failed to group this fact with others in a scientific system. This shows that it is absurd to say 'Science has proved that there are no miracles.' The truth is that the scientific way of looking at a fact is not the way to look at it as a miracle. For imagine whatever fact you may, it is not in itself miraculous in the absolute sense of that term. For we see now that we have been using the word 'miracle' in a relative and an absolute sense. And I will now describe the experience of wondering at the existence of the world by saying: it is the experience of seeing the world as a miracle. Now I am tempted to say that the right expression in language for the miracle of the existence of the world, though it is not any proposition *in* language, is the existence of language itself. But what then does it mean to be aware of this miracle at some times and not at other times? For all I have said by shifting the expression of the miraculous from an expression *by means of* language to the expression *by the existence* of language, all I have said is again that we cannot express what we want to express and that all we *say* about the absolute miraculous remains nonsense. Now the answer to all this will seem perfectly clear to many of you. You will say: Well, if certain experiences constantly tempt us to attribute a quality to them which we call absolute or ethical value and importance, this simply shows that by these words we *don't* mean nonsense, that after all what we mean by saying that an experience has absolute value *is just a fact like other facts* and that all it comes to is that we have not yet succeeded in finding the correct logical analysis of what we mean by our ethical and religious expressions. Now when this is urged against me I at once see clearly, as it were in a flash of light, not only that no description that I can think of would do to describe what I mean by absolute value, but that I would reject every significant description that anybody could possibly suggest, *ab initio*, on the ground of its significance. That is to say: I see now that these nonsensical expressions were not nonsensical because I had not yet found the correct expressions, but that their nonsensicality was their very essence. For all I wanted to do with them was just *to go beyond* the world and that is to say beyond significant language. My whole tendency and I believe the tendency of all men who ever tried to write or talk Ethics or Religion was to run against the boundaries of language. This running against the walls of our cage is perfectly, absolutely hopeless. Ethics so far as it springs from the desire to say something about the ultimate meaning of life, the absolute good, the absolute valuable, can be no science. What it says does not add to our knowledge in any sense. But it is a document of a tendency in the human mind which I personally cannot help respecting deeply and I would not for my life ridicule it.

★ ★ ★

Christianity is not a doctrine, not, I mean, a theory about what has happened and will happen to the human soul, but a description of something that actually takes place in human life. For 'consciousness of sin' is a real event and so are despair and salvation through faith. Those who speak of such things (Bunyan for instance) are simply describing what has happened to them, whatever gloss anyone may want to put on it.

★ ★ ★

The effect of making men think in accordance with dogmas, perhaps in the form of certain graphic propositions, will be very peculiar: I am not thinking of these dogmas as determining men's opinions but rather as completely controlling the *expression* of all opinions. People will live under an absolute, palpable tyranny, though without being able to say they are not free. I think the Catholic Church does something rather like this. For dogma is expressed in the form of an assertion, and is unshakable, but at the same time any practical opinion *can* be made to harmonize with it; admittedly more easily in some cases than in others. It is not a *wall* setting limits to what can be believed, but more like a *brake* which, however, practically serves the same purpose; it's almost as though someone were to attach a weight to your foot to restrict your freedom of movement. This is how dogma becomes irrefutable and beyond the reach of attack.

* * *

Religious similes can be said to move on the edge of an abyss. Bunyan's for example. For what if we simply add: 'and all these traps, quicksands, wrong turnings, were planned by the Lord of the Road and the monsters, thieves and robbers were created by him'? Certainly, that is not the sense of the simile! But such a continuation is all too obvious! For many people, including me, this robs the simile of its power.

But more especially if this is – as it were – suppressed. It would be different if at every turn it were said quite honestly: 'I am using this as a simile, but look: it doesn't fit here.' Then you wouldn't feel you were being cheated, that someone was trying to convince you by trickery. Someone can be told for instance: 'Thank God for the good you receive but don't complain about the evil: as you would of course do if a human being were to do you good and evil by turns.' Rules of life are dressed up in pictures. And these pictures can only serve to *describe* what we are to do, not *justify* it. Because they could provide a justification only if they held good in other respects as well. I can say: 'Thank these bees for their honey as though they were kind people who have prepared it for you'; that is *intelligible* and describes how I should like you to conduct yourself. But I cannot say: 'Thank them because, look, how kind they are!' – since the next moment they may sting you.

Religion says: *Do this! – Think like that!* – but it cannot justify this and once it even tries to, it becomes repellent; because for every reason it offers there is a valid counter-reason. It is more convincing to say: 'Think like this! however strangely it may strike you.' Or: 'Won't you do this? – however repugnant you find it.'

Predestination: It is only permissible to write like this out of the most dreadful suffering – and then it means something quite different. But for the same reason it is not permissible for someone to assert it as a truth, unless he himself says it in torment. – It simply isn't a theory. – Or, to put it another way: If this is truth, it is not the truth that seems at first sight to be expressed by these words. It's less a theory than a sigh, or a cry.

* * *

The spring which flows gently and limpidly in the Gospels seems to have *froth* on it in Paul's Epistles. Or that is how it seems *to me*. Perhaps it is just my own impurity which reads turbidness into it; for why shouldn't this impurity be able to pollute what is limpid? But to me it's as though I saw human passion here, something like pride or anger, which is not in tune with the humility of the *Gospels*. It's as though he *is* insisting here on his own person, *and doing so moreover as a religious gesture,* something which is foreign to the Gospel. I want to ask – and may this be no blasphemy –: 'What might Christ have said to Paul?' But a fair rejoinder to that would be: What business is that of yours? Attend to making *yourself* more honourable! In your present state you are quite incapable of understanding what may be the truth here.

In the Gospels – as it seems to me – everything is *less pretentious*, humbler, simpler. There you find huts; in Paul a church. There all men are equal and God himself is a man; in Paul there is already something like a hierarchy; honours and official positions. – That, as it were, is what my NOSE tells me.

* * *

Kierkegaard writes: If Christianity were so easy and cosy, why should God in his Scriptures have set Heaven and Earth in motion and threatened *eternal* punishments? – Question: But in that case why is this Scripture so unclear? If we want to warn someone of a terrible danger, do we go about it by telling him a riddle whose solution will be the warning? – But who is to say that the Scripture really is unclear? Isn't it possible that it was essential in this case to 'tell a riddle'? And that, on the other hand, giving a more direct warning would necessarily have had the *wrong* effect? God has *four* people recount the life of his incarnate Son, in each case differently and with inconsistencies – but might we not say: It is important that this narrative should not be more than quite averagely historically plausible *just so that* this should not be taken as the essential, decisive thing? So that the *letter* should not be believed more strongly than is proper and the *spirit* may receive its due. I.e. what you are supposed to see cannot be communicated even by the best and most accurate historian; and *therefore* a mediocre account suffices, is even to be preferred. For that too can tell you what you are supposed to be told. (Roughly in the way a mediocre stage set can be better than a sophisticated one, painted trees better than real ones, – because these might distract attention from what matters.)

The Spirit puts what is essential, essential for your life, into these words. The point is precisely that your are only SUPPOSED to see clearly what appears clearly even in *this* representation. (I am not sure how far all this is exactly in the spirit of Kierkegaard.)

In religion every level of devoutness must have its appropriate form of expression which has no sense at a lower level. This doctrine, which means something at a higher level, is null and void for someone who is still at the lower level; he *can* only understand it *wrongly* and so these words are *not* valid for such a person.

For instance, at my level the Pauline doctrine of predestination is ugly nonsense, irreligiousness. Hence it is not suitable for me, since the only use I could make of the picture I am offered would be a wrong one. If it is a good and godly picture, then it is so for someone at a quite different level, who must use it in his life in a way completely different from anything that would be possible for me.

Christianity is not based on a historical truth; rather, it offers us a (historical) narrative and says: now believe! But not, believe this narrative with the belief appropriate to a historical narrative, rather: believe, through thick and thin, which you can do only as the result of a life. *Here you have a narrative, don't take the same attitude to it as you take to other historical narratives!* Make a *quite different* place in your life for it. – There is nothing *paradoxical* about that!

Nobody can truthfully say of himself that he is filth. Because if I do say it, though it can be true in a sense, this is not a truth by which I myself can be penetrated: otherwise I should either have to go mad or change myself.

Queer as it sounds: The historical accounts in the Gospels might, historically speaking, be demonstrably false and yet belief would lose nothing by this: *not*, however, because it concerns 'universal truths of reason'! Rather, because historical proof (the historical proof-game) is irrelevant to belief. This message (the Gospels) is seized on by men believingly (i.e. lovingly). *That* is the certainty characterizing this particular acceptance-as-true, not something *else*.

A believer's relation to these narratives is *neither* the relation to historical truth (probability), *nor yet* that to a theory consisting of 'truths of reason'. There is such a thing. – (We have quite different attitudes even to different species of what we call fiction!)

I read: 'No man can say that Jesus is the Lord, but by the Holy Ghost.' And it is true: I cannot call him *Lord*; because that says nothing to me. I could call him 'the paragon', 'God' even – or rather, I can understand it when he is called thus; but I cannot utter the word 'Lord' with meaning. *Because I do not believe* that he will come to judge me; because *that* says nothing to me. And it could say something to me, only if I lived *completely* differently.

What inclines even me to believe in Christ's Resurrection? It is as though I play with the thought. – If he did not rise from the dead, then he decomposed in the grave like any other man. *He is dead and decomposed.* In that case he is a teacher like any other and can no longer *help*; and once more we are orphaned and alone. So we have to content ourselves with wisdom and specu- lation. We are in a sort of hell where we can do nothing but dream, roofed in, as it were, and cut off from heaven. But if I am to be REALLY saved, – what I need is *certainty* – not wisdom, dreams or speculation – and this certainty is faith. And faith is faith in what is needed by my *heart*, my *soul*, not my speculative intelligence. For it is my soul with its passions, as it were with its flesh and blood, that has to be saved, not my abstract mind. Perhaps we can say: Only *love* can believe the Resurrection. Or: It is *love* that believes the Resurrection. We might say: Redeem- ing love believes even in the Resurrection; holds fast even to the Resurrection. What combats doubt is, as it were, *redemption*. Holding fast to *this* must be holding fast to that belief. So what that means is: first you must be redeemed and hold on to your redemption (keep hold of your redemption) – then you will see that you are holding fast to this belief. So this can come about only if you no longer rest your weight on the earth but suspend yourself from heaven. Then *everything* will be different and it will be 'no wonder' if you can do things that you cannot do now.

(A man who is suspended looks the same as one who is standing, but the interplay of forces within him is nevertheless quite different, so that he can act quite differently than can a standing man.)

* * *

A miracle is, as it were, a *gesture* which God makes. As a man sits quietly and then makes an impressive gesture, God lets the world run on smoothly and then accompanies the words of a saint by a symbolic occurrence, a gesture of nature. It would be an instance if, when a saint has spoken, the trees around him bowed, as if in reverence. – Now, do I believe that this happens? I don't.

The only way for me to believe in a miracle in this sense would be to be *impressed* by an occurrence in this particular way. So that I should say e.g.: 'It was *impossible* to see these trees and not to feel that they were responding to the words.' Just as I might say 'It is impossible to see the face of this dog and not to see that he is alert and full of attention to what his master is doing'. And I can imagine that the mere report of the *words* and life of a saint can make someone believe the reports that the trees bowed. But I am not so impressed.

When I came home I expected a surprise and there was no surprise for me, so, of course, I was surprised.

People are religious to the extent that they believe themselves to be not so much *imperfect*, as *ill*.

Any man who is half-way decent will think himself extremely imperfect, but a religious man thinks himself *wretched*.

Go on, believe! It does no harm.

* * *

Wisdom is cold and to that extent stupid. (Faith on the other hand is a passion.) It might also be said: Wisdom merely *conceals* life from you. (Wisdom is like cold grey ash, covering up the glowing embers.)

Don't *for heaven's sake*, be afraid of talking nonsense! But you must pay attention to your nonsense.

* * *

It strikes me that a religious belief could only be something like a passionate commitment to a system of reference. Hence, although it's *belief*, it's really a way of living, or a way of assessing life. It's passionately seizing hold of *this* interpretation. Instruction in a religious faith, therefore, would have to take the form of a portrayal, a description, of that system of reference, while at the same time being an appeal to conscience. And this combination would have to result in the pupil himself, of his own accord, passionately taking hold of the system of reference. It would be as though someone were first to let me see the hopelessness of my situation and then show me the means of rescue until, of my own accord, or not at any rate led to it by my *instructor*, I ran to it and grasped it.

★ ★ ★

If God really does choose those who are to be saved, there is no reason why he should not choose them according to nationality, race or temperament. Or why the choice should not find expression in the laws of nature. (Certainly he was *able* so to choose that his choice should follow a law.)

I have read excerpts from the writings of St John of the Cross where he says that people have fallen into the pit because they did not have the good fortune to find a wise spiritual director at the right moment.

And if that is so, how can anyone say that God does not try men beyond their strength?

What I really feel like saying here is that distorted concepts have done a lot of mischief, but the truth is that I just *do not know* what does good and what does mischief.

★ ★ ★

'God has commanded it, therefore it must be possible to do it.' That means nothing. There is no *'therefore'* about it. At most the two expressions might mean the *same*.

In this context 'He has commanded it' means roughly: He will punish anybody who doesn't do it. And nothing follows from that about what anybody can or cannot do. And *that* is what 'predestination' means.

But that doesn't mean that it's right to say: 'He punishes you even though you *cannot* do otherwise.' – Perhaps, though, one might say: in this case punishment is inflicted in circumstances where it would be impermissible for men to inflict it. And then the whole concept of 'punishment' changes. For now you can no longer use the old illustrations, or else you have to apply them quite differently. Just look at an allegory like 'The Pilgrim's Progress' and notice how nothing is right – in human terms. – But isn't it right all the same? I.e.: can't it be applied? Indeed, it has been applied. (On railway stations there are dials with two hands; they show when the next train leaves. They look like clocks though they aren't; but they have a use of their own.) (It ought to be possible to find a better simile.)

If anyone gets upset by this allegory, one might say to him: Apply it differently, or else leave it alone! (But there are *some* whom it will confuse far more than it can help.)

★ ★ ★

Suppose someone were taught: there is a being who, if you do such and such or live thus and thus, will take you to a place of everlasting torment after you die; most people end up there, a few get to a place of everlasting happiness. – This being has selected in advance those who are to go to the good place and, since only those who have lived a certain sort of life go to the place of torment, he has also arranged in advance for the rest to live like that.

What might be the effect of such a doctrine?

Well, it does not mention punishment, but rather a sort of natural necessity. And if you were to present things to anyone in this light, he could only react with despair or incredulity to such a doctrine.

Teaching it could not constitute an ethical upbringing. If you wanted to bring someone up ethically while yet teaching him such a doctrine, you would have to teach it to him *after* having educated him ethically, representing it as a sort of incomprehensible mystery.

'Out of his goodness he has chosen them and he will punish you' makes no sense. The two halves of the proposition belong to different ways of looking at things. The second half is ethical, the first not. And taken together with the first, the second is absurd.

★ ★ ★

If someone who believes in God looks round and asks 'Where does everything I see come from?', 'Where does all this come from?', he is *not* craving for a (causal) explanation; and his question gets its point from being the expression of a certain craving. He is, namely, expressing an attitude to all explanations. – But how is this manifested in his life?

The attitude that's in question is that of taking a certain matter seriously and then, beyond a certain point, no longer regarding it as serious, but maintaining that something else is even more important.

Someone may for instance say it's a very grave matter that such and such a man should have died before he could complete a certain piece of work; and yet, in another sense, this is not what matters. At this point one uses the words 'in a deeper sense'.

Actually I should like to say that in this case too the *words* you utter or what you think as you utter them are not what matters, so much as the difference they make at various points in your life. How do I know that two people mean the same when each says he believes in God? And just the same goes for belief in the Trinity. A theology which insists on the use of *certain particular* words and phrases, and outlaws others, does not make anything clearer (Karl Barth). It gesticulates with words, as one might say, because it wants to say something and does not know how to express it. *Practice* gives the words their sense.

A proof of God's existence ought really to be something by means of which one could convince oneself that God exists. But I think that what *believers* who have furnished such proofs have wanted to do is give their 'belief' an intellectual analysis and foundation, although they themselves would never have come to believe as a result of such proofs. Perhaps one could 'convince someone that God exists' by means of a certain kind of upbringing, by shaping his life in such and such a way.

Life can educate one to a belief in God. And *experiences* too are what bring this about; but I don't mean visions and other forms of sense experience which show us the 'existence of this being', but, e.g., sufferings of various sorts. These neither show us God in the way a sense impression shows us an object, nor do they give rise to *conjectures* about him. Experiences, thoughts, – life can force this concept on us.

* * *

How God judges a man is something we cannot imagine at all. If he really takes strength of temptation and the frailty of nature into account, whom can he condemn? But otherwise the resultant of these two forces is simply the end for which the man was predestined. In that case he was created so that the interplay of forces would make him either conquer or succumb. And that is not a religious idea at all, but more like a scientific hypothesis.

So if you want to stay within the religious sphere you must *struggle*.

Note on Sources

Chapter one is an abridgement by myself of the *Tractatus Logico-Philosophicus*. I have used the translation by Ramsey and Ogden, first published in 1922 (Routledge and Kegan Paul) because in spite of its Germanism it has a special authority as having been revised by Wittgenstein himself. In making my abridgement I have been guided, though not exclusively, by the decimal numbering Wittgenstein attached to the sections of the work. He explained it as follows: 'the decimal figures as numbers of the separate propositions indicate the logical importance of the propositions, the emphasis laid upon them in my exposition. The propositions *n*.1, *n*.2, *n*.3, etc., are comments on proposition No. *n*; the propositions *n*.*m*1, *n*.*m*2, etc., are comments on the proposition No. *n*.*m*; and so on. A line has been left blank in the text whenever a section of the original has been omitted.

The remaining chapters are drawn from Wittgenstein's posthumous published works, as follows.

Chapter 2: *Philosophical Grammar* (ed. R. Rhees, trs. A. Kenny, Blackwell 1969), pp. 202–7, 210–19; *Blue and Brown Books* (Blackwell 1958), pp. 16–17: *Philosophical Investigations* (trs. G. E. M. Anscombe, Blackwell 1953), I, 23, 65–7.

Chapter 3: *Philosophical Investigations* I, 1, 26–32; *Blue and Brown Books*, pp. 1–5; *Philosophical Grammar*, sections 6–8, 10–13.

Chapter 4: *Philosophical Grammar*, sections 62, 91–2, 94–6, 98–101; *Blue and Brown Books*, pp. 30–1, 35–9.

Chapter 5: *Philosophical Investigations* I, 145–55, 179–92, 195–219; *Zettel* (ed. G. E. M. Anscombe and G. H. von Wright, trs. G. E. M. Anscombe, Blackwell 1967), 278–80, 293–314.

Chapter 6: *Philosophical Investigations* I, 36–349; *Blue and Brown Books*, pp. 24–5; *Philosophical Investigations* I, 354–61; *Zettel*, 100–30.

Chapter 7: *Philosophical Investigations* I, 587–94, 611–29; *Remarks on the Philosophy of Psycholgy* (ed. G. H. von Wright and H. Nyman, trs. C. G. Luckhardt and M. A. E. Aue, Blackwell 1980), I, 840–52; 897–902.

Chapter 8: *Philosophical Investigations* I, 243–314; *Lecture on Private Experience,* (ed. R. Rhees, *Philosophical Review, LXXVII,* 1968) pp. 278–81, 284–5, 288–91, 295–7, 316–18.

Chapter 9: *Remarks on the Philosophy of Psychology* II, 59–101; *Philosophical Grammar* II, pp. 193–7, 213–15; *Remarks on the Philosophy of Psychology* I, 899–900.

Chapter 10: *Blue and Brown Books,* pp. 61–2, 66–70; *Philosophical Investigations* I, 398–417; II, pp. 187–92.

Chapter 11: *Philosophical Investigations* II, pp. 222–4; *Remarks on the Philosophy of Psychology,* I, 563–86, 903–22, 927–39.

Chapter 12: *Zettel,* 320–32; *Remarks on the Foundations of Mathematics* (ed. G. H. von Wright, R. Rhees and G. E. M. Anscombe, Blackwell, 1956 and later editions), I, 113–31; III, 29–42, 52–7, 60.

Chapter 13: *On Certainty* (ed. G. E. M. Anscombe and G. H. von Wright, trs. D. Paul and G. E. M. Anscombe, Blackwell 1969) 35–7, 51–6, 79–83, 118–23, 126–35, 161–215, 233–62, 279–84.

Chapter 14: MS 213 (*The Big Typescript*), newly translated by myself, pp. 406–35; *Philosophical Investigations* I, 89–92, 106–33; *Zettel,* 447–60.

Chapter 15: *Lecture on Ethics, Culture and Value* (ed. G. H. von Wright, trs. P. Winch, Blackwell 1966), remarks from pp. 28–33, 45, 56, 64, 72, 77, 81, 85–6

Index

a priori truth, 7
ABC, 89
ability, 63, 92
absolute good, 290–2
absolute safety, 292–3
absolute value, 294
acquaintance, 215–17
"ad inf." 100, 102
aeroplanes, 250
aesthetics, 29
agreement with reality, 6, 42–3, 59–60, 255
analogies, 264–5
analysis, 8, 40–2, 280
anchor, 267
angina, 118
apples, 46, 195
application, 106
architecture, 263
ascetic, 267
aspect, 136, 181–7
aspect-blindness, 185–7
association, 59
assumption, 47
atomic facts, 3, 6, 13
Augustine, St, 53, 56, 65, 132, 279, 286
Australia, 252
authority, 252
auxiliary activities, 122

Ballard, 116–17, 123
banjo, 58
Barth, K., 304
bearer of a name, 71
bearer of property, 38
bedrock, 102, 257

beetle in box, 153
behaviourism, 155
belief, 23–4, 203–7, 218, 250–7, 300–4
bewitchment, 282
blindness, 167, 176
blueprint, 42–3
body, 191, 221
boxer, 47
brain, 106, 199–200, 217–19, 249, 254
brake, 73–4
bumps of understanding, 274

calculus, 119
Catholics, 256
causal nexus, 19
causality, 27, 96
certainty, 112–13, 213, 223, 247–59
chair thinking, 120, 125
character, 191–2
chart, 59
chess, 44–5, 49, 55–6, 66, 98–9, 111, 236, 285
children, 252–9, 273, 276
Christianity, 296–301
circle, 39–40
clockwork, 111
code, 186
cogito, ergo sum, 196
colour inversion, 160–2, 167
colour-impressions, 148–9, 157–62, 168
colours, 29, 44
combination lock, 269
complaint, 203

complexes, 3, 8
compositeness, 13
compulsion of logic, 230–2
concatenation, 15
concepts, 35–8, 236–9
confession, 211
consciousness, 199–201, 211, 221–3
conservation, 27
contradiction, 16–19, 242–3, 284
conviction, 114, 205, 221
cookery, 227
counting, 106
criteria vs symptoms, 118
criterion of identity, 36–7, 112,
    143, 162, 237
crystalline purity, 281
cylinder, 92

dance, 116
deaf mutes, 117
death, 30, 278
definitions, 8, 10, 54–9,
descriptions, 8, 39, 41, 152, 202
determinateness of sense, 8
determining, 95–6
diary, 144–7
dictionary, 146
diet, 130
digestion, 77
dog, 120, 142, 221, 293
doing, 132
dolls, 150, 183
doubt, 247–59
dreams, 76, 212, 222–3
duck-rabbit, 181
duration, 173

electric shock, 199
elementary propositions, 15–19,
    23, 40–3
empirical propositions, 247–9
epistemology, 23
equations, 27, 39
Ernst, P., 277
essence, 241, 264, 280, 283
ethics, 29, 289–306
evidence, 252–5
exclamations, 54, 112, 203

existence, 9, 36
existential quantifier, 36–7
expectation, 71–3
experience, 249–53
explanation vs description, 107,
    270, 281
explorer, 99, 141
explosion, 291
expression, 9, 73, 78, 111–15,
    144–9, 164, 173, 215

facial expression, 221
facts, 3–5, 7, 12, 79, 82–3, 290–4
fairy-tale, 149
faith, 129, 296–305
family resemblances, 49
fancy, 180
fear, 202–3
film, 275
fingers, 131–2,
fitting, 92, 102
flame, 125, 169
flower, 58
fly, 150
fly-bottle, 155
form of representation, 5–6
form vs content, 7
formula, 88–91, 95
Frazer, J. G., 270, 277
Frege, G., 10, 21, 23, 35, 47, 238
French politician, 115
fulfilment, 71
functions, 20
fury, 221

Galton, J., 289
games, 48–9, 104, 194
general form of proposition, 17,
    45, 48, 282
generality, 23, 44
giddiness, 200
God, 18, 30, 296–305
goodness, 289
Gospels, 297–9
grammar, 119, 153, 155, 211,
    266–72, 279
grasping in a flash, 96, 236
grief, 201–2

ground vs cause, 250
guessing thoughts, 212

hair on tongue, 264
Hamlet, 291
hands, 248–50
headache, 157
Heraclitus, 265, 275
Hertz, H. R., 28, 271
hesitancy, 207
hidden propositions, 40–1

"I", 25, 70, 166, 191–207
ice, 281
identity, 23, 36, 102, 143, 266
idols, 267
images, 60–1, 69, 174–80, 197, 236
imagination, 135–6, 174–80
imagining the opposite, 142–3
immortality, 30
incorporeal process, 116
induction, 27–8, 112–13,
inexpressible, 31, 61–2
inference, 229–32
infinity, 102
inner eye, 174
inner picture, 183
inner process, 155
intention, 73–8, 115, 129–30,
    142, 186, 213
intentionality, 67–83
internal relations, 19
interpretation, 58–9, 75, 97–9,
    101, 181
intuition, 101
"is", 9, 273

James, W., 116, 123, 200
Jastrow, 181
Jekyll and Hyde, 192
Jesus, 256, 300
jokes, 266
jotting, 219
judgement, 24

Kierkegaard, S., 298
kinaesthetic sensations, 132
King's College, 83

knots, 272
knowledge, 63–5, 89, 221, 256–9,
    285

labels, 54
ladder, 31
language, 24, 53, 59, 72, 98,
    227–8, 272–4, 282, 295
language-games, 42, 46–9, 87–93,
    151–2, 175, 194, 213, 228, 248,
    284
laws of inference, 229–32
learning, 53
Lichtenberg, G. C., 272
life, problem of, 31, 271
limits of language, 24, 228, 265–6,
    271, 296
lion, 213
logic, 21–7, 248, 279–80
logical constants, 13, 18, 21–2
logical form, 6, 14
logical machine, 321–2
logical picture, 6, 13
logical space, 3, 6, 11
logical syntax, 10–11
looking, 175
loom, 200
love, 129
Luther, M., 129
lying, 158, 164

Macbeth, 177
machine as symbol, 233–4
machine thinking, 120
manometer, 147
map, 124
mathematical multiplicity, 13
mathematics, 27, 240, 269
meaning, 12, 53–7, 94–5
measuring, 113–14, 231
memory, 69, 117, 135, 147
mental activity, 83, 104, 124
mental mechanism, 60, 131
mental process, 90–1, 155
mental undertone, 130
metaphysics, 79, 265, 283
miracles, 300
mirror, 22

mistake, 87, 179, 247–9, 251–2
moaning, 165, 194
moon, 256
Moore, G. E., 23, 204–5, 248–51, 289
motor cars, 258
mountains, 255
multiplying, 103–5, 242
musical ear, 186
must, logical, 233
mystical, 30

names, 8, 9, 13, 24, 35–8, 53–4, 141–7
Napoleon, 70, 83, 252
natural science, 14, 26, 295
necessity, 28–9, 227–43
negation, 22–3
New York, 254
Nobody, 195
numbers, 54–5, 87–93
nursing, 173

objective certainty, 252
objects, 3–5, 35–8, 53–4
observation, 201–3, 220
omniscience, 290
operations, 20–2
ostensive definition, 35–6, 53–9, 145–7, 162

pain, 91, 132, 141–57, 194–9
pain-behaviour, 141–57
patch, 38
patience, 142
Paul, St, 297
pedal note, 65
personal identity, 191, 198
personality, 192
perspicuity, 269
phenomenology, 44
philosophy, 14, 31, 144, 153, 177, 192, 228, 263–86
pi, 100
picture by similarity, 80–1
pictures, 4–6, 11–13, 42–3, 69
pin game, 193
plans, 69

Plato, 273, 278, 285
portrait, 69, 77
possibility, 234–5
predestination, 297, 299, 302–4
predicate, 35–8
prediction, 213, 239
primary colours, 228
private experience, 141–69
private language, 141–53
privacy, 142, 214–17
probability, 18–19
process, 78, 91, 97
projection, 7, 38–40, 42–3, 81
proof, 238–41, 256, 299–300
property, 38
proposition, 7–31, 70
proposition-radical, 47
propositional sign, 7–11, 21
psycho-physical parallelism, 218
psychoanalysis, 265
psychological verbs, 173
puzzle picture, 183

queerness, 60, 82, 104

rage, 132, 136–7
rails, 102, 229, 265
reality, 273
redemption, 300
regularity, 100–1
relations, 7
religion, 293–305
remembering, 155
renunciation, 263
reporting, 204
representation, 69
representing relation, 5
rest vs motion, 135
resurrection, 300
retinal image, 220
right road, 291–2
rigidity, 232–3
rivers, 36
ruler, 74
rules, 87–107
Russell, B., 10, 21, 23–4, 35, 286

safety, 292–3
samples, 74

sawdust, 258
saying vs showing, 28, 161
scapegoat, 278
scepticism, 30, 247–59
schematic cube, 181, 184–5
Schlemiehl, 116
search, 71
seas of language, 234
secrecy, 214–17
seeds, 218
seeing, 173–87
self, 200
sensation S, 144–7
sensations, 141–69, 173–4
sense, 12, 15, 80
sense-data, 158–67, 197
series, 88–91
shadow, 79–81, 116
Siamese twins, 143
signpost, 98
signs vs symbols, 9–11
silence, 31
simple signs, 8, 15
slaves, 123
society, 267
solipsism, 25, 166, 197
soul, 24, 217
speaking, 113–17
sphere, 42
spider's web, 280
states of affairs, 3, 6, 7, 13
states, 64, 92
stone, 150–1
structure, 4
struggle, 305
subject, 35–8
subjective certainty, 252
substance, 4
supernatural, 291
symbols, 9–11
symptoms, 118
synthetic *a priori*, 241

tailor, 97, 235
talking to oneself, 117, 141, 211, 217
tautology, 16–19, 25–7, 293
tense, 70
testimony, 130

theses, 270
thinking, 46–7, 56, 78–83,
    111–25, 211–17
thought, 6–7, 11, 23
thought-reading, 217
time, 43–6
timetable, 76, 146
Tolstoy, L., 263
tools, 65, 193
toothache, 61, 159–60
"tove", 57–8
Tractatus, 40–2, 254
translation, 12
trisection of angle, 238–40
truth and falsehood, 6, 13, 253
truth-conditions, 16
truth-functions, 17–18, 22, 25, 41,
    45
truth-grounds, 18
truth-operations, 20
truth-possibilities, 15
truth-tables, 16
truthfulness, 211
trying, 131–2
tune, 93, 114, 134, 176

unconscious, 64, 89,
understanding, 61–6, 88–107, 212
use, 10, 60

value, 29, 289–94
visual room, 196–7
vivacity, 174
voluntary action, 131–7

walking, 93
water boiling, 153
will, 28–9, 129–37, 176–8, 263–4
willing, 131–2
wisdom, 301
wish, 71, 78, 81
wonder, 292
word order, 115
wordless thought, 113–17, 121
world, 3–4, 24, 28–31

yardstick, 76
yes or no, 12, 43